Contemporary American Slang

Richard A. Spears

Orbis Verlag

ABOUT THE AUTHOR

Richard A. Spears, Ph.D., Associate Professor of Linguistics, Northwestern University. Specialist in lexicography; English language structure; phonetics; language standardization and codification; English as a second language; American culture.

Sonderausgabe 1992 Orbis Verlag für Publizistik GmbH, München
Published by National Textbook Company, a division of NTC Publishing Group.
© 1991 by NTC Publishing Group, 4255 West Touhy Avenue,
Lincolnwood (Chicago), Illinois 60646-1975 U.S.A.
Druck und Einband: Mohndruck Graphische Betriebe GmbH, Gütersloh
Printed in Germany
ISBN 3-572-00581-7

ABOUT THIS DICTIONARY

This dictionary is a resource cataloging the meaning and usage of frequently used slang expressions in the U.S.A. It contains expressions that are familiar to many Americans and other expressions that are used primarily within small groups of people. These expressions come from movies, novels, newspaper stories, and everyday conversation. The entries represent the vocabulary found in many places, such as the college campus and urban streets. We hear from surfers, weight lifters, and young people in general.

There is no standard test that will decide what is slang and what is not. Expressions that are identified as slang are sometimes little more than entertaining wordplay, and much slang is little more than an entertaining, alternative way of saying something. Slang is rarely the first choice of careful writers or speakers or anyone attempting to use language for formal, persuasive, or business purposes. Nonetheless, expressions that can be called slang make up a major part of American communication in movies, television, radio, newspapers, magazines, and informal spoken conversation.

Young people are responsible for a high proportion of the fad expressions and collegiate wordplay found here. And strangely, there are a large number of clever expressions for vomiting from this source. Clever or insulting nicknames for types of people are the major linguistic product of this subgroup. Matters of social taboo have provided many slang expressions. Although, strictly speaking, taboo words are not slang, the major taboo words have been included in this dictionary.

Some slang expressions are not standardized in spelling or punctuation. This dictionary usually represents slang expressions in the form in which they were found, except for the following. Entry heads made up of initials that are pronounced as one word—acronyms—are spelled without periods, e.g., "GAPO." Entry heads that are to be pronounced as one or more letter names, e.g., "L.I.Q.," have a period after each letter. Rhyming compounds, e.g., "fender-bender, fling-wing," are always hyphenated.

The entries come from many sources. Many have been collected by college students and other individuals. Much of the recent material has come directly from television and a lesser amount from contemporary radio and journalism. Standard reference works have been used to verify the meanings and spellings of older material. Most of the examples are concocted and have been edited to exemplify an expression's meaning as concisely as possible. The examples are to be taken as representative of slang usage, not of standard, formal English usage. They are included to illustrate meaning, not to prove the earliest date of print or broadcast dissemination.

Guide to the Use of This Dictionary

1. Entry heads are alphabetized according to an absolute alphabetical order that ignores all punctuation, spaces, and hyphens.

2. Entry heads appear in **boldface type**. When words or expressions that are not entries in this dictionary are cited, they appear in *italics*. Function codes [see 9 below] and examples appear in *italics*.

3. An entry head may have one or more alternative forms. The alternatives are printed in **boldface type** and are preceded by "AND." Alternative forms containing commas are separated by semicolons, otherwise by commas. For an example, see *blow a fuse*.

4. An entry head enclosed in square brackets, e.g., **[head]**, leads to other entry heads that contain the word in brackets. Entry heads in square brackets do not have definitions.

5. Definitions are in roman type. Alternative or closely related definitions are separated by semicolons. For an example, see *bucko*.

6. Some definitions contain restrictive comments in square brackets that help to make the definition more clear. These comments limit the context in which the expression can be used. For an example, see *crash*, sense three.

7. Sometimes the numbered senses refer only to people or things, but not both. In such cases the numeral is followed by "[with *someone*]" or "[with *something*]." For an example, see *jack someone or something up*.

8. A definition may be followed by comments in parentheses. These comments give additional information about the expression, including cautions, comments on origins, or cross-referencing. Each numbered sense can have its own comments. For an example, see *cakewalk*.

9. Every expression is followed by a function code that indicates the grammatical or syntactic function of the expression. These codes are in *italics*. The function codes provide a way of determining the grammatical or syntactic function of a particular expression as it occurs in its examples. Expressions functioning as nominals (nouns, noun phrases, etc.) are marked *n*. Expressions serving to modify, restrict, or qualify (adjectives, adjective phrases, adverbs, adverb phrases, etc.) are marked *mod*. Expressions that are transitive verbs or transitive verb phrases (a transitive verb, its auxiliaries, object[s], and modifier[s]) are marked *tr*. Expressions that are intransitive verbs or intransitive verb phrases (an intransitive verb, its auxiliaries, and modifiers) are marked *in*. Other abbreviations are explained in the section titled TERMS AND ABBREVIATIONS.

10. Some expressions that are modifiers (marked *mod.*) can occur before or after the things they modify. Other modifiers can occur both before and after the things they modify. The possible orders of each modifier are illustrated in the examples.

11. Many expressions have more than one major sense or meaning. These meanings are numbered with boldface numerals. For an example, see *cream puff*.

12. Sometimes a numbered sense will have an alternative form that does not apply to the other senses. In such cases the AND and the alternative forms follow the numeral. For an example, see *deduck*.

13. Entry heads that contain unfamiliar words or whose spelling is misleading have an indication of pronunciation in IPA symbols. See the symbols and their values in the PRONUNCIATION GUIDE.

14. In some entries, comments direct the user to other entries for additional information through the use of the terms "compare to," "see," "see also," or "see under." The expressions mentioned are in *slanted sans serif type*.

15. When additional forms of an expression are to be found at another entry head, a comment beginning with "more at ..." is found at the end of the entry. For an example, see *frost*.

16. Many of the examples utilize "eye-dialect" spelling to indicate that certain words are contracted or shortened in the slangy speech style of the examples. These words are *gimme* "give me," *gonna* "going to," *kinda* "kind of," *lemme* "let me," *oughtta* "ought to," *outa* "out of," *sorta* "sort of," *wanna* "want to," and *ya* "you."

PRONUNCIATION GUIDE

Some expressions in the Dictionary are followed by a phonetic transcription in the International Phonetic Alphabet (IPA) symbols. These expressions include words whose pronunciation is not predictable from their spellings, difficult or unfamiliar words, and words where the stress placement is contrastive or unique. The style of pronunciation reflected here is informal and tends to fit the register in which the expression would normally be used. The transcriptions distinguish between [a] and [ɔ] even though not all Americans do so. In strict IPA fashion, [j] rather than the [y] substitute is used for the initial sound in "yellow." The most prominent syllable in a multisyllabic word is *preceded* by the stress mark, ['].
There may be additional prominent or stressed syllables in compounds and phrases, but their weight and placement varies from speaker to speaker and utterance to utterance.

The use of spaces, hyphens, AND, or OR in phonetic transcriptions echoes the use of spaces, hyphens, AND, or OR in the preceding entry heads. The use of "..." in a transcription indicates that easy-to-pronounce words have been omitted from the transcription. Parentheses used in a transcription either correspond to parentheses in the preceding entry head or indicate optional elements in the transcription. For instance, in ['ɑrtsi 'kræf(t)si] "artsy-craftsy," the "t" may or may not be pronounced.

The following chart shows the American English values for each of the IPA symbols used in the phonetic transcriptions. To use the chart, first find the phonetic symbol whose value you want to determine. The two English words to the right of the symbol contain examples of the sound for which the phonetic symbol stands. The letters in boldface type indicate where the sound in question is found in the English word.

[a] { stop / top	[ɚ] { bird / turtle	[m̩] { bottom / chasm	[t] { top / pot
[æ] { sat / track	[f] { feel / if	[n] { new / funny	[tʃ] { cheese / pitcher
[aʊ] { cow / now	[g] { get / frog	[n̩] { button / kitten	[θ] { thin / faith
[aɪ] { bite / my	[h] { hat / who	[ŋ] { bring / thing	[u] { food / blue
[b] { beet / bubble	[i] { feet / leak	[o] { coat / wrote	[U] { put / look
[d] { dead / body	[ɪ] { bit / hiss	[oɪ] { spoil / boy	[v] { save / van
[ð] { that / those	[j] { yellow / you	[ɔ] { caught / yawn	[w] { well / wind
[dʒ] { jail / judge	[k] { can / keep	[p] { tip / pat	[ʌ] { wheel / while
[e] { date / sail	[l] { lawn / yellow	[r] { rat / berry	[z] { fuzzy / zoo
[ɛ] { get / set	[l̩] { bottle / puddle	[s] { sun / fast	[ʒ] { pleasure / treasure
[ə] { but / nut	[m] { family / slam	[ʃ] { fish / sure	['] { 'water / ho'tel

TERMS AND ABBREVIATIONS

□ (a box) marks the beginning of an example.

AND indicates that an entry head has variant forms that are the same or similar in meaning as the entry head. One or more variant forms are preceded by AND.

acronym is a set of initials pronounced as a single word, like *UNESCO*.

black describes an expression typically used by or originated by black Americans.

blend is an expression made up of sounds from two other words, like *smoke + fog = smog*.

California describes an expression originating among the young people of California.

catchphrase describes an expression meant to catch attention because of its cleverness or aptness.

collegiate describes an expression that is typically heard on college campuses.

combining form is a form of a word used only in combination with another word.

compare to   means to consult the entry indicated and examine its form or meaning in relation to the entry head containing the "compare to" instruction.

derogatory   describes an expression that insults, mocks, or abuses someone or a class of people.

elaboration   is an expression that is built on, or is an expansion of, another expression.

entry head   is the first word or phrase, in boldface, of an entry; the word or phrase that the definition explains.

euphemism   is a *euphemistic* expression. See the following.

euphemistic   describes an expression that is used as a substitute for a less acceptable expression.

exclam.   exclamation.

eye-dialect   is a class of spelling variants that attempts to capture colloquial pronunciation or indicates that the person who uttered the words or phrases is illiterate.

function code   is an indication of the grammatical or syntactic potential of a particular sense of an expression. See item 9 in the GUIDE TO THE USE OF THE DICTIONARY   and *exclam., in., interj., interrog., mod., n., phr., prep., pro., sent.,* and *tr.* in this section.

in.   intransitive. Expressions that are intransitive verbs or intransitive verb phrases (an intransitive verb, its auxiliaries, and modifiers) are marked *in.*

interj.   interjection.

interrog.   interrogative.

jocular   describes an expression that is intended to be humorous.

military   describes expressions that are, or were originally, used in the U.S. military services.

mod.   modifier. Expressions serving to modify, restrict, or qualify (adjectives, adjective phrases, adverbs, adverb phrases, etc.) are marked *mod.*

more at   means that an additional, frequently used form of the entry head has its own separate entry. Consult the indicated entry for additional examples or explanation.

n.   nominal. Expressions functioning as nominals (nouns, noun phrases, etc.) are marked *n.*

phr.   phrase.

Pig Latin   is a type of wordplay in which the first consonant of a word or syllable is shifted to the end of the word or syllable and followed by "ay" (phonetic [e]). For example: eep-kay our-yay outh-may ut-shay. [ˈip-ke ˈɚ-je ˈɑʊθ-me ˈət-ʃe]. "Keep your mouth shut!"

play on   refers to wordplay that is based on a particular expression. For instance, "monolithic" is a play on "stoned."

prep.   preposition.

pro.   pronoun.

see   means to turn to the entry indicated.

see also   means to consult the entry indicated for additional information or to find expressions similar in form or meaning to the entry head containing the "see also" instruction.

see under   means to turn to the entry head indicated and look for the phrase you are seeking *within* the entry indicated.

sent.   sentence.

standard English   is the widely known and accepted style or register of English taught in schools.

streets   describes an expression originating in the streets of urban America.

taboo   indicates an expression that is regarded as out of place in public use.

teens   describes an expression used typically—but not exclusively—by teenagers.

term of address   describes an expression that is used to address someone directly.

tr.   transitive. Expressions that are transitive verbs or transitive verb phrases (a transitive verb and its auxiliaries, object[s], and modifier[s]) are marked *tr.*

verbal weapon   describes an expression that is typically used to insult or malign someone.

A

abs [æbz] *n.* the abdominal muscles. (Bodybuilding.) □ *Look at the abs on that guy.* □ *I do sit-ups to harden my abs.*

ace **1.** *mod.* most competent; the best; top-rated. (Said of persons.) □ *She is an ace reporter with the newspaper.* □ *Frank is an ace swimmer.* **2.** *tr.* to pass a test easily, with an A grade. □ *Man, I really aced that test.* □ *I knew I wouldn't ace it, but I never thought I'd flunk it!* **3.** *tr.* to surpass someone or something; to beat someone or something; to ace someone out. □ *The Japanese firm aced the Americans by getting the device onto the shelves first.* □ *Fred aced Tom in the contest for the best beard.* (More at **aced**.)

aced [est] *mod.* outmaneuvered; outscored. □ *Rebecca really got aced in the track meet.* □ *"You are aced, sucker!" shouted Rebecca as she passed Martha in the 100-yard sprint.*

ace in(to something) *in.* to happen onto something good; to manage to get into something. □ *I hope I can ace into the afternoon physics class.* □ *I don't know how I aced in. I guess I was just lucky.*

ace out *in.* to be fortunate or lucky. □ *I really aced out on that test in English.* □ *Freddy aced out at the dentist's office with only one cavity.*

ace someone out AND **ace out someone** *tr.* to maneuver someone out; to win out over someone. (See also ace.) □ *Martha aced*

1

out Rebecca to win the first-place trophy. □ *I plan to ace you out in the first lap.* (More at **aced**.)

action **1.** *n.* excitement; activity in general; whatever is happening. □ *This place is dull. I want some action.* □ *How do I find out where the action is in this town?* **2.** *n.* a share of something; a share of the winnings or of the booty. □ *I did my share of the work, and I want my share of the action.* □ *Just what did you do to earn any of the action?*

adios muchachos [adi'os mu'tʃatʃos] *phr.* "the end"; "good-bye, everyone." (Spanish. See examples.) □ *If you step out in front of a car like that again, it's adios muchachos.* □ *I've got a gun aimed at your navel. If you move so much as one muscle, you can just say adios muchachos.*

aggie ['ægi] **1.** *mod.* agricultural. □ *She spent a year at some aggie college, but didn't like it.* □ *Her aggie interests faded fast.* **2.** *n.* a student of an agricultural (college) training program. (Specifically, Texas A. and M. University.) □ *More and more aggies are going back for their M.B.A.s.* □ *What kind of a job can an aggie get these days?*

air-bags *n.* the lungs. □ *Fill those air-bags with good Colorado air!* □ *I've had a cold or something in my air-bags for about three days now.*

air ball *n.* a basketball throw that misses everything, especially the goal. □ *Old Fred has become a master with the air ball. The net will never get worn out.* □ *Another air ball for Fred Wilson. That's his fourth tonight.*

airbrain See *airhead*.

air guitar *n.* an imaginary guitar, played along with real music or instead of real music. □ *Dave stood near the window while his roommate played air guitar in front of the mirror.* □ *Jed, who sees himself as some sort of rock star, plays air guitar when he's happy or sad.*

airhead AND **airbrain** *n.* a stupid person. (Someone with air where there should be brains. Compare to *smurfbrain*.) □ *What is that loony airhead doing there on the roof?* □ *Some airbrain put mustard in the ketchup squeezer.*

air hose *n.* invisible socks; no socks. □ *All these kids run around campus in air hose. You'd think they'd get blisters.* □ *How do you like my new air hose? One size fits all.*

alley apple **1.** *n.* a lump of horse manure. (See also *road apple*.) □ *The route of the parade was littered with alley apples after about 20 minutes.* □ *Harry is collecting alley apples for his garden. It's great fertilizer.* **2.** *n.* a brick or stone found in the rubble of the streets. (Especially a stone that might be thrown.) □ *"Drop it!" the cop called to the kid with an alley apple in his hand.* □ *Kelly kicked an alley apple so that it struck a garbage can with a metallic crash.*

all-nighter **1.** *n.* something that lasts all night, like a party or study session. □ *After an all-nighter studying, I couldn't keep my eyes open for the test.* □ *Sam invited us to an all-nighter, but we're getting a little old for that kind of thing.* **2.** *n.* a place of business that is open all night. (Usually a cafe or similar place.) □ *We stopped at an all-nighter for a cup of coffee.* □ *I worked in an all-nighter for a month. I just couldn't keep those hours though.* **3.** *n.* a person who stays up all night often or habitually. □ *Fred is an all-nighter. He's not worth much in the mornings though.* □ *I'm no all-nighter. I need my beauty sleep, for sure.*

all wet *mod.* completely wrong. □ *Wrong again! You're really all wet.* □ *If you think I'm going to take that kind of talk from you, you're all wet.*

amigo [ə'migo] *n.* a friend. (Spanish. Also a term of address.) □ *Me and my amigo here want to rent a couple of horses.* □ *Hey, amigo, let's go somewhere for a drink.*

ammo ['æmo] **1.** *n.* ammunition. □ *There they were, trapped in a foxhole with no ammo, enemy all over the place. What do you* *think happened?* □ *I don't know. They sent out for ammo, maybe?* **2.** *n.* information or evidence that can be used to support an argument or a charge. □ *I want to get some ammo on the mayor. I think he's a crook.* □ *Try to keep my traffic tickets a secret. The opposition will use them as ammo in the next election.*

ammunition **1.** *n.* toilet tissue. □ *Could somebody help me? We're out of ammunition in here!* □ *The ammunition in Europe is better these days than it used to be.* **2.** *n.* liquor. (See also **shot**.) □ *The cowboy walked in, downed a shot, and called for more ammunition.* □ *He's had about all the ammunition he can hold.*

animal *n.* a male who acts like a beast in terms of manners, cleanliness, or sexual aggressiveness. (Also a term of address.) □ *You are nothing but an animal!* □ *Stop picking your nose, animal.*

ankle **1.** *n.* an attractive woman. (Typically with *some.* More in appreciation than derogation.) □ *Now, there's some ankle I've never seen around here before.* □ *Do you get ankle like that around here all the time?* **2.** *in.* to walk away from one's employment; to leave or quit work permanently. (Compare to *walk.*) □ *One more day like this, and I'm gonna ankle.* □ *I didn't fire her. I told her she could ankle if she wanted.*

antifreeze *n.* liquor; any legal or illegal alcohol. □ *With enough antifreeze, I can stand the cold.* □ *Here's some antifreeze to stop your teeth from chattering.*

A-number-one See *A-one.*

A-O.K. ['e'o'ke] *mod.* in the best of condition. □ *I really feel A-O.K.* □ *Show me the most A-O.K. canary you have.*

A-one AND **A-number-one** ['e-'wən AND 'e-'nəmbɚ-'wən] *mod.* of the highest rating. □ *This steak is really A-one!* □ *I would like to get an A-number-one secretary for a change.*

ape hangers *n.* long steering handles on a bicycle or motorcycle. □ *Who is that guy riding the bike with ape hangers?* □ *Aren't ape hangers sort of dangerous?*

apple *n.* a baseball. □ *Jim slammed the apple over the plate, but the ump called it a ball.* □ *Just when I raised my arm to throw to second, the damn apple slipped out of my hand and rolled down my arm. Now, explain that!*

ark [ɑrk] *n.* an old car, especially a big one. □ *Why don't you get rid of that old ark and get something that's easier to park?* □ *This ark is the most comfortable car I've ever had. I'll drive it till it falls apart.*

armpit *n.* any undesirable place, described as a human armpit. (A nickname for an undesirable town or city.) □ *Who wants to spend a weekend in an armpit?* □ *I won't stay another minute in this armpit!*

[artist] See *con artist, off artist, rip-off artist.*

asphalt jungle *n.* the paved landscape of the city; the city viewed as a savage place. □ *I don't look forward to spending the rest of my days in an asphalt jungle.* □ *I want to go back to Kansas. I hate the asphalt jungle.*

ass **1.** *n.* the buttocks. (Caution with **ass**. There are additional taboo meanings.) □ *Careful! You'll fall on your ass!* □ *Shut up or I'll kick you in the ass!* **2.** *n.* a worthless person; a despised person. □ *You can be such an ass!* □ *Who is that stupid ass with the funny hat?*

attic *n.* the head, thought of as the location of one's intellect. □ *She's just got nothing in the attic. That's what's wrong with her.* □ *Ken has an attic full of fear and resentment he needs to clean out before he will feel comfortable again.*

avs [ævz] *n.* chance; the law of averages. (Streets. Always with the.) □ *The avs say that I ought to be dead by now.* □ *It looks like the avs finally caught up with him.*

awesome **1.** *exclam.* "Great!"; "Excellent!" (Usually **Awesome!** Standard English, but slang when overused.) □ *You own that gorgeous car? Awesome!* □ *Awesome! I'm impressed.* **2.** *mod.* impressive. □ *Let me have a look at this awesome new stereo of yours.* □ *That thing is really awesome.*

B

(baby) boomer *n.* someone born during the baby boom—from the last years of World War II until the early 1960s. □ *When the baby boomers get around to saving up for retirement, you're going to see a lot more investment scams.* □ *At about age 45 the boomers will start putting money away.*

back-ender See *rear-ender.*

back up *in.* to refuse to go through with something; to back out (of something). □ *Fred backed up at the last minute, leaving me with 20 pounds of hot dogs.* □ *Don't back up now, man. It's too late.*

bacon *n.* the police; a police officer. (Black. Compare to *pig.* See also *What's shakin' (bacon)?*) □ *Keep an eye out for the bacon.* □ *The bacon's hassling me!*

bad **1.** *mod.* powerful; intense. (Black.) □ *Man, that is really bad music!* □ *This grass is bad!* **2.** *mod.* suitable; excellent. (Black.) □ *I got some new silks that are really bad.* □ *That is a bad man dancing there.*

bad rap **1.** *n.* a false criminal charge. □ *Freddy got stuck with a bad rap.* □ *All those guys get nothing but bad raps. Nobody's ever guilty.* **2.** *n.* a bad reputation. □ *This car has gotten a bad rap, and I don't know why.* □ *Butter has been getting sort of a bad rap lately.*

bagged 1. AND **in the bag** *mod.* alcohol intoxicated. □ *How can anybody be so bagged on four beers?* □ *She just sat there and got bagged.* **2.** *mod.* arrested. □ *"You are bagged," said the officer, clapping a hand on the suspect's shoulder.* □ *"I'm not bagged yet, copper," said the crook.*

Bag it! **1.** *exclam.* "Drop dead!" (California. See also *Bag your face!*) □ *You are not rad, and you are not awesome, so, like, bag it!* □ *Bag it yourself!* **2.** *exclam.* "Shut up!" □ *Bag it! I'm reading.* □ *Oh, bag it! I've heard enough.*

bag some rays See *catch some rays.*

Bag your face! *exclam.* "Go away!" (See also *Bag it!*) □ *You outrage me. Bag your face!* □ *You are always in the way. Beat it! Bag your face!*

ball (See the entry that follows and *B-ball, V-ball, air ball, drop the ball, eyeball, goofball, sleazeball, slimeball, sludgeball, whole ball of wax.*) **1.** *n.* a wild time at a party; a good time. □ *We really had a ball. Good-bye.* □ *Your birthday party was a ball!* **2.** *in.* to enjoy oneself. □ *The whole crowd was balling and having a fine time.* □ *We balled the whole evening.* **3.** *n.* a testicle. (Usually plural. Caution with *ball.*) □ *He got hit right in the balls.* □ *The teacher preferred "testicles" to "balls," if they had to be mentioned at all.*

balled up AND **balled-up** *mod.* confused; mixed up. □ *That dame is so balled up she doesn't know anything.* □ *This is really a balled-up mess you've made.*

bang **1.** *n.* a bit of excitement; a thrill; some amusement. □ *We got a bang out of your letter.* □ *What a bang the party was!* **2.** *n.* the degree of potency of the alcohol in liquor. □ *This stuff has quite a bang!* □ *The bang is gone from this wine.*

bang for the buck *n.* value for the money spent; excitement for the money spent; the cost-to-benefit ratio. □ *I didn't get anywhere near the bang for the buck I expected.* □ *How much bang* *for the buck did you really think you would get from a 12-year-old car—at any price?*

bang-up   *mod.* really excellent. □ *We had a bang-up time at your bash.* □ *I like to throw a bang-up party once or twice a year.* □ *Another bang-up day at the factory!*

banjaxed   ['bændʒækst] **1.** *mod.* demolished; ruined. □ *My car is totally banjaxed. What a mess!* □ *Everything I worked for is now banjaxed.* **2.** *mod.* alcohol intoxicated. □ *She just sat there and got banjaxed.* □ *All four of them went out and got banjaxed.*

barf   [barf] **1.** *in.* to empty one's stomach; to vomit. □ *I think I'm going to barf!* □ *Don't barf here.* **2.** *n.* vomit. □ *Is that barf on your shoe?* □ *Whatever it is, it looks like barf.* **3.** *in.* [for a computer] to fail to function. □ *The whole system barfed about noon, and all the data was lost.* □ *My little computer barfs about once a day. Something is wrong.*

Barf out!   *exclam.* "This is awful!"; "This is unacceptable!" (California.) □ *Look at that jerk! Barf out!* □ *Barf out! Get a life!*

barf-out   *n.* an unpleasant person or thing. □ *What a barf-out! I want my money back.* □ *That guy is a real barf-out.*

barf someone out AND **barf out someone**   *tr.* to disgust someone. (California.) □ *This whole scene like, so, like, barfs me out.* □ *The movie barfed out everybody in the theater.*

base   *mod.* rude; *gross.* (California.) □ *You are so, like, base!* □ *What a base creep!* □ *Oh, how base!*

bashed   [bæʃt] **1.** *mod.* crushed; struck. □ *His poor car was bashed beyond recognition.* □ *Give me that bashed one, and I'll straighten it out.* **2.** *mod.* alcohol intoxicated. □ *All four of them went out and got bashed.* □ *I've never seen anybody so bashed.*

bashing *n.* criticizing; defaming. (A combining form that follows the name of the person or thing being criticized.) □ *I am sick of your college-bashing!* □ *I hope you'll excuse the quarterback-bashing, but some of these guys don't play fair.* □ *On T.V. they had a long session of candidate-bashing, and then they read the sports news.*

bazillion [bəˈzɪljən] *n.* an indefinite enormous number. □ *Ernie gave me a bazillion good reasons why he shouldn't do it.* □ *Next year's bazillion-dollar budget should make things even worse.*

bazoo [ˈbɑˈzu OR bəˈzu] **1.** *n.* a jeer; a *raspberry*. □ *They gave Ted the old bazoo when he fumbled the ball.* □ *A chorus of bazoos and hoots rebuked the coach when he threw the chair on the court.* **2.** *n.* the mouth. □ *You would have to open your big bazoo and tell everything.* □ *Don't talk with a full bazoo.*

B-ball *n.* basketball; a basketball. (See also *hoops*. Compare to *V-ball*.) □ *Let's go play some B-ball.* □ *Toss me the B-ball, huh?*

bean **1.** *n.* the head. (See also *biscuit*.) □ *I got a bump right here on my bean.* □ *Put your cap on your bean and cruise.* **2.** *tr.* to hit someone on the head. □ *Some lady beaned me with her umbrella.* □ *A board fell off the scaffold and beaned the worker below.*

bean-counter *n.* a statistician; an accountant. □ *When the bean-counters get finished with the numbers, you won't recognize them.* □ *The bean-counters predict a recession sometime in the next decade.*

beans **1.** *n.* nothing. □ *You act like you don't know beans about it.* □ *I have nothing I can give you. Nothing, zotz, beans!* **2.** *n.* nonsense. □ *Come on, talk straight. No more beans!* □ *Stop feeding me beans.*

bean time *n.* dinnertime. □ *Hey, you guys! It's bean time!* □ *I'm hungry. When's bean time around here?*

beast **1.** *n.* an ugly person. □ *Who is that beast with the big hat?* □ *That beast should give the monkey back its face before it bumps into something.* **2.** *n.* a crude, violent, or sexually aggressive male; an *animal*. □ *That beast scares the hell out of me.* □ *Oh, Martin, you're such a beast!* **3.** *n.* liquor. □ *I feel a little overcome by the beast.* □ *Pour me some more of that beast.*

beasty *mod.* undesirable; *yucky*. (California.) □ *You are like, so like, beasty!* □ *I can't stand that gross beasty jerk!*

beat **1.** *mod.* exhausted; worn-out. □ *I'm just beat!* □ *The whole family was beat after the game.* **2.** *mod.* down and out; ruined. (From *beat up*.) □ *This thing is beat. I don't want it.* □ *Who wants a beat hat?* **3.** *mod.* broke. □ *Man, I'm beat. I got no copper, no bread.* □ *All we need is another beat mouth to feed.*

beat box *n.* the person who provides the (verbal) rhythmic beat in a rap song. □ *What makes him sound so good is his beat box.* □ *Let me be the beat box this time.*

beater *n.* a junky old car. □ *I like my old beater even if it has no bumpers.* □ *I want an old beater that doesn't cost more than 800 bucks.*

beautiful *mod.* very satisfying; excellent. □ *This wine is really beautiful!* □ *Man, this place is beautiful. You got your own sink and toilet right in the room and good strong bars to keep the riff-raff out.*

beefcake **1.** *n.* a display of the male physique. (Compare to *cheesecake*.) □ *There was some beefcake at the party just to liven things up.* □ *There was one calendar showing beefcake rather than the usual cheesecake.* **2.** *n.* a muscularly handsome male. □ *She's been going out with a real beefcake.* □ *I prefer skinny guys to a beefcake.*

beemer ['bimɚ] *n.* a B.M.W. automobile. □ *I had to sell my beemer when the stock market crashed.* □ *Tiffany's beemer was leased, but no one was supposed to know.*

beerbong ['bɪrbɔŋ] **1.** *n.* a can of beer prepared for drinking in one gulp. (An opening is made in the bottom of a can of beer. The can, with the opening placed in the mouth, is turned upright, and the tab opener is pulled, releasing all the beer directly into the mouth.) □ *Do you know how to make a beerbong?* □ *A beerbong is a great way to liven up a party.* **2.** *in.* to drink beer as described in sense 1. □ *Those guys who were beerbonging all barfed after it was over.* □ *I tried beerbonging once, just once.*

begathon *n.* a televised appeal for contributions, especially as conducted by U.S. public television stations. □ *It seems like this station is one long begathon all year long.* □ *They made two million in the begathon last month.*

beige [beʒ] *mod.* boring; insipid. (California. See also *vanilla.*) □ *The party is beige. Let's cruise.* □ *Let's blow this beige joint!* □ *This day is way beige! Bag it!*

belly-up **1.** *mod.* alcohol intoxicated. □ *Sylvia was boiled— belly-up—glassy-eyed.* □ *After four beers, I was belly-up, for sure.* **2.** *mod.* dead. (See also *turn belly-up.*) □ *That's the end. This company is belly-up.* □ *After the fire, the firm went belly-up.*

bench **1.** *tr.* to take someone out of a ball game. □ *The coach benched Jim, who injured his arm.* □ *If you don't stop fouling, I'll bench you!* **2.** *tr.* to retire someone; to withdraw someone from something. □ *I worked as a bridge painter for 25 years until they benched me.* □ *The manager benched the entire sales staff for cheating on their expense reports.*

bench jockey *n.* a player who sits on the bench and calls out advice. □ *The coach told all the bench jockeys to shut up.* □ *Do what you are told, or be a bench jockey for the rest of the season!*

bench warmer *n.* a ballplayer who spends most of the game on the bench waiting to play; a second-rate player. □ *You'll never be anything but a bench warmer.* □ *I do what I'm told so I can play every game. I don't want to be a bench warmer.*

benies *n.* benefits. □ *The salary is good, but the benies are almost nonexistent.* □ *Are retirement contributions one of your benies?*

bent 1. *mod.* alcohol or drug intoxicated. □ *I've never seen two guys so bent.* □ *I can get bent on a glass of wine.* 2. *mod.* dishonest; crooked. □ *I'm afraid that Paul is a little bent. He cheats on his taxes.* □ *A lot of those officeholders get bent in office—if they weren't before.* 3. *mod.* angry. □ *He was so bent there was steam coming out of his ears.* □ *Come on, don't get bent. I was only kidding.*

biffy ['bɪfi] *n.* a toilet. □ *Where's the biffy?* □ *The house we toured has a pink biffy. Can you believe it?*

biggie 1. *n.* something or someone important. □ *This one's a biggie. Treat him well.* □ *As problems go, this one's a biggie.* 2. *n.* copulation. (Usually with *the.*) □ *But I don't think I'm ready for the biggie.* □ *He wanted to do the biggie!*

big gun *n.* an important and powerful person, such as the officers of a company. (Often with *bring in* as in the example.) □ *It went up to the big guns, who said no immediately.* □ *I knew they would bring in the big guns at the last minute.*

big iron *n.* a large, mainframe computer. (Computers. See *iron.*) □ *We'll have to run this job on the big iron over at the university.* □ *What kind of big iron do they have over there?*

big mouth 1. *n.* a person who talks too much or too loudly; someone who tells secrets. (Also a term of address.) □ *Okay, big mouth! Shut up!* □ *Tell that big mouth to shut up.* 2. *tr.* to spread secrets around. □ *Why do you always have to big mouth everything around?* □ *Don't you big mouth this to anyone, but I'm going to have a baby.*

big noise 1. *n.* an important person. □ *If you're such a big noise, why don't you get this line moving?* □ *She's the big noise in Washington right now.* 2. *n.* the important current news; the current scandal. ☐ *What's the big noise around town now?* ☐ *There's a big noise up on Capitol Hill. Something about budget cuts.*

big stink *n.* a major issue; a scandal; a big argument. ☐ *There was a big stink made about my absence.* ☐ *Don't make such a big stink about it.*

biker *n.* a motorcycle rider. ☐ *Four bikers roared by and woke up the baby.* ☐ *That biker is wearing about a dozen earrings.*

billie AND **bill(y)** ['bɪli] *n.* a piece of paper money. (California.) ☐ *Do you have any billies on you?* ☐ *Nope, no billies on me.*

bill(y) See the previous entry.

bimbo ['bɪmbo] **1.** *n.* a clown-like person. ☐ *What a silly bimbo!* ☐ *If that bimbo doesn't keep quiet, I'll bop him.* **2.** *n.* a giddy woman; a sexually loose woman. ☐ *So she's a bimbo. She still has rights. Have a heart!* ☐ *Now the bimbo is a star in the movies.*

bird-dog **1.** *tr.* to take away another man's girlfriend. ☐ *Why'd you have to go and bird-dog me, your best buddy?* ☐ *I didn't bird-dog you. I'm just more lovable, that's all.* **2.** *tr.* to supervise someone; to tail someone. ☐ *I wish you would stop bird-dogging me!* ☐ *Marlowe knew somebody was bird-dogging him, but he was too smart to show it.*

birdseed **1.** *n.* a small amount of money. ☐ *That's just birdseed compared to what I spend.* ☐ *Forty billion is birdseed to a government with a 600 billion dollar budget.* **2.** *n.* nonsense. (Based on the *B.S.* of birdseed.) ☐ *Cut the birdseed. I'm not stupid, you know.* ☐ *I've heard enough birdseed here to last for a lifetime.*

biscuit ['bɪskət] *n.* the head. (See also *bean*.) ☐ *She got a nasty little bump on the biscuit.* ☐ *He wears a helmet on his biscuit in case he tumbles.*

bit-bucket *n.* the imaginary place where lost computer data goes. (Computers.) □ *I guess my data went into the bit-bucket.* □ *I bet the bit-bucket is filled with some of the best stuff in the world.*

bitch 1. *n.* a derogatory term for a woman. (A verbal weapon.) □ *The stupid bitch doesn't know from nothing.* □ *You bitch! Stop it!* **2.** *in.* to complain. (Caution with *bitch.* See also *pitch a bitch.*) □ *You are always bitching!* □ *If I couldn't bitch, I would blow my top.* **3.** *n.* a difficult thing or person. (Caution with *bitch.*) □ *Life's a bitch.* □ *This algebra problem is a real bitch.*

(bitchen-)twitchen ['bɪtʃn̩'twɪtʃn̩] *mod.* excellent. (California.) □ *This is a bitchen-twitchen way to boogie.* □ *She is like, twitchen!*

bitchin' AND **bitchen** ['bɪtʃn̩] **1.** *mod.* excellent; great; classy. □ *This is a totally bitchin' pair of jeans!* □ *This is a way bitchen rally, my man!* **2.** *exclam.* "Terrific!" (Usually **Bitchin'!**) □ *Bitchin'! Let's do it again!* □ *Four of them? Bitchen!*

bitch of a someone or something *n.* a really difficult person or thing. (Caution with *bitch.*) □ *What a bitch of a day!* □ *He is really a bitch of a boss.*

bitch session *n.* an informal gathering where people gripe and air their grievances. (Caution with *bitch.*) □ *The bitch session went on for 40 minutes.* □ *I learned never to open my mouth in those office bitch sessions.*

bitchy ['bɪtʃi] *mod.* spiteful; moody; rude; complaining. (Caution with *bitch.*) □ *Don't be so bitchy!* □ *Who needs a house full of bitchy kids?*

Bite the ice! *exclam.* "Go to hell!" □ *If that's what you think, you can just bite the ice!* □ *Get a life! Bite the ice!*

blade 1. *n.* a knife. □ *Bring your blade over here and cut this loose.* □ *What are you carrying a blade for?* **2.** *n.* a young man, witty and worldly. □ *One of those blades kept winking at me.* □

A couple of blades from the international jet set ordered vintage wine for everyone.

blaster, (ghetto) See *(ghetto) blaster.*

blimp *n.* a nickname for an obese person. (Cruel.) □ *Look at that blimp who just came in.* □ *This enormous blimp managed to get on the plane, but couldn't get into a seat.*

blimp out *in.* to overeat. □ *I love to buy a bag of chips and just blimp out.* □ *I only blimp out on weekends.*

blinkers *n.* the eyes. □ *As I opened my blinkers, guess who I saw?* □ *Look at those sexy blinkers!*

blissed (out) AND **blissed-out** [blɪst...] **1.** *mod.* in a state of emotional bliss. □ *After the second movement, I was totally blissed out.* □ *What a blissed-out dame!* □ *I know a gal who can get blissed from a sunset.* **2.** *mod.* alcohol or drug intoxicated. □ *She is more than blissed. She is stoned.* □ *My friend is a little blissed out. Can she rest here?*

bliss ninny ['blɪs 'nɪni] *n.* a giddy and disoriented person; a *blissed-out* person. (See *blissed (out).*) □ *You silly bliss ninny! Who watches over you, anyway?* □ *Tiffany is such a bliss ninny —all heart though.*

bliss out *in.* to become euphoric. □ *I blissed out just because it is spring and I am with you.* □ *I always bliss out from talk like that, but I still love Wally.* (More at *blissed (out).*)

blitz [blɪts] **1.** *n.* a devastating attack. □ *After that blitz from the boss, you must feel sort of shaken.* □ *That's my second blitz this week. I feel like London.* **2.** *tr.* to attack and defeat someone or something. □ *Two of your friends came by and blitzed my refrigerator.* □ *The team from downstate blitzed our local team for the third year in a row.*

blitzed (out) [blɪtst…] *mod.* alcohol or drug intoxicated. □ *To say she is blitzed out is putting it mildly!* □ *I want to go out and get totally blitzed. I'll show her who's in charge!*

blivit ['blɪvət] *n.* someone or something annoying and unnecessary. □ *The dame's a blivit. She adds up to one too many.* □ *Don't be a blivit. Just calm down.*

blixed ['blɪkst] *mod.* mildly drug intoxicated. □ *He was a little blixed when I last saw him.* □ *He has been blixed for hours.*

blooey ['bluɪ] **1.** *mod.* gone; destroyed. □ *Everything is finished, blooey!* □ *All my plans are blooey!* **2.** *mod.* alcohol intoxicated. □ *Reggie is totally blooey. He can't even open his eyes.* □ *Man, I'm blooey. I'm stoned to the bones.*

blotto ['blɑdo] *mod.* alcohol intoxicated; dead drunk. □ *Let's get some beer and get blotto.* □ *She just lay there—blotto.*

blow **1.** *tr. & in.* to leave (someplace) in a hurry. □ *It's late. I gotta blow.* □ *They blew this place before you got here.* **2.** *tr.* to ruin something; to ruin an opportunity. □ *You really blew it!* □ *It was my last chance, and I blew it.* **3.** *tr.* to waste money; to spend money. □ *Mary blew 40 bucks on a second-hand radio.* □ *We blew it all at a fancy restaurant.*

blow a fuse AND **blow one's fuse, blow a gasket, blow one's cork, blow one's lid, blow one's top** *tr.* to explode with anger; to lose one's temper. □ *Come on, don't blow a fuse.* □ *Go ahead, blow a gasket! What good will that do?*

blow a hype *tr.* to overreact; to **spaz out.** □ *I was afraid she would blow a hype about the broken window.* □ *Come on, don't blow a hype. It's only a car.*

blow beets *tr.* to empty one's stomach; to vomit. □ *What was in that stew? I feel like I gotta blow beets.* □ *She wasted a few minutes blowing beets, just to make things worse.*

blow chunks *tr.* to empty one's stomach; to vomit. (Collegiate.) □ *Wilson Food Service strikes again. Time to blow chunks.* □ *The stuff makes me blow chunks every time I get near it.*

Blow it out your ear! *exclam.* "Go away!"; "I don't believe it!" □ *Oh, blow it out your ear, you twit!* □ *You are not way rad, you're just way out, jerk! Blow it out your ear!*

blown away *mod.* overwhelmed; greatly impressed. (Often with *with* or *by*.) □ *We were just blown away by your good words.* □ *Like it? I was blown away.*

blow off **1.** *in.* to goof off; to waste time; to procrastinate. □ *You blow off too much.* □ *All your best time is gone—blown off.* **2.** *n.* a time-waster; a *goof-off.* (Usually **blow-off.**) □ *Fred is such a blow-off!* □ *Get busy. I don't pay blow-offs around here.* **3.** *n.* the final insult; an event that causes a dispute. (Usually **blow-off.**) □ *The blow-off was a call from some dame named Monica who asked for Snookums.* □ *When the blow-off happened, nobody was expecting anything.*

blow one's cookies *tr.* to empty one's stomach; to vomit. □ *I think I'm going to blow my cookies.* □ *Okay, if any of you guys gotta blow your cookies or something, do it outside, not here!*

blow one's cool *tr.* to become angry. (Compare to *keep one's cool.*) □ *Now, now, don't blow your cool.* □ *I almost blew my cool when the dog wet on my pants leg.*

blow one's doughnuts AND **lose one's doughnuts** [... 'donəts] *tr.* to empty one's stomach; to vomit. □ *The stuff was so vile, I thought I would blow my doughnuts.* □ *Who lost their doughnuts in the hall?*

blow one's groceries *tr.* to empty one's stomach; to vomit. □ *I gotta blow my groceries. Look out!* □ *She blew her groceries all over the front seat.*

blow (one's) lunch AND **lose one's lunch** *tr.* to empty one's stomach; to vomit. □ *I almost lost my lunch, I ran so hard.* □ *I wanted to blow my lunch, that's how rotten I felt.*

Blow on it! *exclam.* "Cool it!"; "Take it easy!" (As if one were trying to cool something by blowing on it.) □ *It's all right, Tom. Blow on it!* □ *Hey, man. Relax. Blow on it!*

blow smoke *tr.* to state something in a way that conceals the truth. □ *She is a master at blowing smoke. She belongs in government.* □ *When they began to figure him out, he began to blow smoke.*

blow someone away AND **blow away someone** *tr.* to overwhelm someone. □ *The music about blew me away.* □ *The whole idea just blew her away.*

blow someone or something off AND **blow off someone or something** **1.** *tr.* to neglect or ignore someone or something. □ *Get it done now. Don't blow it off!* □ *Don't blow me off. Listen! I want it done now!* **2.** *tr.* [with *someone*] to cheat someone; to deceive someone. □ *They blew off a young couple and conned a hundred bucks out of them.* □ *Don't try to blow me off! I know what's what.*

blow someone's doors off *tr.* to defeat someone; to surpass someone. (As if someone were going by another vehicle on the highway at such a high speed that the doors would be blown off in passing.) □ *We're gonna really blow your doors off in the next game.* □ *They blew our doors off in sales last year.*

blow Z's [...ziz] *tr.* to sleep. (See also *catch some Z's, cut some Z's.*) □ *I got to blow Z's for a while; then we'll talk.* □ *Him? Oh, he's in the back blowing Z's.*

boat **1.** *n.* a big shoe. □ *Whose boat is that under the coffee table?* □ *Those boats are special made, in fact.* **2.** *n.* a big car; a full-size car. □ *I don't want to drive a big boat like that.* □ *How do you stop that boat? Throw out an anchor?*

bod [bɑd] **1.** *n.* a body, especially a nice body. □ *You got a nice bod, Tom.* □ *If you got a good bod and enough money, why are you so depressed?* **2.** *n.* a person. □ *How many bods are coming over tonight?* □ *Who's the bod with the tight slacks?*

boff [bɑf] **1.** *tr.* to punch someone. □ *I was afraid she was going to boff me.* □ *Ted boffed Harry playfully.* **2.** *in.* to empty one's stomach; to vomit. (See also *barf*.) □ *She boffed and boffed, until she was exhausted.* □ *I think I'm gonna boff!*

boffo [ˈbɑfo] **1.** *n.* a box-office hit; a successful play, musical, movie, etc. □ *The last one was a tremendous boffo, but we only broke even.* □ *I need a boffo just once in my life.* **2.** *mod.* successful; tremendous. □ *We had a boffo time at your rally.* □ *Another boffo success for Wally!* □ *That was really boffo!*

bogue [bog] *mod.* bogus; fake. □ *Keep your bogue gold watch. I don't want it!* □ *She is so, like, bogue!*

bokoo AND **boku** [ˈboˈku] *mod.* many. (A play on French *beaucoup*.) □ *I've got bokoo things to do today.* □ *There are already boku people invited.*

boku See the previous entry.

bomb **1.** *n.* a bad performance or an inherently bad show. □ *They tried as hard as they could, but the thing was a bomb from act one on.* □ *The latest bomb on Broadway, like all bombs, will only go off once. This one finished to a chorus of boos before the final curtain.* **2.** *in.* to fail. □ *My first try bombed, but things got better.* □ *It bombed the minute the first curtain went up.* **3.** AND **bomb out** *in.* [for a computer program] to fail. □ *You expect a program to bomb a time or two.* □ *The whole thing bombed out at just the wrong time.*

bombed (out) *mod.* alcohol or drug intoxicated. □ *They were bombed and looked nearly dead.* □ *How can I drive when I'm bombed out?*

bomb out See under *bomb*.

bonehead **1.** *n.* a stupid or stubborn person. □ *You are such a bonehead when it comes to buying cars!* □ *Don't be a bonehead! Cooperate!* **2.** AND **boneheaded** *mod.* stupid; stubborn. □ *Of all the boneheaded things to do!* □ *Why am I married to the world's greatest, all-time bonehead klutz?* □ *Don't be so boneheaded!* **3.** *mod.* suitable for a stupid person. □ *Are you signed up for that bonehead course?* □ *I only read bonehead books—and only those with pictures.*

boneheaded See under *bonehead*.

bones **1.** *n.* dice. □ *Toss me the bones and get out your checkbook.* □ *Throw them bones and hope for the best.* **2.** *n.* a nickname for a physician. (From *sawbones*. Also the nickname of the doctor on the starship *Enterprise* of Star Trek fame. Also a term of address.) □ *Look, bones, I just can't lose weight!* □ *This is quite a cut. You'll have to go over to the bones in Adamsville.*

bonkers ['bɔŋkɚz] **1.** AND **crackers** *mod.* insane; crazy. □ *Get this bonkers brother of yours out of here!* □ *I think I am going bonkers.* **2.** *mod.* slightly intoxicated. □ *I'm just a little bonkers, nothing really serious.* □ *She's too bonkers to drive.*

bonzo ['bɑnzo] *mod.* crazy. □ *You are completely bonzo!* □ *I want out of this bonzo place!*

boo-bird ['bubɚd] *n.* a person who boos frequently at games or other public events. □ *It was a big day for the boo-birds at Wrigley Field.* □ *The catcher turned and stared right at the loud-mouthed boo-bird. Everybody knew what he was thinking.*

boo-boo ['bubu] *n.* an error. □ *It's only a small boo-boo. Don't stress yourself.* □ *Another boo-boo like that, and you are through.*

boob-tube ['bubtub] *n.* a television set. □ *You spend too much time in front of the boob-tube.* □ *What's on the boob-tube to-night?*

boody AND **boodie, bootie** ['budi] *n.* the buttocks. (Caution with topic.) □ *Look at the nice little boody on that guy.* □ *Get your boodie out on that dance floor and shake it.*

boogie ['bugi OR 'bʊgi] **1.** *n.* a kind of rock dance. □ *I didn't like the boogie until I learned how to do it right.* □ *The boogie will tire you out, but good.* **2.** *in.* to dance rock-style. □ *I don't like to boogie.* □ *I'm too old to boogie.* **3.** *n.* a party where the *boogie* is danced. □ *There's a boogie over at Steve's tonight.* □ *One more boogie like that one, and I'm through for the year.* **4.** *in.* to get down to work; to get down to business. □ *All right, it's time to boogie. Cool it!* □ *The whistle blew. Time to boogie.*

boogie-board ['bugibord OR 'bʊgibord] **1.** *n.* a surfboard. (California.) □ *Get your boogie-board out there in that tube.* □ *She cracked her boogie-board apart on that big one.* **2.** *n.* a skateboard. (Teens.) □ *He fell off his boogie-board and broke his tailbone.* □ *Can you imagine a boogie-board costing 600 dollars?*

book **1.** *in.* to leave. □ *Time's up. Gotta book.* □ *Let's book. I'm late.* **2.** *tr.* to charge someone with a crime. □ *The cop booked him for vagrancy.* □ *She looked sort of messy, and they wanted to book her for something, but didn't know what.* **3.** *in.* to study. □ *I gotta book. Bye.* □ *I hate to have to book all night.*

boom box *n.* a portable stereo radio. (See also *box.*) □ *Turn down that damn boom box, or I'll kick it in.* □ *Hey, man! Do you even take your boom box to church?*

boom sticks *n.* drumsticks. (Musicians.) □ *He always carries his boom sticks in his back pocket, and he beats on walls, radiators, desks—you name it.* □ *I need new boom sticks. They keep breaking.*

booster *n.* a shoplifter. □ *The cops had hauled in two boosters by noon.* □ *Gary was a part-time booster till he got into dope.*

bootie See *boody.*

booze [buz] **1.** *n.* beverage alcohol. (Slang since the 1500s.) □ *I don't care for booze. It makes me sneeze.* □ *Where's the booze?* **2.** AND **booze up** *in.* to drink alcohol to excess; to go on a bash. □ *Let's go out and booze up!* □ *Stop boozing for a minute and listen up, guys.*

booze up See under *booze.*

bop [bap] **1.** *tr.* to strike someone or something. □ *I bopped the car on the hood and made a dent.* □ *You wanna get bopped in the beezer?* **2.** *n.* a style of jazz popular in the 1940s. □ *We heard some bop in an old movie.* □ *Bop is not popular, but it is by no means dead.* **3.** *n.* a drug in pill form; a dose of a drug. (See *hit.*) □ *Give me a bop of that stuff, will ya?* □ *You gonna drop both of them bops?*

boss *mod.* excellent; powerful. □ *That is a boss tune.* □ *This rally is really boss.*

bounce for something See *spring for something.*

bow to the porcelain altar *in.* to empty one's stomach; to vomit. (The porcelain altar is the toilet bowl.) □ *He spent the whole night bowing to the porcelain altar.* □ *I have the feeling that I will be bowing to the porcelain altar before morning.*

box (See also the two entries that follow and *(ghetto) box, beat box, boom box, doc(s)-in-a-box, go home in a box, thunderbox.*) **1.** *n.* a coffin. □ *I want the cheapest box they sell.* □ *Put him in a box and put the box in a hole. Then the matter is closed.* **2.** *n.* a portable stereo radio; a *(ghetto) box.* (See *(ghetto) blaster, boom box.*) □ *Where did you get that box?* □ *Does that damn box have to be so loud?*

boxed in *mod.* in a bind; having few alternatives. □ *I really feel boxed in around here.* □ *I got him boxed in. He'll have to do it our way.*

boxed (up) 1. *mod.* alcohol or drug intoxicated. □ *I am way boxed, and I feel sick.* □ *She got boxed up on gin.* **2.** *mod.* in jail. □ *I did it, and I was boxed for a long time for it. Now lay off!* □ *Pat was boxed up for two days till we got bond money.*

brassed (off) *mod.* angry; disgusted. □ *You look so brassed off with the world. Smile!* □ *I'm not brassed in the least, really.*

bread *n.* money. □ *I need to get some bread to live on.* □ *You got any bread you can spare?*

break 1. *n.* a chance; an opportunity. □ *Come on, give me a break!* □ *I got my first break in show biz when I was only 12.* **2.** *n.* an escape from prison; a prison breakout. □ *I hear there's a break planned for tonight.* □ *Two prisoners got shot in the break.*

Break a leg! *exclam.* "Good luck!" (A special theatrical way of wishing a performer good luck. Saying "good luck" is a jinx.) □ *"Break a leg!" shouted the stage manager to the star.* □ *Let's all go and do our best. Break a leg!*

Break it up! *exclam.* "Stop it!" (An order to two or more people to stop doing something, such as fighting.) □ *All right, you two, break it up!* □ *She told the boys to break it up or get sent to the principal's office.*

brew 1. *n.* coffee; occasionally, tea. □ *I could use a nice cup of brew.* □ *This is my kind of brew—hot, black, and aromatic.* **2.** *n.* beer; a can, bottle, or glass of beer. □ *Hey, give me a cold brew, will ya?* □ *This is my favorite brew, and it's at just the right temperature.*

brew-ha ['bruhɑ] *n.* beer; a beer. □ *One brew-ha over here, innkeeper!* □ *How 'bout another brew-ha, Mike?*

brew-out *n.* a beer blast. □ *Were you at Tom's brew-out? I was too bombed to see who was there.* □ *Was that Tom's brew-out I was at?*

brewski AND **brewsky** ['bruski] *n.* beer; a beer. □ *Hey, how 'bout a brewski?* □ *I'll take a nice cold brewsky.*

bring-down **1.** *n.* something that depresses someone. □ *The news was a terrible bring-down.* □ *Just to see your face was a bring-down.* **2.** *n.* something that brings someone back to reality. □ *The bill for the week's stay was a real bring-down.* □ *I have had one bring-down after another today.*

browned (off) *mod.* angry. □ *I am really browned off at you!* □ *The boss is browned—to say the least.*

brownout **1.** *in.* [for the electricity] to fade and dim down. □ *The power kept browning out.* □ *The lights started to brownout, and I thought maybe I didn't pay the bill for the juice.* **2.** *n.* a period of dimming or fading of the electricity. (Something less than a blackout.) □ *There was another brownout today.* □ *They keep building all these expensive power stations, and then we still have brownouts.*

brutal *mod.* excellent; powerful. □ *Man, what a brutal tune!* □ *That last wave was brutal to the max.*

B.S. *n.* nonsense; *bullshit.* □ *I've heard enough of your B.S.* □ *Less B.S. and more facts, please.*

buck (See also *bang for the buck, fast buck, kilobucks, megabucks, quick buck.*) **1.** *n.* a dollar. □ *Gimme a buck for a bottle of wine, will you, mister?* □ *Here's a buck; get me some cigarettes.* **2.** *tr.* to resist something. □ *Don't buck it. Do what you are told.* □ *He enjoys bucking the system.* **3.** *n.* a buckskin (leather) shoe. (Usually plural.) □ *Look at my new bucks!* □ *You don't see many red bucks. Are you sure you got the right thing?*

bucket **1.** *n.* the goal (hoop and net) in basketball. (Sports.) □ *Freddy arced one at the bucket and missed.* □ *When he holds his arm up, his hand is as high as the top of the bucket.* **2.** *n.* a goal or basket in basketball. (Sports.) □ *Four buckets in two minutes. Is that a record, or what?* □ *The last bucket put Adamsville ahead by two points.*

bucko ['bəko] *n.* friend; pal. (Also a term of address.) □ *Hey, bucko, come here a minute.* □ *Ask your bucko there if he wants to join us.*

bud [bəd] *n.* a Budweiser™ beer; any beer. (See *budhead*.) □ *How 'bout one of them buds in a green bottle?* □ *I got four kinds of bud here. Which do you want?*

budhead ['bədhɛd] *n.* a beer drinker. (Black. See *bud*.) □ *You're a budhead, and you're getting worse.* □ *Here comes Charlie, my favorite budhead. How about a brew, Charlie?*

bug **1.** *n.* a flaw in a computer program. □ *As soon as I get the bugs out, I can run my program.* □ *There is a little bug still, but it hardly causes any problems.* **2.** *n.* a combining form meaning someone who is enthusiastic about something. □ *Mary is a camera bug.* □ *Al has turned into a real compact disc bug.* **3.** *n.* an obsession or urge. □ *I've got this bug about making money.* □ *I had this bug that made me eat all shapes of pasta.* **4.** *tr.* to annoy someone. □ *Stop bugging me, you twit!* □ *This kind of thing really bugs me.*

Bug off! *exclam.* "Get out!"; "Go away!" □ *Bug off! Get out of here!* □ *Bug off and leave me alone!*

bull **1.** *n.* nonsense; *bullshit*. □ *That's just a lot of bull.* □ *Don't give me that bull! I won't buy it.* **2.** *tr. & in.* to lie to or deceive someone. □ *Stop bulling me!* □ *Is she bulling again?*

bull-pucky ['bʊlpəki] **1.** *n.* bull dung. □ *Why didn't you watch where you were going? Didn't you expect to find bull-pucky in a barnyard?* □ *How can you tell it's bull-pucky?* **2.** *n.* nonsense;

bullshit. □ *Don't give me that bull-pucky!* □ *That's all just bull-pucky. Don't believe a word of it.*

bullshit **1.** *n.* nonsense; lies; deception. (Caution with *shit.*) □ *Don't give me all that bullshit!* □ *That's just bullshit.* **2.** *tr.* to deceive someone; to lie to someone. (Caution with *shit.*) □ *Stop bullshitting me!* □ *You wouldn't bullshit us, would you?*

bummed (out) *mod.* discouraged; depressed. □ *I feel so bummed. I think I need a nice hot bath.* □ *When you're feeling bummed out, think how many problems I have.*

bummer **1.** AND **bum trip** *n.* a bad drug experience. □ *She almost didn't get back from a bum trip.* □ *This bummer comes from mixing pills.* **2.** *n.* a disagreeable thing or person. (Compare to *buzz-kill.*) □ *My coach is a real bummer.* □ *The game was a bummer you wouldn't believe.*

bumming *mod.* down; depressed; suffering from something disagreeable. (Collegiate.) □ *I'm really bumming. I think I need somebody to talk to.* □ *Everybody's bumming. It must be the weather.*

bum someone out AND **bum out someone** *tr.* to discourage someone. □ *The failure of two tires bummed out the race driver.* □ *That darn blowout bummed me out.* (More at *bummed (out).*)

bum something (off someone) *tr.* to beg or borrow something (from someone). □ *Can I bum a cigarette off you?* □ *Can I bum a quarter for a phone call?*

bum trip See under *bummer.*

bunch of fives *n.* the fist, especially when used to strike someone. □ *How would you like a bunch of fives right in the kisser?* □ *He ended up with a bunch of fives in the gut.*

buns *n.* the buttocks. □ *What cute little buns!* □ *His face looks like a mule kicked him, but have you seen his buns!*

burb [bɚb] *n.* a suburb. (Usually plural.) □ *I've lived in the burbs all my life.* □ *Our burb is too far from the city for much pollution.*

burbed out [bɚbd...] *mod.* looking very middle-class and suburban; decked out like a suburban citizen. □ *She's all burbed out with new clothes and a fancy car.* □ *He looks sort of burbed out for a city guy.*

burn **1.** *n.* a cigarette. □ *Gimme a burn, huh?* □ *Fred just stood there with a burn on his lower lip and his hands in his pockets.* **2.** *tr.* to smoke a cigarette. □ *I need to burn a fag. Just a minute!* □ *This nicotine fiend needs to burn one for a fix!* **3.** *tr.* to cheat or rob someone. □ *Tom tried to burn me by selling me a bum watch, but I'm too clever.* □ *He will burn you if you're not careful.*

burn someone down AND **burn down someone** *tr.* to humiliate someone. □ *Man, don't you ever burn me down like that again!* □ *You just want to burn down everybody to make yourself seem better.*

bushed [buʃt] *mod.* exhausted. □ *I am just bushed.* □ *Another hard day! I'm more bushed than ever.*

bust **1.** *n.* a failure. □ *The whole project was a bust from the beginning.* □ *My whole life is a bust!* **2.** *n.* a riotous drinking party. □ *There was a big bust in the park until two in the morning.* □ *There was no beer at the bust. Only wine.* **3.** *n.* a raid by the police. □ *The cops staged a bust on Carl's place.* □ *I knew it was a bust the minute they broke in the door.* **4.** *tr.* [for the police] to raid a place and make arrests. □ *The cops busted Bill's bar and put Bill in the slammer.* □ *We're gonna bust every bookie joint in town.*

bust (some) suds **1.** *tr.* to drink some beer. □ *Let's go out and bust some suds.* □ *I'm tired of busting suds. Let's play cards.* **2.** *tr.* to wash dishes. □ *I don't want to spend the rest of my life busting suds.* □ *You get into that kitchen and bust some suds to pay for your meal!*

butt [bət] **1.** *n.* the buttocks. (Caution with *butt.*) □ *She fell down right on her butt.* □ *The doctor gave him a shot in the butt.* **2.** *n.* a cigarette butt. □ *Whose butts are those in the car ashtray?* □ *Don't leave your butts in the houseplants!* **3.** *n.* a cigarette of any kind. □ *You got a butt I can bum?* □ *What kind of butt is that, anyway?*

button **1.** *n.* the termination of a recitation; the punch line of a joke. (The equivalent of a button that is pressed to signal a response.) □ *When I got to the button, I realized that I had told the whole joke wrong.* □ *When I came to the button, I knew I was really going to insult the guy.* **2.** *n.* a police officer's badge or shield. □ *The guy flashed his button, so I let him in.* □ *Just because you got a button, it doesn't mean you can push innocent citizens around!*

butt, pain in the See *pain in the ass.*

buy it *tr.* to die. □ *For a minute, I thought I was going to buy it.* □ *He lay there coughing for a few minutes, and then he bought it.*

buzz **1.** *n.* a call on the telephone. (Usually with *give.*) □ *I'll give you a buzz tomorrow.* □ *I got a buzz from him yesterday.* **2.** *tr.* to call someone on the telephone. □ *Buzz me about noon.* □ *I'll buzz Mary and see if she can go.* **3.** *tr.* to signal someone with a buzzer. □ *I'll buzz my secretary.* □ *Did you buzz, Gloria?*

buzz-kill *n.* a person or thing that ruins someone's fun; a *bummer.* □ *John is a real buzz-kill.* □ *The news about the suspension was a buzz-kill.*

C

cake (See the entry that follows and *beefcake, cake, cakewalk, cheesecake, cupcake, piece of cake.*) *n.* money. (From *bread.*) □ *I can't scrape together enough cake to do the job.* □ *I don't have cake in my pocket, in the bank, or under my mattress. What am I going to do?*

cakewalk *n.* something very easy. (Compare to *sleepwalk.*) □ *Nothing to it. It's a cakewalk.* □ *The game was a cakewalk from beginning to end.*

calendar *n.* a month. (Black.) □ *Okay, man. I'll see you in one calendar.* □ *One more calendar, then you get your money.*

call **1.** *n.* a decision; a prediction. □ *That was a good call, Mike.* □ *The ship behaved just as you said it would. Good call.* **2.** *tr.* to challenge someone. □ *I called him, but he ignored me.* □ *Are you the guy who called me? Who do you think you are?*

Call my service. *sent.* "Please call me through my answering service." (Not a friendly or encouraging invitation.) □ *Good to talk to ya, babe. Call my service. Love ya!* □ *I can't talk now. Call my service.*

call someone out *tr.* to challenge someone to a fight. □ *Carl wanted to call him out, but thought better of it.* □ *Did you call me out? What are you going to do about it?*

campus ['kæmpəs] *tr.* to restrict someone to the grounds of a college campus. (Collegiate.) □ *The dean threatened to campus the*

30

entire fraternity for a month. □ *"We will campus you for a year, if necessary," shouted the dean, who really didn't understand young people.*

can **1.** *n.* the head. □ *What do you have in your can, anyway? Lard?* □ *Jerry landed one on Frank's can. Frank crumpled.* **2.** *n.* toilet. □ *Hell, I ain't tired! Where's the can?* □ *I gotta use the can before we leave.* **3.** *n.* jail. (Usually with *the.*) □ *I had to spend the night in the can, but it wasn't too bad.* □ *You've seen one can, you've seen 'em all.* **4.** *tr.* to dismiss someone from employment. □ *The jerk canned everybody who played a part in the gag.* □ *I'll can anybody who tries a stunt like that again.*

cans *n.* earphones. (See also *can.*) □ *The guy with the cans on his head is the radio operator.* □ *I bought a new set of cans for my stereo.*

capish [kə'piʃ] *in.* to understand. (Usually a question. From an Italian dialect.) □ *The matter is settled. No more talk. Capish?* □ *Now, if you don't capish, let's get it clear right now.*

capper ['kæpɚ] *n.* the climax or *clincher* of something. □ *The capper of the evening was when the hostess got lathered and couldn't stand up.* □ *When the butler tripped and served Mr. Wilson the entire dessert in his lap, that was the capper to an exciting evening.*

carb [karb] *n.* carburetor. □ *This car needs a new carb.* □ *I learned how to clean and adjust a carb by the time I was in high school.*

carbos ['karboz] *n.* carbohydrates. (Bodybuilding.) □ *You need more protein and less carbos.* □ *Too many carbos will make you fat.*

card **1.** *n.* a funny person. □ *Molly is such a card. She cracks me up.* □ *Gee, Fred. You're a card. Somebody's gonna have to deal with you.* **2.** *tr.* to check people's I.D. cards for age or other eligibility. □ *They card everybody at the football games, even the parents.* □ *The bartender was carding people, so we left quietly.*

carry the stick *tr.* to live as a hobo, on the streets. (Streets. From the stick that supports the hobo's bundle.) □ *I even carried the stick for a while in the sixties.* □ *I was afraid I'd be carrying the stick if I got laid off.*

case of the shorts See *shorts.*

cash cow *n.* a dependable source of money; a good investment. □ *I put most of my money in a dependable cash cow that pays off once a month.* □ *Mr. Wilson turned out to be the cash cow we needed to start our repertoire company.*

cat **1.** *n.* a fellow; a guy; a *dude.* □ *Now, this cat wants to borrow some money from me. What should I do?* □ *Ask the cat what he's got for security.* **2.** *in.* to empty one's stomach; to vomit. □ *I think I'm gonna cat.* □ *Looks like somebody catted in the bushes.*

catch some rays AND **bag some rays** *tr.* to get some sunshine; to tan in the sun. (See *rays.*) □ *We wanted to catch some rays, but the sun never came out the whole time we were there.* □ *I went to Hawaii to bag some rays.*

catch some Z's AND **cop some Z's, cut some Z's** *tr.* to get some sleep. □ *I gotta catch some Z's before I drop.* □ *Why don't you stop a little bit and try to cop some Z's?*

Catch you later. *sent.* "I will talk to you again when I next see you." □ *Can't talk now. Catch you later.* □ *Sorry, gotta rush. Catch you later.*

cazh [kæʒ] *mod.* casual. (California.) □ *Melissa is so, like, so, cazh!* □ *Roger can be so forceful and cazh—all at the same time.*

chain(saw) *tr.* to destroy something; to cut something up severely. □ *The senatorial committee tried to chainsaw the nomi-*

nee, but the full senate voted for confirmation. □ *We didn't think they'd come in and chain all our plans.*

change the channel *tr.* to switch to some other topic of conversation. □ *Just a minute. I think you changed the channel. Let's go back to the part about you owing me money.* □ *Let's change the channel here before there is a fight.*

chap *tr.* to anger or annoy someone. □ *That whole business really chapped me.* □ *I didn't mean to chap you.*

chart *n.* a musical score. (Musicians. See also *map*.) □ *Come on, man! Look at the chart! You're making mistakes everywhere.* □ *Lemme borrow your chart for a while, okay?*

chas AND **chez** [tʃæz AND tʃɛz] *n.* matches. (Collegiate. A clipping of "matches.") □ *Where are my chas?* □ *You got a couple of chez?*

cheaters *n.* sunglasses. (Formerly used for all spectacles. See also *shades, sunshades*.) □ *Get your cheaters on. The sun's really bright.* □ *Somebody sat on my cheaters!*

check *interj.* okay; yes; "yes, it is on the list." □ BILL: *Four quarts of oil.* TOM: *Check.* □ FRED: *Are you ready?* PAUL: *Check.*

check that *tr.* cancel that; ignore that (last remark.) □ *Check that. I was wrong.* □ *At four, no, check that, at three this afternoon, a bomb exploded at the riverside.*

cheese **1.** *n.* vomit. □ *There's cheese on the sidewalk. Look out!* □ *In there, there's cheese on the bathroom floor. So gross!* **2.** *in.* to empty one's stomach; to vomit. □ *Somebody cheesed on the sidewalk.* □ *She popped into the bushes and cheesed soundlessly.*

cheesecake **1.** *n.* a display of the female form, probably wearing little clothing, often in photographs. (Compare to *beefcake*.) □ *Women don't like to see all that cheesecake on the walls when* *they bring their cars in here to be fixed.* □ *Now they're even putting the magazines with cheesecake under the counter.* **2.** *n.* a good-looking woman; good-looking women. □ *Who's the cheesecake in that low-cut job?* □ *Bring on the cheesecake!*

cheesed off *mod.* angry; disgusted. □ *Clare was really cheesed off at the butler.* □ *The butler was cheesed off at the cook.*

cheesy *mod.* cheap; tacky. □ *I wouldn't live in a cheesy place like this if I could afford anything better.* □ *That was a cheesy trick to pull on somebody.*

chewed *mod.* tired; abused. □ *After that argument at the office yesterday, I really felt chewed.* □ *After an interview like that, I am too chewed to even cry.*

chew face *tr.* to kiss. (More jocular than crude.) □ *A couple of kids were in a doorway chewin' face.* □ *Hey, Molly! Wanna go chew face?*

chicken *n.* a coward. □ *Come on, let's go. Don't be a chicken.* □ *He's no fun. He's a chicken.*

chicken out (of something) *in.* to manage to get out of something, usually because of fear or cowardice. □ *Come on! Don't chicken out now!* □ *Freddy chickened out of the plan at the last minute.*

chief [tʃif] *n.* the person in charge. (Also a term of address.) □ *Okay, chief, where to?* □ *You got a couple of bucks to pay the toll with, chief?*

chill 1. AND **chilly** *n.* a cold can of beer. □ *Hey, toss me a chilly, would ya, buddy?* □ *You ready for another chill?* **2.** *tr.* to kill someone. (Underworld.) □ *Walter had orders to chill Marlowe or not to show his face again.* □ *I'll chill you with one blast from my cannon, you creep.* **3.** *tr.* to reject someone. □ *The whole gang chilled him, and this really made him come home.* □ *She chilled me once too often. I won't take that from a dame.*

chill (out) *in.* to calm down; to be *cool*; to get *cool*. □ *All right now, people, chill...chill.* □ *Before we can debate this matter, you're all gonna have to chill out.*

chill someone's action *tr.* to squelch someone; to prevent someone from accomplishing something. (Black.) □ *Freddie is trying to chill my action, and I'm a little steamed about that.* □ *Just wait! I'll chill his action—just you wait.*

chintzy ['tʃɪntsi] **1.** *mod.* cheap; shoddy. □ *Nobody's gonna buy this chintzy stuff. Throw it out.* □ *What a chintzy car! The door fell off!* **2.** *mod.* stingy; miserly. □ *The chintzy guy left me no tip!* □ *Don't be chintzy. Give the man a dollar for a cup of coffee.*

chippy 1. AND **chippie** *n.* a part-time prostitute. □ *Yeah, so I'm a chippie. So what's that make you?* □ *Some little chippie stopped us to ask for a match. How amateurish.* **2.** *in.* to play around sexually. □ *She won't even chippie.* □ *So me and my boyfriend was chippying a little in the hall. Why was you watching?*

chippy around *in.* to be sexually promiscuous. □ *She has been known to chippy around, but not with just anyone and never for money.* □ *She figures it's her right to chippy around.*

chips *n.* money. □ *I managed to put away a few chips when I worked for Acme Systems.* □ *She saved some chips over the years and bought herself a little place on the beach.*

chiz [tʃɪz] *in.* to relax. (Collegiate.) □ *I gotta get back to my room and chiz awhile.* □ *Chiz, guys, things are getting a little rough.*

chop *n.* a rude remark; a cutting remark. □ *Jerry made some chop about the way I dress.* □ *That was a rotten chop! Take it back!*

chow 1. *n.* food. □ *I need some chow before I go out and shovel snow.* □ *What time is chow served around here?* **2.** *tr. & in.* to eat (something). (See also *chow down*.) ☐ *I've been chowing canned tuna and stale bagels to save money.* ☐ *When do we chow?* **3.** See *ciao*.

chow down *in.* to eat; to take a meal. ☐ *Over there is where we chow down.* ☐ *It's past my time to chow down.*

chow something down AND **chow down something** *tr.* to eat something, probably quickly or without good manners. ☐ *We can chow this pizza down in about two minutes!* ☐ *I found a box of cookies and chowed it down before anybody knew what I was doing.*

chuck 1. AND **chuck up** *in.* to empty one's stomach; to vomit. (See also *upchuck*.) ☐ *Look! Somebody chucked.* ☐ *I think I gotta chuck!* **2.** *tr.* to throw something away. ☐ *Chuck this thing. It's no good.* ☐ *The wrinkle-rod was so twisted we had to chuck it.* **3.** *in.* to eat voraciously. ☐ *Don't just chuck, man, enjoy your food.* ☐ *The two guys sat guzzling and chucking till they were full.*

chuck a dummy *tr.* to empty one's stomach; to vomit. ☐ *He left the room—to chuck a dummy, I guess.* ☐ *Somebody chucked a dummy on the patio.*

chuckers AND **chucks** *n.* a great hunger; an enormous appetite. (Usually with *the*.) ☐ *Oh, man, I really got the chucks. What time is chow?* ☐ *The chuckers got my stomach asking if my throat is cut.*

chucks See the previous entry.

chunk *in.* to empty one's stomach; to vomit. (Collegiate.) ☐ *I think I gotta chunk.* ☐ *The cat chunked all over the carpet.*

ciao AND **chow** [tʃɑʊ] "Good-bye"; "Hello." (Italian.) ☐ *See ya. Ciao.* ☐ *Chow, baby. Call my service.*

clanked *mod.* exhausted; pooped. □ *At the end of the race, the chick was totally clanked.* □ *I'm really clanked, man. Gotta take a rest.*

climb *tr.* to scold someone. □ *The boss climbed Harry for being late.* □ *Don't climb me! The train broke down!*

clincher ['klɪntʃɚ] *n.* the final element; the straw that broke the camel's back. (See also *capper*.) □ *The clincher was when the jerk turned up the volume.* □ *His eating garlic by the bushel was the clincher. I had to get a new roommate.*

clinker **1.** *n.* a mistake; [in music] a misplayed note. □ *That was a bad clinker in the middle of the soft passage.* □ *Look at the score, man! That series of clinkers just isn't there.* **2.** *n.* a worthless person or thing. (From the term for a cinder.) □ *This guy is such a clinker. Who needs him?* □ *Ralph has turned out to be a real clinker. We'll have to pink slip him.*

clip **1.** *tr.* to cheat someone. □ *That guy in there clipped me for a fiver.* □ *I didn't clip you or anybody else!* **2.** *n.* a music video; a short film. □ *This next clip is something you'll all recognize.* □ *Stay tuned for more great clips.* **3.** *n.* a fast rate of speed. □ *By traveling at a good clip, we managed to get there before the wedding started.* □ *You were moving at a pretty good clip when you ran into the truck.*

clunk **1.** *tr.* to strike someone or something. □ *A small truck clunked me from behind.* □ *The branch clunked the roof as it fell.* **2.** *n.* a hit; the sound of a hit. □ *I heard a clunk on the roof. Must be reindeer.* □ *The clunk on the roof was a falling branch.*

clunker **1.** *n.* an old car. □ *He drives an old clunker and doesn't have any insurance.* □ *I gotta get rid of this clunker pretty soon.* **2.** *n.* someone or something worthless; a *clinker*. □ *We have to get the clunkers off the payroll.* □ *Fred? There's another clunker we don't need.*

clutched *mod.* nervous. □ *I get so clutched before a test.* □ *George is clutched most of the time. He's in bad shape.*

clutch (up) *in.* to become very tense and anxious; to freeze with anxiety. □ *I have been known to clutch up before a race.* □ *Cool it, babe! Don't clutch!*

coaster *n.* someone who lives near the ocean. (California.) □ *Tiffany is a coaster now, but she was born, like, somewhere else.* □ *The coasters just don't want to be beige, that's all.*

coin *n.* money. (See also *hard coin*.) □ *I'm sort of short of coin right now. Can it wait?* □ *He made a lot of coin on his last job.*

cold **1.** *mod.* [stopping something] suddenly and totally. □ *I stopped cold—afraid to move farther.* □ *That remark stopped her cold.* **2.** *mod.* dead. □ *This parrot is cold—pifted!* □ *When I'm cold and buried, I hope people will think of me fondly.*

cold fish *n.* a dull and unresponsive person. □ *I hate to shake hands with a cold fish like that. He didn't even smile.* □ *I hate going out with a cold fish.*

collar **1.** *tr.* to arrest someone. □ *The cops collared her as she was leaving the hotel.* □ *The officer tried to collar Carl, but Carl moved away too fast.* **2.** *n.* an arrest. □ *It was a tough collar, with all the screaming and yelling.* □ *I made the collar in broad daylight.*

come down **1.** *in.* to happen. □ *Hey, man! What's coming down?* □ *When something like this comes down, I have to stop and think things over.* **2.** *n.* a letdown; a disappointment. (Usually **comedown**.) □ *The loss of the race was a real comedown for Willard.* □ *It's hard to face a comedown like that.* **3.** *in.* to begin to recover from the effects of alcohol or drug intoxication. □ *She came down slow, which was good.* □ *It was hard to get her to come down.*

come home 1. *in.* to return to reality. □ *I'm glad you decided to come home.* □ *Hey, wake up, you spacy clown. Come home!* **2.** AND **come home to haunt someone** *in.* [for some problem] to cause negative consequences. □ *Eventually every single problem you have avoided dealing with will come home.* □ *All these things come home to haunt you sooner or later.*

come home to haunt someone See under *come home.*

Come off it! 1. *exclam.* "Stop acting arrogantly!" □ *Oh, you're just one of us. Come off it!* □ *Come off it, Tiff. You're not the Queen of England.* **2.** *exclam.* "Give up your incorrect point of view!" □ *Come off it! You're wrong, and you know it.* □ *You are arguing from a foolish position. You're dead wrong. Come off it!*

come on ['kəmɔn] **1.** *n.* a lure; bait. (Usually **come-on.**) □ *Forty people responded to the come-on published in the Sunday paper.* □ *It's just a come on. Nobody is giving away a decent color T.V. just for listening to a sales pitch.* **2.** *n.* an invitation; a sexual invitation. (Usually **come-on.**) □ *She stared at him with her bedroom eyes, giving him that age-old come-on.* □ *Who could resist a come-on like that?*

comer ['kəmɚ] *n.* someone with a bright future. □ *Fred is a real comer. You'll be hearing a lot about him.* □ *A comer like that can command a high salary.*

come up for air *in.* to pause for a break. □ *The kissers—being only human—had to come up for air eventually.* □ *They were taking in money so fast at the box office that there wasn't a minute to come up for air.*

comma-counter *n.* a pedantic person. □ *Comma-counters can be such a pain.* □ *When you need a proofreader, you need a comma-counter.*

con 1. *n.* a convict. □ *One of the cons keeps a snake in his cell for a pet.* □ *Is that guy in the gray pajamas one of the escaped cons?*

2. *n.* a confidence scheme. □ *They pulled a real con on the old lady.* □ *This is an okay con you got going.* **3.** *tr.* to swindle or deceive someone. □ *Don't try to con me. I know the score.* □ *Reggie conned him out of his money.*

con artist See *con man.*

conehead **1.** *n.* a fool; an oaf. □ *Some conehead put sugar in the salt shaker.* □ *You can be pretty much of a conehead yourself sometimes, you know.* **2.** *n.* an intellectual; a *pointy-head.* □ *The coneheads have decided that we are all making too much money.* □ *They build fences around universities to keep the coneheads in.*

conk AND **konk** *n.* the head. □ *Put your hat on your conk, and let's cruise.* □ *Where'd you get that nasty bump on your konk?*

conk out **1.** *in.* [for someone] to collapse. □ *I was so tired I just went home and conked out.* □ *I was afraid I would conk out while I was driving.* **2.** *in.* [for something] to break down; to quit running. □ *My car conked out finally.* □ *I hope my computer doesn't conk out.*

con man AND **con artist** *n.* someone who makes a living by swindling people. □ *Gary is a con artist, but at least he's not on the dole.* □ *He looks like a con man, but he's just a sweetie.*

[cookie] See the entry that follows and *blow one's cookies, drop one's cookies, shoot one's cookies, snap one's cookies, throw one's cookies, toss one's cookies.*

cookie-pusher **1.** *n.* a bootlicker; someone who flatters other people for self-serving motives. □ *When you've got a whole office full of cookie-pushers, there's always someone to take you to lunch.* □ *Another cookie-pusher came in today to tell me what a great teacher I am.* **2.** *n.* a lazy do-nothing. □ *Is Martin a couch potato or a cookie-pusher? That is the question!* □ *I'm just looking for a cookie-pusher to fire today.*

cool 1. *mod.* unabashed; unruffled; relaxed. □ *This chick is so cool—no matter what happens.* □ *She is totally cool and easygoing.* 2. *mod.* good; excellent. □ *This is a really cool setup!* □ *Then this, like, cool muscleman comes over and asks Tiffany if she'd like to dance.*

cool down *in.* to calm down. □ *Now, just cool down. Chill, chill. Everything's gonna be real cool.* □ *When things cool down around here, life will be much more livable.*

cooled out *mod.* calm; unabashed. □ *Ted is a really cooled out kind of guy.* □ *When she's cooled out, she's great.*

cooler *n.* jail. (Usually with *the*.) □ *Do you want to talk, or do you want to spend a little time in the cooler?* □ *Let me outa this cooler! I'm innocent!*

Cool it! *exclam.* "Calm down!" □ *Take it easy! Cool it!* □ *Come on, cool it, man!*

cool off *in.* to calm down. □ *Now, it's all right. Cool off!* □ *I knew things would cool off eventually.*

cool out *in.* to calm down; to relax. □ *Now, just cool out, man. This will pass.* □ *Everybody cooled out after the emergency, and everything was fine.*

cool someone out AND **cool out someone** *tr.* to calm someone; to appease someone. □ *The manager appeared and tried to cool out everybody, but that was a waste of time.* □ *Cool yourselves out, you people. We gotta be sensible.*

cop 1. *tr.* to take or steal something. (Originally underworld.) □ *Somebody copped the statue from the town square.* □ *Who copped the salt from this table?* 2. *n.* a police officer. □ *The cop wasn't in any mood to put up with any monkey business.* □ *You call the cops. I've got enough trouble.*

cop an attitude *tr.* to take a negative or opposite attitude about something. (See also *tude*.) □ *Look, chum, don't cop an attitude with me!* □ *I think you're copping an attitude. Not advised, man. Not advised.*

cop a plea *tr.* to plead guilty to a lesser charge. □ *Walter copped a plea and got off with a week in the slammer.* □ *I wanted to cop a plea, but didn't have the chance.*

cop a squat *tr.* to sit down. □ *Hey, man! Come in and cop a squat.* □ *Cop a squat and crack a tube.*

cop a tube *tr.* to catch a perfect tubular wave. (Surfers.) □ *He was a real pro at copping a tube, and always just the right one.* □ *Mark—as drunk as all get out—said he was gonna go out and cop a tube.*

cop out 1. *in.* to plead guilty (to a lesser charge). (Underworld. See *cop a plea*.) □ *Frank copped out and got off with a night in the cooler.* □ *I decided not to cop out and got a lawyer instead.* **2.** *in.* to give up and quit; to *chicken out (of something)*. □ *Why do you want to cop out just when things are going great?* □ *I couldn't cop out on you guys if I wanted to.* **3.** *n.* a poor excuse to get out of something. (Usually **cop-out** or **copout**.) □ *This is a silly copout.* □ *That's not a good reason. That's just a cop-out.*

copped *mod.* arrested. □ *Jed got himself copped—a speeder.* □ *I was copped for doing absolutely nothing at all.*

copper 1. *n.* a police officer. (Originally underworld. Because the *copper* "cops" or "takes." See *cop*.) □ *See that copper over there? He arrested me once.* □ *The coppers will catch up with you some day.* **2.** *n.* money. (From *copper penny*. See also *rivets*.) □ *How much copper you got on you?* □ *That car takes too much copper to run.*

cop some Z's See *catch some Z's*.

cork, blow one's See *blow a fuse*.

corpse **1.** *n.* an empty liquor or beer bottle. (See *dead soldier*.) □ *Sam tossed another corpse out the window.* □ *Throw your corpses in the trash can, you jerk!* **2.** *n.* a cigarette butt. □ *The wino picked up the corpse and put it in a little box of them he carried with him.* □ *He is saving corpses to build a real smoke.*

cosmic *mod.* excellent; powerful. □ *This pizza is absolutely cosmic!* □ *Who wants to see a really cosmic movie?*

couch potato *n.* a lazy, do-nothing television watcher. (See also *sofa spud*.) □ *If there was a prize for the best couch potato, my husband would win it.* □ *You are turning into a perfect couch potato.*

cowboy *n.* a reckless and independent man; a reckless driver. (Also a term of address.) □ *Come on, cowboy, finish your coffee and get moving.* □ *Some cowboy in a new caddy cut in front of me.*

cow chips *n.* dried cow dung. □ *There's a whole field of cow chips out there! Why do you want to buy a bag of the stuff at a nursery?* □ *Break up these cow chips and work them into the soil around the base of the bushes.*

cow flop AND **cow plop** *n.* a mass of cow dung. □ *Mrs. Wilson is out in the pasture gathering cow flops for her garden.* □ *Cow plops are not all the same, you know.*

cow plop See the previous entry.

coyote-ugly ['kɑɪot 'əgli OR 'kɑɪoti 'əgli] *mod.* extremely ugly. (Said of people. See *double-bagger*. Supposedly, if one woke up and found one's arm around a *coyote-ugly* person, one would chew off one's arm—in the manner of a coyote escaping from a steel-jaw trap—rather than pull it back away from this person.) □ *Is that your pet monkey, or is your date just coyote-ugly?* □ *Isn't that the most coyote-ugly creep you've ever seen?*

cozy up (to someone) *in.* to become overly friendly with someone in hope of gaining special favors. □ *Molly cozied up to the prof, hoping for a good grade at least.* □ *She failed to read the syllabus, which advised students not to cozy up to the professor or call him at home.*

crab *n.* a louse. (Usually plural.) □ *He's scratching like he's got crabs.* □ *The old wino and his crabs wandered into the flophouse for a little peace and quiet.*

crack **1.** *n.* a joke; a smart-aleck remark. □ *Another crack like that and your nose will be a little flatter than it is.* □ *Who made that crack?* **2.** *n.* a try (that may or may not succeed.) □ *Have another crack at it.* □ *One more crack and I'll have it.* **3.** *n.* a unit of something (for a particular price); a use (of something). (See examples.) □ *You would think twice, too, if you remembered that it's seven dollars a crack.* □ *At two dollars a crack, this is the best game on the midway.*

crack a book *tr.* to open a book to study. (Usually in the negative. See also *book*.) □ *I never cracked a book and still passed the course.* □ *Sally didn't crack a book all semester.*

crack a tube *tr.* to open a can of beer. (See *tube*.) □ *Why don't you drop over this evening, and we'll crack a few tubes?* □ *Would you crack a tube for me? My hands are too cold.*

cracked *mod.* crazy. □ *You're cracked if you think I'll agree to that.* □ *You gotta be cracked if you think I'm going back in there.*

crackers See under *bonkers*.

crack open a bottle AND **crack a bottle open** *tr.* to open a bottle of liquor. (Also with *the*.) □ *Let's crack open a bottle and celebrate.* □ *He cracked the bottle open and poured a little for everyone to try.*

crack someone up AND **crack up someone** *tr.* to make someone laugh. □ *She giggled, and that cracked us all up.* □ *The lecturer would talk along sort of boring like, and then all of a sudden he would crack up everybody with a joke.*

cram *in.* to study hard at the last minute for a test. □ *She spent the night cramming for the test.* □ *If you would study all the time, you wouldn't need to cram.*

crank **1.** *n.* a bothersome person who telephones with a bogus message. □ *A crank called with a bomb threat.* □ *A crank came in and offered to punch me in the nose for a quarter.* **2.** *mod.* bogus. □ *We had four crank calls threatening to blow up the Eiffel Tower.* □ *A crank letter promised us a million dollars if we would play "My Blue Heaven" for two hours each morning.* **3.** *n.* a crabby person. (Collegiate.) □ *Why are you such a crank? Is something wrong in your life?* □ *The prof is such a crank; he jokes only about once a semester.*

cranking *mod.* exciting; excellent. □ *This record is really cranking!* □ *We had a massively cranking time at your party.*

crap [kræp] **1.** *n.* junk; worthless matter. □ *Why don't you just throw this crap away?* □ *Get your crap off my bed!* **2.** *n.* dung. (Crude. Caution with topic.) □ *There's dog crap on the lawn.* □ *Don't step in that crap.* **3.** *n.* nonsense; lies. □ *I've had enough of your crap. Now talk straight, or out you go.* □ *Cut the crap!* **4.** *in.* to defecate. (Crude. Caution with topic.) □ *Your dog crapped on my lawn!* □ *I have to crap; then I'll be right with you.*

crap out *in.* to evade something; to *chicken out (of something).* □ *Now, don't crap out on me at the last minute.* □ *Fred crapped out, so there are only three of us.*

crash **1.** *tr. & in.* to attend a party or other event uninvited. □ *Some clown tried to crash the rally, but my dad called the cops.* □ *The boys who tried to crash also broke a window.* (More at *crasher.*) **2.** *in.* to spend the night. □ *I crashed at a friend's place* *in the city.* □ *You have a place I can crash?* **3.** *in.* [for a computer] to stop working. □ *This thing crashes every time I hit a certain key.* □ *My machine hasn't crashed since I got it.*

crash and burn *in.* [for a young man] to fail brilliantly with a romance. (Collegiate. See *go down in flames.*) □ *I knew I would crash and burn with her.* □ *It stands to reason that if Ken hadn't shot me down, I wouldn't have crashed and burned.*

crasher *n.* a person who attends a party uninvited. (See *crash.*) □ *The crashers ruined the party, and my dad called the cops.* □ *The crashers were no more rude than the guests.*

crate *n.* a dilapidated vehicle. □ *Where'd you get that old crate?* □ *This crate gets me to work and back. That's good enough.*

crater *n.* an acne scar. □ *Ted has a nasty crater on his cheek.* □ *Walter was always sort of embarrassed about his craters.*

crater face *n.* someone with an acne-scarred face. (Cruel. Collegiate.) □ *Who's the crater face putting the moves on Sally?* □ *Crater face over there is talking sort of loud.*

crazy 1. *n.* a crazy person. □ *The guy's a crazy, and he keeps coming in here asking for money.* □ *I think the crazies are taking over the world.* **2.** *mod.* cool. □ *This stuff is really crazy, man. I love it!* □ *What a crazy dress. It makes you look like a million.*

cream *tr.* to beat someone; to outscore someone. □ *The other team creamed us, but we had better team spirit.* □ *We'll cream 'em next week.*

cream puff 1. *n.* a weakling; a *wimpy* person. □ *Don't be a cream puff all your life! Join a health club!* □ *We're having a cream puff special this week for you clowns who can't climb stairs without panting.* **2.** *n.* a used car that is in very good condition. □ *This one is a real cream puff. Only driven to church by a little old lady.* □ *This cream puff is loaded, air and everything.*

creased *mod.* exhausted. □ *What a day. I am totally creased.* □ *Here is one creased football player. Let him hit the rack.*

crib **1.** *n.* a location where thieves gather to plot; a dwelling for thieves, prostitutes, etc. (Underworld.) □ *The police busted a crib over on Fourth Street.* □ *They use a basement over there for a crib.* **2.** *n.* a dwelling. (Black.) □ *Where's your crib, man?* □ *My good threads are back at my crib.*

crisco ['krɪsko] *n.* a fat person. (Cruel. Also a rude term of address. The brand name of a baking shortening.) □ *Some crisco came in and ordered 10 large fries.* □ *Hey, crisco! Go on a diet!*

croak **1.** *in.* to die; to expire; to succumb. □ *I was afraid I'd croak.* □ *The parrot croaked before I got it home.* **2.** *tr.* to kill someone. □ *The car croaked the cat just like that.* □ *Somebody croaked my parrot.*

cromagnon [kro'mægnən] *n.* an ugly male. (Collegiate.) □ *Who is that cromagnon you were with last night?* □ *That was no cromagnon. That was your blind date for next weekend.*

crowd **1.** *tr.* to pressure or threaten someone. □ *Don't crowd me!* □ *Carl began to crowd Reggie—which was the wrong thing to do.* **2.** *tr.* to gang up on someone. (Black.) □ *Some guys were crowding Tod, so we chased them off.* □ *They moved in from all sides, carrying clubs, and began to crowd us.*

crud [krəd] **1.** *n.* nastiness; junk; worthless matter. □ *This is just crud. Get rid of it.* □ *Get all that old crud out of the attic so we can have room for newer stuff.* **2.** *n.* a repellent person. (Also a term of address.) □ *Don't be such a crud!* □ *That crud kept trying to paw me!*

crud(d)y AND **cruddie** ['krədi] *mod.* nasty; awful. □ *What is this cruddy stuff on my plate?* □ *It's just chocolate mousse, and it's not cruddie.*

cruise **1.** *in.* to travel at top speed. □ *This old caddy can really cruise.* □ *We cruised all the way to Philly.* **2.** *in.* to drive around looking for friends or social activity. □ *We went out cruising, but didn't see anybody.* □ *Let's go cruise for a while.* **3.** *in.* to move on; to leave. □ *Listen, I gotta cruise.* □ *Time to cruise. Got a test tomorrow.*

crunchers *n.* the feet. □ *My crunchers are sore from all this walking.* □ *New shoes can be hard on your crunchers.*

crunchie *n.* a soldier; a marching infantry soldier. (Military. See *crunchers*.) □ *A couple of crunchies were complaining about the Army.* □ *Crunchies have a pretty hard life.*

cry hughie ['kraɪ 'hjui] *in.* to empty one's stomach; to vomit. □ *He is in the john crying hughie.* □ *I think I gotta go cry hughie.*

cry ruth ['kraɪ 'ruθ] *tr.* to empty one's stomach; to vomit. (See *ruth*.) □ *Someone is in the bushes crying ruth.* □ *He looks like he's gonna cry ruth! Stop the car!*

cube [kjub] **1.** *n.* a very **square** person. □ *This nerd was the most unbelievable cube you have ever seen.* □ *Not just an L7, a real cube.* **2.** *n.* a die, one of a pair of dice. (Usually in the plural.) □ *Toss me the cubes.* □ *She shook the cubes, saying "Baby needs shoes!"*

cuff *tr.* to put a charge on one's bill. □ *Would you cuff this for me, please?* □ *Sorry, I can't cuff any more charges.*

cuffs *n.* handcuffs. □ *I felt the cuffs tighten and snap shut on my wrists.* □ *The cuffs carried the cold of the night to my bare skin. Of course, I was innocent, but that's not the way it works in real life.*

cull *n.* a socially unacceptable person. □ *Who's the cull driving the Edsel?* □ *This place is filled with culls. Let's split.*

cum(e) [kjum] *n.* a cumulative average, such as a grade-point average. □ *My cume is not high enough to get into law school.* □ *My cum is a straight A.*

cupcake *n.* an attractive woman. (Also a term of address.) □ *Hey, cupcake, what ya doing?* □ *Who is that cupcake driving the beemer?*

cushy ['kuʃi] *mod.* soft; easy. (From *cushion*.) □ *He's got sort of a cushy job.* □ *That's a cushy kind of life to lead.*

cuss someone out AND **cuss out someone** *tr.* to rebuke someone; to scold someone severely. □ *Don't cuss me out! I can't take it.* □ *You can't cuss out people you don't know!*

cut **1.** *tr.* to dilute something. □ *She always cuts her eggnog with cola. Yuck!* □ *You can cut the saltiness with a little sugar.* **2.** *n.* a share of the loot or the profits. (Originally underworld.) □ *I want my cut now!* □ *You'll get your cut when everybody else does.* **3.** *n.* a single song or section of music on a record. □ *This next cut is one everybody likes.* □ *Let's listen to another cut of the same album.*

cut and run *in.* to stop what one is doing and flee. □ *The cops were coming, so we cut and run.* □ *At the first warning, we cut and run.*

cut no ice (with someone) *tr.* to have no influence on someone; to fail to convince someone. □ *I don't care who you are. It cuts no ice with me.* □ *So you're the mayor's daughter. It still cuts no ice.*

cut one's wolf loose *tr.* to go on a drinking bout; to get drunk. □ *I'm gonna go out and cut my wolf loose tonight.* □ *You're going to cut your wolf loose too often and really get into trouble.*

cut out *in.* to leave; to run away. □ *It's late. I think I'll cut out.* □ *Don't cut out now. The night is young.*

cut-rate *mod.* cheap; low-priced. □ *I don't want any cut-rate stuff.* □ *Where are your cut-rate sweaters?*

cut someone in (on something) *tr.* to permit someone to share something. □ *You promised you would cut me in on this caper.* □ *We can't cut you in. There's not enough.*

cut some Z's See *catch some Z's.*

Cut the crap! *exclam.* "Stop the nonsense!" □ *I've heard enough. Cut the crap!* □ *Cut the crap. Talk straight or get out.*

cut up (about someone or something) *mod.* emotionally upset about someone or something. □ *She was all cut up about her divorce.* □ *You could see how cut up she was.*

D

damage   *n.* the cost; the amount of the bill (for something). □ *Okay, waiter. What's the damage?* □ *As soon as I pay the damage, we can go.*

dap   [dæp] *mod.* well-dressed. (From *dapper*.) □ *Who is that dap-looking dude?* □ *Man, you look dap!*

darb   [dɑrb] *n.* an excellent person or thing. □ *Carl is a real darb. I'm glad to know him.* □ *What a swell darb of a car!*

dead   **1.** *mod.* quiet and uneventful. □ *The day was totally dead.* □ *What a dead day!* □ *Things were sure dead around this town this summer.* **2.** *mod.* very tired. □ *I am just dead from all that jogging.* □ *I went home from the office, dead as usual.* **3.** *mod.* dull; lifeless; flat. □ *This meal is sort of dead because I am out of onions.* □ *The pop went dead because someone left it open.* □ *Who wants dead pop?*

dead man   See the following entry.

dead soldier AND **dead man, dead marine, dead one**   **1.** *n.* an empty liquor or beer bottle. □ *Toss your dead soldiers in the garbage, please.* □ *A dead marine fell off the table and woke up all the drunks.* **2.** *n.* a cigarette butt. (Less common than sense 1.) □ *The bum found a dead soldier on the ground and picked it up.* □ *He collected dead soldiers to use in building a whole smoke.*

deck   **1.** *tr.* to knock someone to the ground. □ *Fred decked Bob with one blow.* □ *I was so mad I almost decked him.* **2.** *n.* a pack of cigarettes. □ *Can you toss me a deck of fags, please?* □ *Why don't you stop in there and buy a deck?*

deduck ['didək] **1.** *n.* a tax deduction. (From *deduct*.) □ *Interest is no longer a deduck.* □ *I need a few more deducks this year.* **2.** AND **duck** *n.* a deduction from one's paycheck. □ *More of my pay goes to deducks than I get myself.* □ *What's this duck for?*

deejay See *disk jockey*.

deep, in See *in deep*.

deep pockets **1.** *n.* a good source of money. □ *We need to find some deep pockets to finance this venture.* □ *Deep pockets are hard to find these days.* **2.** *n.* a rich person. □ *The lawyer went after the doctor who was the deep pockets of the organization.* □ *I want to find the deep pockets who arranged all this.*

def [dɛf] *mod.* better; *cool*. (Black. From *definitive*.) □ *Man, that yogurt is def!* □ *What a def set of threads!*

defrosted *mod.* "even" with someone who has insulted, embarrassed, or angered one. (Black. See *chill*.) □ *He yelled at her till he was defrosted, and then things settled down.* □ *Bob was finally defrosted when he insulted Alice.*

delish [də'lɪʃ] *mod.* delicious. □ *Oh, this cake is just delish.* □ *What a delish meal.*

delts [dɛlts] *n.* the deltoid muscles. (Bodybuilding.) □ *Look at the delts on that dame!* □ *How do you get delts like that?*

desk jockey *n.* someone who works at a desk in an office. (Patterned on *disc jockey*.) □ *I couldn't stand being a cooped-up desk jockey.* □ *The desk jockeys at our place don't get paid very well.*

dialog *tr.* to attempt to deceive someone; to attempt to seduce someone. □ *Just let me dialog her for a while; then you'll see some action.* □ *Ron was dialoging some dame when her brother came in.*

dicey ['daɪsi] *mod.* touchy; chancy; touch and go. □ *Things are just a little dicey right now.* □ *I'm working on a dicey deal with the city right now.*

dick 1. *n.* a detective; a police officer. (Underworld. From *detective*.) □ *Some dicks were around looking for you.* □ *Marlowe is a private dick who has to keep one step ahead of the cops.* 2. *n.* the penis. (Caution with *dick* and topic.) □ *She told some dirty joke about a dick, but everybody just sat there and looked straight ahead.* □ *He covered his dick and stooped down, then reached up to pull down the shade.* 3. *n.* a stupid person, usually a male. (Caution with *dick*. Also a provocative term of address.) □ *You stupid dick!* □ *What stupid dick put this thing here in the way?*

dicty ['dɪkti] *mod.* snobbish. (Black.) □ *Those people can be so dicty!* □ *That dicty lady told me I could come to the back to get a tip if I wanted.*

diddly-squat AND **(doodly-)squat** ['dɪdliskwɑt AND 'dudliskwɑt] *n.* nothing. (Folksy. Originally black or southern.) □ *This contract isn't worth diddly-squat.* □ *I get paid almost doodly-squat for a full day's work.*

dig 1. *tr. & in.* to understand something. □ *I just don't dig what you are saying.* □ *Sorry. I just don't dig.* 2. *tr.* to appreciate something; to like something. □ *He really digs classical music.* □ *Do you dig chocolate?*

digs *n.* a dwelling; a dwelling and its furnishings. □ *You got some pretty swell digs here.* □ *Nice digs. You like it here?*

Dig up! *exclam.* "Listen up!"; "Pay attention!" (Black.) □ *Dig up, man! This is important.* □ *Shut up and dig up!*

dinero [dɪˈnɛro] *n.* money. (Spanish.) □ *I don't have as much dinero as I need, but other than that, I'm doing okay.* □ *You got some dinero I can borrow?*

ding *tr.* to shoot, dent, or knock something. □ *The rock dinged my left fender.* □ *The bullet dinged Walter's right arm.*

dingy [ˈdɪŋi] *mod.* loony; giddy. □ *That friend of yours sure does act dingy sometimes.* □ *Tell the dingy drip to forget it.* □ *I'm not dingy, I'm just in love.*

dirt **1.** *n.* low, worthless people. □ *He is just dirt.* □ *I am not dirt. I'm just temporarily financially embarrassed.* **2.** *n.* scandal; incriminating secrets. □ *What's the dirt on Molly?* □ *I don't want to know about anybody's dirt!*

dirty **1.** *mod.* obscene. □ *You have a dirty mind.* □ *The movie was too dirty for me.* □ *How would you know what's dirty and what's not?* **2.** *mod.* low and sneaky. □ *What a dirty trick!* □ *That was really dirty!* □ *What a dirty thing to do!*

(dirty) dozens *n.* a game of trading insulting remarks about relatives. (Black. Always with *the*. See also *play the dozens*.) □ *Man, what's with you? Always the dirty dozens. You just gotta start something all the time.* □ *Freddy is out giving the dozens to Marty.*

dish the dirt *tr.* to spread gossip; to gossip. □ *Let's sit down, have a drink, and dish the dirt.* □ *David goes down to the tavern to dish the dirt.*

disk jockey AND **deejay, disc jockey, D.J.** *n.* a radio announcer who introduces music from phonograph records. (Compare to *desk jockey*.) □ *The disk jockey couldn't pronounce the name of the singing group.* □ *I was a D.J. for a while, but I didn't like it.*

ditch **1.** *tr.* to dispose of someone or something; to abandon someone or something. □ *The crooks ditched the car and continued on foot.* □ *The pilot ditched the plane in the lake and waded* ashore. **2.** *tr. & in.* to skip or evade someone or something. □ *Tod ditched class today.* □ *If you ditch too often, they'll throw you out of the organization.*

ditsy AND **ditzy** ['dɪtsi] *mod.* pretentious; haughty; snobbish. □ *Who is that ditsy old girl who just came in?* □ *This table is too ditzy with all this fancy silver stuff.*

ditz [dɪts] *n.* a giddy, absentminded person. □ *You silly ditz!* □ *I'm getting to be such a ditz!*

divot ['dɪvət] *n.* a toupee; a partial toupee. (See also *rug*.) □ *I think that Sam is wearing a little divot.* □ *His divot slipped, but no one laughed.*

D.J. See *disk jockey.*

do a fade *tr.* to leave; to sneak away. □ *Carl did a fade when he saw the cop car.* □ *It's time for me to do a fade.*

do a job on someone or something *tr.* to ruin someone or something; to give someone or something a thorough working over. □ *The cops did a job on Walter, but he still wouldn't talk.* □ *There's no need to do a job on me, man, I'll tell you everything I know—which is zip.* □ *That punch sure did a job on my nose.*

do a slow burn *tr.* to be quietly angry. □ *I did a slow burn while I was getting my money back.* □ *I was doing a slow burn, but I didn't let it show.*

do a snow job on someone *tr.* to deceive or confuse someone. □ *Don't try to do a snow job on me. I know all the tricks.* □ *She thought she did a snow job on the teacher, but it backfired.*

doc(s)-in-a-box *n.* a walk-in emergency health care center, as found in shopping centers. □ *I was cut and went immediately to the docs-in-a-box in the mall.* □ *The doc-in-the-box finally closed because of lack of customers.*

dog 1. *n.* a foot. (Usually plural.) ☐ *My dogs are killing me.* ☐ *I gotta get home and soak my dogs.* 2. *n.* an ugly girl or woman. ☐ *I'm no dog, but I could wish for some changes.* ☐ *So she's not a movie star; she's not a dog either!* 3. *n.* something undesirable or worthless; merchandise that no one wants to buy. ☐ *Put the dogs out on the sale table so people will see them.* ☐ *People even bought all the dogs this year. Sales were great.*

dog meat *n.* a dead person. (Typically in a threat. See examples.) ☐ *Make one move, and you're dog meat.* ☐ *They pulled another hunk of gangland dog meat out of the river.*

dome-doctor *n.* a psychologist or psychiatrist. ☐ *They sent Reggie to a dome-doctor, but it didn't help.* ☐ *The dome-doctor lets me talk while he keeps score.*

done over *mod.* beaten; outscored. ☐ *The other team was done over, and they knew it.* ☐ *Reggie felt that Carl would get the idea if he was done over a little.*

(doodly-)squat See *diddly-squat.*

doofer AND **dufer** ['dufɚ] *n.* a (found or borrowed) cigarette saved for smoking at another time. (It will "do for" later.) ☐ *Sam always has a doofer stuck behind his ear.* ☐ *He takes two fags, one to smoke and a dufer.*

dope 1. *n.* a stupid person. ☐ *I'm not such a dope.* ☐ *That dope has done it again!* 2. *n.* drugs in general; marijuana. ☐ *Lay off the dope, will ya?* ☐ *How much dope do you do in a week anyway?* 3. *n.* news; gossip. ☐ *What's the dope on the new mayor?* ☐ *I got some dope on the tavern fire if you want to hear it.*

dope something out AND **dope out something** *tr.* to figure out something from the *dope* or information available. ☐ *I think I can dope this thing out from the evidence available.* ☐ *We can dope out the truth from her testimony if we have to.*

dorf [dorf] *n.* a stupid person; a weird person. □ *You are a prize-winning dorf.* □ *Is there a convention of dorfs here today or something?*

dork [dork] **1.** *n.* a *jerk*; a strange person. (See also *dorky, mega-dork.*) □ *Ye gods, Sally! You are a dork!* □ *Here comes the king of dorks again.* **2.** *n.* the penis. (Caution with topic.) □ *Paul told a joke about a dork, but everybody just sat there and looked straight ahead.* □ *He covered his dork and squatted down; then he reached up and pulled down the shade.*

dorky ['dorki] *mod.* strange; weird; undesirable; typical of a *dork,* [sense 1]. □ *That is a real dorky idea. Just forget it.* □ *It's just too dorky.* □ *Let me out of this dorky place!*

double-bagger **1.** *n.* a hit good for two bases in baseball. □ *Wilbur hit a nice double-bagger in the top of the fourth.* □ *The hit was good for a double-bagger.* **2.** *n.* a very ugly person. (With a face so ugly that it takes two paper bags to conceal it. See *Bag your face!* See also *coyote-ugly.*) □ *Fred is what I would call a double-bagger. What a mug!* □ *I am no double-bagger! I just have strong features.*

double buffalo See *double nickels.*

double-deuces *n.* the number 22. □ *The National Weather Service says it's going down to the double-deuces tonight.* □ *He hit the old double-deuces today. That's right, 22 years old!*

double nickels AND **double buffalo** *n.* the number 55; the 55-mile-per-hour speed limit. (Originally citizens band radio. The buffalo is on one side of the nickel.) □ *You'd better travel right on those double nickels in through here. The cops are out.* □ *The double buffalo is enforced on this road.*

douche bag *n.* a repellent person; a disliked person. (Crude.) □ *Oh, shut up, you old douche bag!* □ *Don't be a douche bag!*

dough [do] *n.* money. (See *bread*.) □ *I got a lot of dough for that ring I found.* □ *I need some dough to buy groceries.*

down 1. *tr.* to eat or drink something down quickly. □ *He downed a can of soda and burped like a thunderclap.* □ *She downed her sandwich in record time.* 2. *mod.* behind in a score. □ *We're three points down with two minutes to play.* □ *They're 20 points down, and it looks like the Adamsville team has won.* 3. *mod.* finished; completed; behind one. □ *Well, I've got the test down. Now what?* □ *One down and three to go.*

downbeat *mod.* *cool*; easygoing. □ *He is sort of a downbeat character—no stress.* □ *I wish I was downbeat like he is.* □ *I had sort of a downbeat day. Not your typical Monday.*

downer AND **down(ie)** 1. *n.* a barbiturate or a tranquilizer. □ *She favors downers.* □ *Too much booze with those downers, and you're dead.* 2. *n.* a bad drug experience; a *down trip*. □ *That stuff you gave me was a real downer.* □ *Dust is a downer for most people.* 3. *n.* a depressing event; a bad situation; a *down trip*. □ *These cloudy days are always downers.* □ *My birthday party was a downer.*

down(ie) See the previous entry.

down trip 1. *n.* a bad and depressing drug experience. (Compare to *downer*.) □ *Tod is still suffering from that down trip he had.* □ *For some of them, one down trip is enough.* 2. *n.* any bad experience. (Compare to *downer*.) □ *Today was a classic down trip.* □ *My vacation was a down trip.*

[dozens] See *(dirty) dozens, play the dozens, shoot the dozens*.

D.Q. *n.* "Dairy Queen," a trade name for a franchise fast-food store specializing in frozen desserts. (Teens and collegiate.) □ *Let's go to D.Q., okay?* □ *The D.Q. is closed for the winter.*

drafty *n.* a draft beer; beer. □ *How about a cold drafty?* □ *You about ready for another drafty, Tom?*

drag **1.** *n.* something dull and boring. □ *This day's a drag.* □ *What a drag. Let's go someplace interesting.* **2.** *n.* an annoying person; a burdensome person. (Compare to *s(c)hlep.*) □ *Gert could sure be a drag when she wanted.* □ *Clare was a drag whether she wanted to be or not.* **3.** *n.* a puff of a cigarette. □ *He took a big drag and scratched at his tattoo.* □ *One more drag and he coughed for a while and stubbed out the fag.* **4.** *tr.* to pull or puff on a cigarette. □ *She dragged a couple and sat in the funk for a while.* □ *When she dragged a fag, you could see her relax and get straight.*

dragged out *mod.* exhausted; worn-out. □ *I feel so dragged out. I think I need some vitamins.* □ *After the game, the whole team was dragged out.*

drain the bilge *in.* to empty one's stomach; to vomit. □ *Fred left quickly to drain the bilge.* □ *Who drained the bilge in the bushes?*

dreck [drɛk] *n.* dirt; garbage; feces. (From German via Yiddish.) □ *What is all this dreck in the corner?* □ *I've had enough of this dreck around here. Clean it up, or I'm leaving.*

drinkies ['drɪŋkiz] *n.* drinks; liquor. □ *Okay, kids, it's drinkies all around.* □ *What time is drinkies around here?*

Drink up! *exclam.* "Finish your drink!"; "Finish that drink, and we'll have another!" □ *Okay, drink up! It's closing time.* □ *Drink up, and let's get going.*

drinkypoo ['drɪŋkipu] *n.* a little drink of liquor. □ *Wouldn't you like just one more drinkypoo of Madeira?* □ *Just a little drinkypoo, my dear.*

drive the big bus AND **drive the porcelain bus, ride the porcelain bus** *tr.* to vomit into the toilet. □ *Harry's in the john driving the big bus.* □ *Who do I hear driving the porcelain bus in the john?*

drive the porcelain bus See the previous entry.

droid [drɔɪd] *n.* a robot-like person; a *nerd*. (From *android*.) □ *Merton is as close to a droid as we'll ever see.* □ *The droids are taking over this campus.*

droob AND **drube** [drub] *n.* a dullard; an oaf. □ *Who's the droob standing by the punch bowl?* □ *That drube is my brother!*

drop **1.** *tr.* to knock someone down. □ *Jim dropped Willard with a punch to the shoulder.* □ *The swinging board hit him and dropped him.* **2.** *tr.* to take a drug, specifically L.S.D. □ *Ted dropped some stuff and went on a trip.* □ *Now he doesn't drop even once a month.*

drop one's cookies *tr.* to empty one's stomach; to vomit. (See *toss one's cookies*.) □ *The runner went off to the side and dropped her cookies.* □ *If you feel like you're going to drop your cookies, don't do it on the carpet.*

drop the ball *tr.* to fail at something; to allow something to fail. □ *I didn't want to be the one who dropped the ball, but I knew that someone would flub up.* □ *Sam dropped the ball, and we lost the contract.*

drube See *droob*.

ducats AND **duc-ducs** ['dəkəts AND 'dəkdəks] *n.* money. (See also *gold*.) □ *Who's got enough ducats to pay for the tickets?* □ *I've got duc-ducs galore!*

duc-ducs See the previous entry.

duck See under *deduck*.

ducks *n.* tickets. □ *You got the ducks for Friday?* □ *There were no ducks left.*

duck-squeezer *n.* someone with strong concerns about the environment and conservation, especially rescuing oil-covered ducks. (See *eagle freak*.) □ *Some duck-squeezers were complaining about what the new dam might do.* □ *The duck-squeezers were picketing the dam site.*

ducky *mod.* okay; good. (Often used sarcastically.) □ *Now, isn't that just ducky?* □ *That's a ducky idea!*

dude [dud] *n.* a male friend; a guy. (Also a term of address.) □ *Who's the dude with the big car?* □ *Hey, dude, what's happening?*

dude up *in.* to dress up. □ *Let's get all duded up and go out.* □ *I got to dude up a little before we go.*

dufer See *doofer.*

duffer ['dəfɚ] **1.** *n.* a foolish oaf; a bumbler. □ *Some old duffer is weeding our garden for us. He's lost, I think.* □ *Tod's just a duffer—he's not really serious at it.* **2.** *n.* an unskilled golfer. □ *Those duffers up ahead are holding up the game.* □ *Don't call me a duffer!*

duke **1.** *in.* to empty one's stomach; to vomit. (Collegiate. Rhymes with *puke*.) □ *He left to duke. I saw how green he was.* □ *She's in the john, duking like a goat.* **2.** a fist. (Always plural.) □ *Okay, brother, put your dukes up.* □ *The guy's got dukes like hams.* **3.** *n.* one's knee. (Always plural.) □ *He went down on his dukes and prayed for all sorts of good stuff.* □ *He cracked one of his dukes on the railing.*

duke someone out AND **duke out someone** *tr.* to knock someone out with the fist. (See *duke*.) □ *Bob duked out the mugger with a jab to the cheek.* □ *Wilbur tried to duke the guy out first.*

dumbski ['dəmski] **1.** *n.* a stupid person. □ *He's not the dumbski he seems to be.* □ *They used to think Gert was a dumbski.*

2. *mod.* stupid; dumb. □ *What a dumbski jerk!* □ *It is not a dumbski idea!*

dummy 1. *n.* an empty liquor or beer bottle. □ *Toss your dummies over here, and I'll put them in the bin.* □ *That was a sixty dummy party. I counted.* **2.** *n.* a cigarette butt. □ *The tramp collected dummies until he had enough for a smoke.* □ *The guy tossed a dummy out the window of his car.* **3.** *n.* a stupid person. □ *Don't be such a dummy.* □ *I'm no dummy!*

dupe 1. *n.* a potential victim of a confidence trick. □ *The crooks found a good dupe and started their scheme.* □ *I don't want to be a dupe for anybody.* **2.** *tr.* to trick someone; to swindle someone. □ *You tried to dupe me!* □ *I did not try to dupe you. It was an honest mistake.* **3.** *n.* a duplicate; a copy. □ *Make a dupe of this before you send it off.* □ *I've got a dupe in the files.*

dust 1. *in.* to leave; to depart. □ *Well, it's late. I gotta dust.* □ *They dusted out of there at about midnight.* **2.** *tr.* to defeat someone; to win out over someone. □ *We dusted the other team, 87 to 54.* □ *In the second game, they dusted us.*

dust someone off AND **dust off someone** *tr.* to give someone a severe pounding or beating. □ *Reggie threatened to dust Carl off.* □ *Bob dusted off Larry; then he started for Tom.*

dust-up *n.* a fight. □ *Carl got in a dust-up with Reggie.* □ *There was a dust-up at the party that ruined the evening for everyone.*

dweeb [dwib] **1.** *n.* an earnest student. (Collegiate.) □ *Don't call Merton a dweeb! Even if he is one.* □ *The dweebs get all the A's, so why work?* **2.** *n.* a strange or eccentric person; a *nerd.* □ *This place is filled with dweebs of all sizes.* □ *Here comes a dweeb. Ask him for some money.*

dynamite [ˈdaɪnəmaɪt] **1.** *n.* anything potentially powerful: a drug, news, a person. □ *This chick is really dynamite!* □ *The story about the scandal was dynamite and kept selling papers for a month.* **2.** *mod.* excellent; powerful. □ *I want some more of your dynamite enchiladas, please.* □ *These tacos are dynamite, too.*

E

eagle freak *n.* someone with strong concerns about the environment and conservation, especially the preservation of the eagle. (Jocular and slightly derogatory.) □ *The eagle freaks oppose building the dam.* □ *They call me an eagle freak, which doesn't bother me at all.*

ear candy *n.* soft and pleasant popular music; music that is sweet to the ear. □ *I find that kind of ear candy more annoying than loud rock.* □ *People joke about it, but ear candy is restful.*

ear-duster *n.* a gossipy person. □ *Sally is sort of an ear-duster, but she's all heart.* □ *I can be an ear-duster, I know, but have you heard about Sally and her you-know-what?*

earful ['irʊl] **1.** *n.* a tremendous amount of gossip. □ *I got a big earful about Sally.* □ *I can give you an earful about the mayor.* **2.** *n.* a scolding. □ *Her mother gave her an earful when she finally got home.* □ *Tom got an earful for his part in the prank.*

earp AND **urp** [ərp] **1.** *in.* to empty one's stomach; to vomit. □ *Somebody earped here!* □ *I wish people could urp silently.* **2.** *n.* vomit. □ *There's earp on your shoe.* □ *Throw something over the urp in the flower bed.*

easy mark *n.* a likely victim. □ *Merton looks like an easy mark, but he's really quite careful.* □ *Mary is an easy mark because she is so unsuspecting.*

eat **1.** *tr.* [for something] to bother or worry someone. □ *What's eating you, Bill?* □ *Nothing's eating me. I'm just the nervous type.* **2.** *tr.* to absorb the cost or expense of something. □ *It was our mistake, and we'll have to eat it.* □ *We'll eat the costs on this one. It's the least we can do.*

eat up *in.* to eat what is prepared for one. (Usually a command.) □ *Come on, now. Sit down and eat up!* □ *Eat up! There's plenty more where this came from.*

eco freak AND **eco nut** ['iko frik AND 'iko nət] *n.* someone with strong concerns about the environment and conservation. (From *ecology.*) □ *They call me an eco freak, which is okay with me.* □ *It's we eco nuts who think about the future of our planet.*

eco nut See the previous entry.

eggbeater **1.** *n.* an outboard boat motor. □ *My eggbeater has been acting up, so I didn't go out on the lake today.* □ *By the time you get about 20 eggbeaters on the lake at once, it's really pretty noisy.* **2.** *n.* a helicopter. (See also *rotorhead.*) □ *The egg-beater landed on the hospital roof.* □ *I would think that eggbeaters all over the place would disturb the patients.*

el cheapo [ɛl 'tʃipo] **1.** *n.* the cheap one; the cheapest one. (Mock Spanish.) □ *I don't want one of those el cheapos.* □ *I can only afford el cheapo.* **2.** *mod.* cheap. □ *The el cheapo brand won't last.* □ *Is this the el cheapo model?*

em [ɛm] *n.* an empty liquor bottle. □ *Put your ems in the garbage, not on the floor.* □ *Whose ems are all these?*

ends **1.** *n.* money. (Streets.) □ *You got enough ends to get you through the week?* □ *We don't have enough ends to pay the gas bill.* **2.** *n.* shoes. □ *You even got holes in your ends.* □ *Could you use some new ends?*

enforcer   *n.* a bully; a thug or bodyguard. □ *Reggie is the perfect enforcer. Meaner than all get out.* □ *Walter is too tenderhearted to be a good enforcer.*

evil   *mod.* excellent. (See *wicked*.) □ *This wine is really evil!* □ *Man, what evil fronts!*

Excellent!   *exclam.* "Fine!" (Like *awesome*, this expression is a standard word used frequently in slang contexts.) □ *A new stereo? Excellent!* □ *Excellent! Way rad!*

eyeball   *tr.* to look hard at someone or something. □ *I eyeballed the contract and saw the figures.* □ *The two eyeballed each other and walked on.*

eyepopper   *n.* someone or something visually astonishing. □ *The picture of the proposed building was a real eyepopper.* □ *What an eyepopper of a house!* □ *Isn't that foxy lady an eyepopper?* □ *I may not be an eyepopper, but my virtue is exemplary.*

F

fab [fæb] *mod.* fabulous. □ *Man, what a fab stereo!* □ *Your pad is not what I'd call fab. Just okay.*

[face] See the four entries that follow and *Bag your face!, Get out of my face!, chew face, crater face, get face, kissyface, mace someone's face, mess someone's face up, suck face.*

face card *n.* an important person; a self-important person. (As with the royal characters in playing cards.) □ *Who's the face card getting out of the benz?* □ *Reggie is the face card in the local mob.*

faced **1.** *mod.* alcohol intoxicated. □ *Lord, is he faced!* □ *Who is that guy on the corner who looks so faced?* **2.** *mod.* rejected by a member of the opposite sex. (Collegiate.) □ *I've been faced again, and I hate it!* □ *Sally was faced by Tod, and she won't speak to him or anybody else.*

face man *n.* a good-looking young man with no personality. (Collegiate.) □ *Harry is just a face man and as dull as dishwater.* □ *Norm is the perfect face man—all looks and no brains.*

face-off ['fesɔf] *n.* a confrontation. (From hockey.) □ *For a minute it looked like we were headed toward a nasty face-off.* □ *The face-off continued for a few moments till both of them realized that there was no point in fighting.*

fack [fæk] *in.* to state the facts; to tell (someone) the truth. (Black.) □ *That dude is not facking with me.* □ *Now is the time to start facking. Where were you?*

fade **1.** *in.* to leave. □ *I think that the time has come for me to fade. See ya.* □ *Hey, man, let's fade.* **2.** *in.* [for someone] to lose power or influence. □ *Ralph is fading, and someone else will have to take over.* □ *The mayor is fading and won't run for re-election.*

fake off *in.* to waste time; to *goof off.* □ *Hey, you guys, quit faking off!* □ *All you clowns do is fake off. Now, get busy!*

fanny-bumper *n.* an event that draws so many people that they bump into one another. □ *The fire on 34th Street turned into a real fanny-bumper.* □ *There was a typically dull fanny-bumper in the village last night.*

fanny-dipper *n.* a swimmer, as opposed to a surfer. (California.) □ *The fanny-dippers are not supposed to go out that far.* □ *It's too windy for fanny-dippers, let alone surfers.*

far-out **1.** *mod.* cool; great; extraordinary. □ *This jazz is really far-out!* □ *You want to hear some far-out heavy metal?* **2.** *mod.* very hard to understand; arcane; highly theoretical. □ *This stuff is too far-out for me.* □ *I can't follow your far-out line of reasoning.*

fart (Caution with word and topic in all senses.) **1.** *in.* to release intestinal gas through the anus. □ *Okay, who farted?* □ *I think I heard one of you fart.* **2.** *n.* a release of intestinal gas. □ *Wow, what a fart!* □ *Who is responsible for that vile fart?* **3.** *n.* a totally disgusting person. (Also a term of address.) □ *Look here, you stupid fart!* □ *Don't act like such a fart all the time.*

fast buck See *quick buck.*

fat *mod.* well supplied; having an overabundance of something. □ *When it comes to bad food, this place is fat.* □ *We're fat with paper, but there's not a printer ribbon in sight.*

feeb [fib] *n.* an oaf; a stupid person. (From *feebleminded*.) □ *Don't be a feeb. Wake up!* □ *You are such a feeb!*

feeby AND **feebee** ['fibi] *n.* the F.B.I., the Federal Bureau of Investigation. □ *The locals were going to call in the feebies, but the prosecutor said to wait.* □ *The feeby is in on this already.*

fenced *mod.* angry. (California.) □ *Boy, was that old man fenced!* □ *Too many people around here are fenced all the time.*

fender-bender ['fɛndɚbɛndɚ] **1.** *n.* a minor accident. (Compare to *rear-ender*.) □ *There are a couple of fender-benders on the expressway this morning, so be careful.* □ *A minor fender-bender blocked traffic for a while.* **2.** *n.* a reckless driver who may cause minor accidents. □ *I can't get insurance on my 17-year-old, who is a hopeless fender-bender.* □ *Don't give up on young fender-benders.*

fink [fɪŋk] **1.** *n.* a guard hired to protect strikebreakers. (From *Pinkerton*.) □ *Management called in the finks.* □ *We would've settled if the finks hadn't showed up.* **2.** *n.* a strikebreaker. □ *The finks moved in with clubs.* □ *Reggie used to be a fink. He'd do anything for money.* **3.** *n.* an informer. (See also *rat fink*.) □ *Molly has turned into a fink.* □ *Wally doesn't think much of finks.* **4.** *n.* any strange or undesirable person. □ *You are being such a fink. Stop it!* □ *Merton is a strange kind of fink.*

fish-kiss **1.** *tr. & in.* to kiss (someone) with puckered-up lips. (Collegiate.) □ *He can fish-kiss like an expert, which is like being an expert at nothing.* □ *He fish-kissed me, then ran back to his car.* **2.** *n.* a kiss made with puckered-up lips. (Collegiate.) □ *One more fish-kiss tonight, and I am going to scream.* □ *The actor planted a big fish-kiss right on her lips and frightened her.*

[five]   See the entry that follows and *Give me five!, Slip me five!, bunch of fives, give someone five, hang five, high five, low five, slip someone five, take five.*

five-finger discount   *n.* the acquisition of something by shoplifting. □ *Reggie used his five-finger discount to get the kind of gift Molly wanted.* □ *I got this candy with my five-finger discount.*

fix   1. AND **fix-up**   *n.* a dose of a drug, especially for an addict who is in need of drugs. (Drugs. It fixes or eases the suffering of withdrawal.) □ *It was clear that the prisoner needed a fix, but there was nothing the cops would do for him.* □ *Carl arranged to get a fix-up into the con.* **2.** *n.* a bribe. □ *Walter never took a fix in his life.* □ *The agent paid a fix to the cops.*

fla(c)k   [flæk] **1.** *n.* complaints; criticism; negative feedback. □ *Why do I have to get all the flak for what you did?* □ *We're getting a lot of flack for that news broadcast.* **2.** *n.* publicity; hype. □ *Who is going to believe this flack about being first-rate?* □ *It's all flak and no substance.* **3.** *n.* a public relations agent or officer. □ *The flak made an announcement and then disappeared.* □ *There were flacks all over the place telling lies and making false promises.*

flack (out)   *in.* to collapse in exhaustion; to go to sleep. □ *I just have to go home now and flack out.* □ *Betsy flacked out at nine every night.*

flag   [flæg] **1.** *tr.* to fail a course. □ *Pat flagged English again.* □ *I'm afraid I flagged algebra.* **2.** *n.* the grade of F. □ *I'll get a flag on algebra for the semester.* □ *I got three flags and an A.* **3.** *tr.* to arrest someone. □ *The cop flagged Molly for soliciting.* □ *They flagged Bob for speeding even though he was a judge.*

flake   [flek] *n.* a person who acts silly or giddy. □ *Sally is such a flake!* □ *Who's the flake in the plaid pants?*

flake down *in.* to go to bed; to go to sleep. □ *Look at the time. I gotta go home and flake down.* □ *After I flake down for about three days, I'll tell you about my trip.*

flake (out) *in.* to pass out from exhaustion; to fall asleep. □ *I just flaked out. I had had it.* □ *After jogging, I usually flake for awhile.*

flaky ['fleki] *mod.* unreliable. □ *She's too flaky to hold the job.* □ *He's a flaky dude.* □ *I'm getting so flaky. Must be old age.*

flash [flæʃ] **1.** *n.* something suddenly remembered; something suddenly thought of. □ *I had a flash and quickly wrote it down.* □ *After we talked awhile, a flash hit me. Why don't we sell the house?* **2.** *n.* a very short period of time; an instant. □ *I'll be there in a flash.* □ *It was just a flash between the time I said I'd be there and when I showed up.* **3.** *tr.* to display something briefly. □ *You'd better not flash a wad like that around here. You won't have it long.* □ *The cop flashed her badge and made the pinch.*

flashback *n.* a memory of the past; a portrayal of the past in a story. (Almost standard English.) □ *Suddenly, Fred had a wonderful flashback to his childhood.* □ *The next scene in the film was a flashback to the time of Ivan the Terrible.*

flash on something *in.* to remember something suddenly and vividly. □ *Then I flashed on a great idea.* □ *I was trying to flash on it, but I couldn't bring it to mind.*

flash the hash *tr.* to empty one's stomach; to vomit. □ *Dave left quickly to go out and flash the hash, I think.* □ *Who's in there flashing the hash?*

flexed out of shape *mod.* very angry. □ *The boss was completely flexed out of shape.* □ *I am truly flexed out of shape.*

flick [flɪk] *n.* a movie. □ *That was a pretty good flick, right?* □ *Let's go see that new Woody Allen flick.*

fling up *in.* to empty one's stomach; to vomit. □ *I was afraid I was going to fling up.* □ *Who flung up on the sidewalk?*

fling-wing *n.* a helicopter. (See also *eggbeater*.) □ *The fling-wing from the radio station is hovering over the traffic jam.* □ *There must be a dozen fling-wings up there making all that noise.*

flip *in.* to go crazy. □ *Wow, I've got so much to do, I may just flip.* □ *The guy flipped. He was the nervous type.*

flip (out) *in.* to lose control of oneself. □ *Wow, I almost flipped out when I heard about it.* □ *He got so mad that he flipped.*

flip side **1.** *n.* the "other" side of a phonograph record. □ *On the flip side, we have another version of "Love Me Tender" sung by Sally Mills.* □ *Give a listen to the flip side sometime.* **2.** *n.* the "other" side of something, such as an argument. □ *I want to hear the flip side of this before I make a judgment.* □ *On the flip side, he is no bargain either.* **3.** *n.* the return trip of a long journey. (Citizens band radio.) □ *See ya. Catch you on the flip side, maybe.* □ *Didn't I talk to you on the flip side last week?*

flub something up AND **flub up something** *tr.* to do something incorrectly; to mess up a procedure. □ *Now don't flub this up.* □ *I never flub up anything.*

flub (up) **1.** AND **flub-up** *n.* an error; a blunder. □ *I tried not to make a flub, but I did.* □ *Who is responsible for this flub-up?* **2.** *in.* to make a confused mess of something. □ *You are flubbing up again, aren't you?* □ *I do my best to keep from flubbing.*

fluff-stuff ['fləfstəf] *n.* snow. □ *There is supposed to be an inch of fluff-stuff tonight.* □ *Fluff-stuff looks pretty, but it's no fun to shovel it.*

fly *mod.* knowledgeable; alert and in the know. □ *This dude is fly; there's no question about it.* □ *We don't need any more fly birds around here.*

foam *n.* beer. □ *How about some more foam?* □ *All the guy thinks about is foam.*

fomp [fɑmp] *in.* to play around sexually. (Collegiate.) □ *Who are those two over there fomping?* □ *Jerry wanted to fomp, and I wanted to get him out of my sight.*

fooey See *phooey*.

foot it *tr.* to go somewhere on foot; to walk or run. (Compare to *ankle, shank it.*) □ *I have to foot it over to the drugstore for some medicine.* □ *I'm used to footing it wherever I go.*

fossil **1.** *n.* an old-fashioned person. □ *Some old fossil called the police about the noise.* □ *Oh, Tad, you are such a fossil.* **2.** *n.* a parent. (See also *rent(al)s.*) □ *My fossils would never agree to anything like that.* □ *Would your fossils permit that?*

fox *n.* an attractive person, typically a young woman. □ *Man, who was that fox I saw you with?* □ *That fox was my sister. Next question?*

fox trap *n.* an automobile customized and fixed up in a way that will attract women. □ *I put every cent I earned into my fox trap, but I still repelled women.* □ *To you it's a fox trap; to me it's a sin-bin.*

foxy ['fɑksi] **1.** *mod.* sexy, especially having to do with a woman. □ *Man, isn't she foxy!* □ *What a foxy dame!* (More at *foxy lady.*) **2.** *mod.* smelly with perspiration odor. □ *Somebody in this taxi is a little foxy.* □ *Who's got the foxy pits?* □ *Subway cars can sure get foxy in the summer.*

foxy lady *n.* a sexually attractive young woman. □ *You are really a foxy lady, Molly.* □ *A couple of foxy ladies stopped us on the street.*

fragged [frægd] *mod.* destroyed; ruined. □ *Why does your room look so fragged?* □ *My clothes are fragged, and I need a haircut.*

frantic *mod.* great; wild. □ *We had a frantic time at Chez Freddy.* □ *That party was really frantic.*

freaked (out) AND **freaked-out** **1.** *mod.* shocked; disoriented. □ *I was too freaked out to reply.* □ *Man, was I freaked.* **2.** *mod.* tired out; exhausted. □ *I'm too freaked out to go on without some rest.* □ *The chick is really freaked. Let her rest.*

freaker ['frikɚ] **1.** *n.* an incident that causes someone to *freak out.* (Collegiate.) □ *Wasn't that weird? A real freaker.* □ *Did you see that near miss? What a freaker!* **2.** *n.* a *freaked-out* person. (Collegiate.) □ *Some poor freaker sat in the corner and rocked.* □ *Who's the freaker over there?*

freaking *mod.* damned; unsuitable or unacceptable. □ *Get your freaking socks off my bed.* □ *What is this freaking mess on my plate?*

freak (out) **1.** [frik('aʊt)] *in.* to panic; to lose control. □ *I was so frightened, I thought I would freak.* □ *Come on, relax. Don't freak out.* **2.** ['frikaʊt] *n.* a wild party of any type; any exciting happening. (Usually **freak-out** or **freakout.**) □ *There is a big freak-out at Freddy's joint tonight.* □ *What a frantic freakout!* **3.** ['frikaʊt] *n.* a *freaked-out* person. (Usually **freak-out** or **freakout.**) □ *Some poor freak-out sat in the corner and rocked.* □ *Who's the freakout in the corner?*

freak someone out AND **freak out someone** *tr.* to shock or disorient someone. □ *The whole business freaked me out.* □ *I didn't mean to freak out everybody with the bad news.*

freebee See the following entry.

freebie AND **freebee, freeby** ['fribi] *n.* something given away free. □ *They gave me a freebie with my purchase.* □ *I expect a freebee when I spend a lot of money like that.*

freeze **1.** *n.* the act of ignoring someone. (Usually with *the*.) □ *Everybody seems to be giving me the freeze.* □ *I got the freeze from Julie. What did I do wrong?* **2.** *tr.* to ignore someone; to give someone the cold shoulder. □ *Don't freeze me, gang! I use a mouthwash!* □ *They froze him because he didn't act like a civilized human being.*

French kiss **1.** *n.* kissing using the tongue; open-mouth kissing. □ *What's French about a French kiss?* □ *I didn't know whether I was going to get a French-kiss or a fish-kiss.* **2.** *tr.* to kiss someone, using the tongue. (Usually **French-kiss**.) □ *Kids like to try to French-kiss each other at an early age. It's part of growing up.* □ *He tried to French-kiss me, but I stopped him.*

from (the) git-go *mod.* from the very start. (See *git-go, jump (street)*.) □ *This kind of thing has been a problem from the git-go.* □ *I warned you about this from git-go.*

fronts *n.* clothing; a sports jacket. (Black.) □ *You got some good-looking fronts there.* □ *I need some new fronts.*

froody ['frudi] *mod.* grand; wonderful. □ *The curtains parted to the most froody funky set I've ever seen.* □ *Man, is this froody!* □ *Oh, you have some froody ideas, all right. But can you carry them out?*

frost *tr.* to make someone angry. □ *That really frosts me.* □ *The little car frosted me by zooming into my parking place.* (More at *frosted (over)*.)

frosted (over) *mod.* angry; annoyed. □ *The clerk was really frosted over when I asked for a better one.* □ *Why was he so frosted?*

frosty 1. AND **frosty one** *n.* a beer; a cold beer. □ *Hey, toss me a frosty, will ya?* □ *I need a frosty one after all that work.* **2.** *mod.* cool; really cool and mellow. □ *That music is really frosty.* □ *We had a frosty time, didn't we?*

froth *n.* a beer. □ *Would you like some froth?* □ *How about another pitcher of froth, innkeeper?*

fugly ['fəgli] *mod.* "fat and ugly." (Collegiate.) □ *Man, is that dog of yours ever fugly! What or who did it eat?* □ *This is a real fugly problem we're facing.*

funk [fəŋk] **1.** *n.* a bad odor; a stench. □ *What is that ghastly funk in here?* □ *Open the windows and clear out this funk.* **2.** *n.* a depressed state. □ *I've been in such a funk that I can't get my work done.* □ *As soon as I get out of my winter funk, I'll be more helpful.*

funky 1. *mod.* strange; far-out. □ *I like your funky hat.* □ *Isn't he funky?* □ *He's such a funky guy.* **2.** *mod.* basic and simple; earthy. □ *Everything she does is so funky.* □ *I like to be around funky people.* **3.** *mod.* smelly; obnoxious. □ *Get your funky old socks outa here.* □ *This place is really funky. Open some windows.*

funky-drunk *mod.* alcohol intoxicated; stinking drunk. □ *The guy is funky-drunk, and I think he's going to be sick.* □ *Wow, is she ever funky-drunk!*

fur *n.* the police. (See *fuzz.*) □ *I think the fur is on to you, Walter.* □ *No fur ain't never gonna get me!*

fuse, blow a See *blow a fuse.*

futz See *phutz.*

fuzz [fəz] **1.** AND **fuzz man, fuzzy (tail)** *n.* the police; a jail keeper; a detective. □ *The fuzz is on to you.* □ *See if you can distract the fuzz man while I lift his keys.* **2.** AND **fuzzle** *in.* to get drunk. □ *They were just sitting there fuzzling away the day.* □ *Stop fuzzing and listen.*

fuzzle   See under *fuzz.*

fuzz man   See *fuzz.*

fuzz station   *n.* a police station. (See *fuzz.*) □ *He had to spend about an hour at the fuzz station, but nothing happened to him.* □ *Drop by the fuzz station and pick up a copy of the driving rules.*

fuzzy (tail)   See *fuzz.*

G

G. See *grand*.

Gag me with a spoon! *exclam.* "I am disgusted!" (A catchphrase initiated by Moon Unit Zappa in a phonograph recording about "Valley Girls" in California.) □ *So gross! Gag me with a spoon!* □ *Gag me with a spoon! You are way gross!*

GAPO AND **gapo** ['gæpo] *n.* "giant armpit odor"; a bad underarm odor. □ *Who's got the gapo in here?* □ *That cab driver really has the GAPO.*

garbage something down AND **garbage down something** *tr.* to gobble something up; to bolt something down. □ *Don't garbage your food down!* □ *That guy will garbage down almost anything.*

gasket, blow a See *blow a fuse*.

gaucho ['gaʊtʃo] *tr. & in.* to expose the buttocks (at someone), usually through a car window; to *moon*. □ *Wally gauchoed the cops as they went by.* □ *Victor would gaucho at the drop of a hat —so to speak.*

gazoo [gə'zu] *n.* the buttocks; the anus. □ *He fell down flat, smack on his gazoo.* □ *Look at the monstrous gazoo on that guy.*

gear 1. *mod.* excellent. □ *This jazz is really gear!* □ *Man, what a gear pizza!* **2.** *n.* "*"; an asterisk. □ *Why is there a gear after this word?* □ *The gear stands for anything you want it to stand for.*

gee [dʒi] **1.** *exclam.* "Wow!" (An abbreviation of *Jesus!*, although not always recognized as such. Usually **Gee!**) □ *Gee! What a mess!* □ *Golly gee, do I have to?* **2.** *mod.* "gross"; disgusting. (From the initial letter of *gross*.) □ *This is just too gee!* □ *Tiffany is acting way gee lately.*

geedunk [giˈdəŋk OR ˈgidəŋk] *n.* ice cream. □ *Let's go out and get some geedunk for dessert.* □ *Pineapple on chocolate geedunk? Yuck!*

geek AND **geke** [gik] **1.** *n.* a disgusting and repellent person. □ *The convention was a seething morass of pushy sales geeks and glad-handers.* □ *Who's the geek who just came in?* **2.** *n.* an earnest student; a hardworking student. □ *Merton is a geek, but he will go places with his brains.* □ *It looks like the geeks are taking over this campus. How gross!*

Get a life! *exclam.* "Change your life radically!" (Compare to **Get real!**) □ *You are such a twit! Get a life!* □ *Get a life, you clown!*

get down **1.** *in.* to lay one's money on the table. (Gambling.) □ *Okay, everybody get down.* □ *Get down, and let's get going!* **2.** *in.* to concentrate; to do something well. □ *I'm flunking two subjects, man. I gotta get down.* □ *Come on, Sam, pay attention. Get down and learn this stuff.* **3.** *in.* to copulate. (Black.) □ *Hey, let's get down!* □ *All Steve wants to do is get down all the time.*

get face *tr.* to gain respect; to increase one's status. (The opposite of *lose face*.) □ *He's doing his best in life to get face.* □ *Let's do something to help her get face.*

get into something *in.* to become deeply involved with something. □ *I got into computers when I was in junior high school.* □ *When did you get into foreign films?*

get it **1.** *tr.* to understand a joke; to understand a point of information. □ *Sorry. I don't get it.* □ *Don't you get it?* **2.** *tr.* to get punished. □ *I just know I'm going to get it when I get home.* □ *You're going to get it all right!*

get it on 1. *tr.* to begin something. □ *Time to go back to work. Let's get it on!* □ *Get it on, you guys! Time to start your engines.* 2. *tr.* to begin dancing. □ *Let's go out there and get it on!* □ *He wanted to get it on, but my feet hurt.* 3. *tr.* [for people] to copulate. (Caution with topic.) □ *Come on, baby, let's get it on.* □ *I don't want to get it on with you or any other creep.* 4. *tr.* to undertake to enjoy oneself. □ *I can really get it on with that slow jazz.* □ *Let's go listen to some new-age stuff and get it on.*

get it up *tr.* to get excited about something. (Other taboo meanings, also.) □ *I just couldn't get it up about going off to college.* □ *Paul just couldn't get it up about life in general.*

get lip *tr.* to get some kissing; to neck. (Teens.) □ *Jim's been out getting lip again. Look at the lipstick.* □ *These kids talk about getting lip. Ye gods, how crude!*

get naked *in.* to enjoy oneself thoroughly; to relax and enjoy oneself. □ *Let's all go out and get naked tonight.* □ *Man, I feel like getting naked!*

get off 1. *in.* to reach an understanding with someone. (Not slang.) □ *We just weren't getting off well at all.* □ *How well do you get off with Ralph?* 2. See the following entry.

get off (on something) 1. *in.* to get pleasure from something. □ *I don't get off on music anymore.* □ *I listen, but I just don't get off.* 2. *in.* to take a drug and experience a *rush.* □ *Carl likes to get off, but he's got his business to run.* □ *Molly likes getting off on grass better than anything else.*

get off the dime *in.* [for something or someone] to start moving. (To get off the dime that one stopped on in "stop on a dime" or turned on in "turn on a dime.") □ *I wish this organization could get off the dime.* □ *If this project gets off the dime, we'll be okay.*

get one's rocks off (on something) *tr.* to enjoy something. (Other taboo meanings, also.) □ *I really get my rocks off on rock and roll.* □ *I've listened to the stuff, but I sure don't get my rocks off on it.*

get one's ticket punched *tr.* to die; to be killed. (Literally, to be canceled.) □ *Poor Chuck got his ticket punched while he was waiting for a bus.* □ *Watch out there, or you'll get your ticket punched.*

Get out of my face! *exclam.* "Stop arguing with me!"; "Stand back! Don't confront me with your arguments and challenges!" □ *Beat it! Get out of my face!* □ *Get outa my face if you know what's good for you.*

Get real! *exclam.* "Start acting realistically!" (Compare to *Get a life!*) □ *Hey, chum! You are way off base! Get real!* □ *Get real! Wake up to reality!*

get someone's motor running **1.** *tr.* to get someone excited. □ *What'll I have to do to get your motor running about algebra?* □ *I've got some news that'll really get your motor running.* **2.** *tr.* to get someone sexually aroused. □ *She knows how to get his motor running.* □ *It's funny how that wild music gets her motor running.*

get with it **1.** *in.* to modernize one's attitudes and behavior. □ *Get with it, Merton. Get real!* □ *You really have to get with it, Ernie.* **2.** *in.* to hurry up and get busy; to be more industrious with something. □ *Get with it; we've got a lot to do.* □ *Let's get with it. There's a lot of work to be done.*

(ghetto) blaster AND **(ghetto) box** ['gɛdo blæstɚ AND 'gɛdo baks] *n.* a portable stereo radio. (Often carried on the shoulder, especially by blacks.) □ *Hey, turn down that ghetto blaster in here!* □ *You can't bring that box on this bus!*

(ghetto) box See the previous entry.

giffed [gɪft] *mod.* alcohol intoxicated. (From *T.G.I.F* "Thank God it's Friday." Said of people who celebrate the end of the workweek by drinking liquor.) □ *He left the tavern pretty giffed.* □ *She was pretty giffed for just a few beers.*

gig **1.** *n.* a onetime job; an engagement. (Musicians.) □ *I had a gig out on the west side, but I couldn't get there.* □ *The gig was canceled because of the snow.* **2.** *in.* to play or perform. (Musicians.) □ *I didn't gig at all last week. I'm getting hungry for a job.* □ *I'm happiest when I'm gigging.* **3.** *n.* any job of an assignment nature; a onetime job such as when a newspaper reporter is assigned to write a particular story. □ *I didn't want that election gig, but I got it anyway.* □ *Wally is tired of getting the crime gigs.*

git-go ['gɪtgo] *n.* the very beginning. (Black. See also *from (the) git-go*.) □ *Clear back at the git-go, I told you this wouldn't work.* □ *He's been gritching ever since git-go.*

Give it a rest! *exclam.* "Shut up!" (The "it" is a mouth. Compare to *Give me a rest!*) □ *I've heard enough. Give it a rest!* □ *Give it a rest! You talk too much.*

Give it up! *exclam.* "Quit now!"; "Stop, you will continue to fail!" □ *Oh, give it up! You can't do it right.* □ *Give it up! You can't pitch!*

Give me a rest! *exclam.* "Lay off!"; "That is enough!" (Compare to *Give it a rest!*) □ *Haven't I told you everything you need to know? Give me a rest!* □ *Give me a rest! I've heard enough.*

Give me five! See the following entry.

Give me (some) skin! AND **Give me five!, Slip me five!** *exclam.* "Shake [or slap] my hand!" (A request for some form of hand touching in greeting. See also *give someone five, high five*.) □ *Hey, man! Give me some skin!* □ *Give me five, my man!*

give someone five **1.** *tr.* to give someone a helping hand. □ *Hey, give me five over here for a minute, will ya?* □ *I gotta give this* *guy five with the crate. Be right with you.* **2.** *tr.* to slap hands in greeting. (See *high five.*) □ *Jerry gave John five as they passed in the corridor.* □ *Don tried to give me five in class, but missed.*

give someone the gate *tr.* to get rid of someone. □ *The guy was a pest, so I gave him the gate.* □ *He threatened to give me the gate, so I left.*

give someone the go-by *tr.* to bypass someone; to ignore someone. (See *go-by.*) □ *Gert gave us all the go-by when she got rich.* □ *I didn't mean to give you the go-by. I'm preoccupied, that's all.*

glad-hand *tr.* to greet someone effusively. □ *The senator was glad-handing everyone in sight.* □ *He glad-handed Ernie and got a real earful.*

glad-hander *n.* someone who displays effusive friendship. □ *What a hoard of eager glad-handers and glitz!* □ *The glad-handers were out in full force at the Independence Day parade.*

glad rags *n.* fancy clothes; best clothing. □ *You look pretty good in your glad rags.* □ *I'll get on my glad rags, and we'll go out tonight.*

glitch [glɪtʃ] *n.* a defect; a bug. □ *There is a glitch in the computer program somewhere.* □ *I'm afraid there's a glitch in our plans.*

glitz [glɪts] *n.* flashiness and glamour. □ *The place was nothing but eager sales geeks and phony glitz.* □ *The glitz was blinding, and the substance was invisible.*

glitzy ['glɪtsi] *mod.* fashionable; glamorous. □ *It was a real glitzy place to hold a meeting.* □ *Some glitzy blonde sang a couple of songs, and then the band played again.*

gnarly AND **narly** ['narli] *mod.* excellent; great. (California.) □ *This pizza is too gnarly for words!* □ *Who is that narly guy in the white sweater?*

go 1. *n.* a try (at something). □ *Let me have a go at it this time.* □ *I'd like to have another go at it, if I can.* 2. *n.* a drink of liquor; a dose of a drug. □ *She had one go and then sat back for a while.* □ *Another go and she was essentially stoned.*

go ape (over someone or something) *in.* to become very excited over something. □ *I just go ape over chocolate.* □ *Sam went ape over Mary.*

goat *n.* a fast and powerful car; a Pontiac GTO. □ *Hey, man, where'd you get that goat?* □ *His goat conked out on him.*

gob [gab] 1. *n.* a blob or mass of something. □ *I'd like a big gob of mashed potatoes, please.* □ *Take that horrid gob of gum out of your mouth!* 2. *n.* a large amount of something. (Usually in the plural.) □ *I've just got gobs of it if you need some.* □ *I need gobs of money to get through school.*

go bananas *in.* to go mildly crazy. □ *Sorry, I just went bananas for a minute.* □ *I thought he was going to go bananas.*

go belly-up See *turn belly-up.*

go blooey AND **go flooey** [go 'blui AND go 'flui] *in.* to fall apart; to go out of order. □ *Suddenly, all my plans went blooey.* □ *I just hope everything doesn't go flooey at the last minute.*

go-by ['gobaɪ] *n.* an instance of ignoring or passing by (someone). (See *give someone the go-by.*) □ *I got the go-by from her every time I saw her.* □ *I find the go-by very insulting.*

Go chase yourself! AND **Go climb a tree!**, **Go fly a kite!**, **Go jump in the lake!**, **Go soak your head!** *exclam.* "Beat it!"; "Go away!" □ *Oh, go chase yourself! Get out of my face!* □ *Go soak your head! You're a pain in the neck.*

go down 1. *in.* to happen. □ *Hey, man! What's going down?* □ *Something strange is going down around here.* **2.** *in.* to be accepted. (See *swallow.*) □ *We'll just have to wait awhile to see how all this goes down.* □ *The proposal didn't go down very well with the manager.* **3.** *in.* to be arrested. (Underworld.) □ *Lefty didn't want to go down for a job he didn't do.* □ *Wally said that somebody had to go down for it, and he didn't care who.*

go down in flames *in.* to fail spectacularly. □ *The whole team went down in flames.* □ *I'd hate for all your planning to go down in flames.*

go down the chute See the following entry.

go down the tube(s) AND **go down the chute** *in.* to fail totally; to be ruined. □ *The whole project is likely to go down the tubes.* □ *All my plans just went down the chute.*

gofer See *gopher.*

go flooey See *go blooey.*

Go for it! *exclam.* "Do it!"; "Try it!" □ *Go for it! Give it a try!* □ *It looked like something I wanted to do, so I decided to go for it.*

go home in a box *in.* to be shipped home dead. □ *Hey, I'm too young to go home in a box.* □ *You had better be careful on this camping trip, or you'll go home in a box.*

gold *n.* money. (See also *ducats.*) □ *Do you have enough gold to pay the bill?* □ *There's no gold in my pockets.*

gomer ['gomɚ] **1.** *n.* a stupid oaf; a social reject. (From the television character Gomer Pyle.) □ *Who's that gomer in the overalls?* □ *That gomer is my Uncle Ben.* **2.** AND **goomer** ['gumɚ] *n.* a person unwelcome in a hospital. (Supposedly an acronym for "Get out of my emergency room.") □ *That goomer with the al-*

lergy is back in E.R. □ *I don't want that goomer back in the emergency room.*

gone 1. AND **gone under** *mod.* unconscious. □ *He's gone. Prop his feet up and call an ambulance.* □ *He's gone under. You can begin the procedure now.* **2.** AND **gone under** *mod.* alcohol or drug intoxicated. □ *Those chicks are gone—too much to drink.* □ *Ted is really gone under.* **3.** *mod.* cool. □ *This ice cream is gone, man, gone!* □ *She is one real gone chick.*

gonzo ['gɑnzo] **1.** *n.* a silly or foolish person. □ *Some gonzo is on the phone asking for the president of the universe.* □ *Tell the gonzo I'm out.* **2.** *mod.* crazy; wild and uncontrollable. □ *The guy is totally gonzo!* □ *Who drew this gonzo picture of me?*

goo [gu] *n.* some sticky substance; *gunk.* □ *What is this goo on my shoe?* □ *There is some sort of goo on my plate. Is that meant to be my dinner?*

goob [gub] *n.* a pimple. (Short for *guber.*) □ *The goobs are taking over my whole face.* □ *I have the world's greatest goob right on the end of my nose.*

goober See *guber.*

goober-grease ['gubɚgris] *n.* peanut butter. □ *Pass me some of that goober-grease, will ya?* □ *This goober-grease is stale.*

good trip 1. *n.* a good session with L.S.D. or some other drug. □ *Paul said he had a good trip, but he looks like the devil.* □ *She said she had a good trip, but I think she hates the stuff.* **2.** *n.* any good time. □ *This meeting was a good trip.* □ *Compared to the last class, this one is a good trip.*

goof [guf] **1.** *n.* a foolish oaf; a *goofy* person. □ *Sometimes I'm such a goof. I really messed up.* □ *Don't be a goof. Get with it.* **2.** AND **goof up** *in.* to make a blunder. □ *Whoops, I goofed!* □ *This time, you goofed.* **3.** *n.* a blunder; an error. □ *Who made this silly goof?* □ *This goof is yours, not mine.*

goof around   See under *goof off*.

goofball AND **goofer**   *n.* a stupid person; a fool. □ *You are such a silly goofball.* □ *Chuck acts like a goofer, but he's really with it.*

goofed (up)   **1.** *mod.* messed up; out of order. □ *All my papers are goofed up.* □ *Everything on my desk is goofed. Who's been here?* **2.** *mod.* confused; distraught. □ *I'm sort of goofed up today. I think I'm coming down with something.* □ *I was up too late last night, and now I'm all goofed up.*

goofer   See *goofball*.

goof off   **1.** AND **goof around**   *in.* to waste time. □ *Quit goofing off.* □ *Get busy. Stop goofing around.* **2.** *n.* a time-waster; a jerk. (Usually **goof-off**.) □ *Tod is such a goof-off!* □ *I'm no goof-off, but I am no scholar either.*

goof on someone   *in.* to play a prank on someone; to involve someone in a deception. □ *Hey, don't goof on me. I'm your buddy!* □ *The kid goofed on Chuck, and he thought it was a pretty good joke.*

goof something up AND **goof up (on) something**   *tr.* to mess something up. □ *Now don't goof it up this time.* □ *I hope I don't goof up the report again.*

goof up   See under *goof*.

goofus   ['gufəs] **1.** *n.* a gadget. □ *Where is that little goofus I use to pry open these cans?* □ *Here's just the little goofus you're looking for.* **2.** AND **goopus**   *n.* a foolish oaf. (Also a term of address.) □ *You're just acting like a goofus. Be serious!* □ *Hey, goopus! Come here!*

goofy   ['gufi] *mod.* silly. □ *Stop acting so goofy! What will the neighbors say?* □ *You are really a goofy chick.*

goombah [ˈgumbɑ] *n.* a buddy; a trusted friend. (Also a term of address. Ultimately from Italian.) □ *Hey, goombah! How goes it?* □ *He's my goombah. I can trust him.*

goomer See under *gomer.*

goophead [ˈguphɛd] *n.* an inflamed pimple. (Patterned on *blackhead*.) □ *Ye gods! I'm covered with goopheads.* □ *You ought to see the goophead on your nose.*

goopus See under *goofus.*

goose egg **1.** *n.* a score of zero. □ *We got a goose egg in the second inning.* □ *It was double goose eggs for the final score.* **2.** *n.* a bump on the head. □ *You've got quite a goose egg there.* □ *I walked into a door and got a big goose egg on my forehead.* **3.** *n.* a failure; a zero. (Similar to sense 1.) □ *The outcome was a real goose egg. A total mess.* □ *The result of three weeks' planning is one big goose egg.*

goozlum [ˈguzləm] *n.* any gummy, sticky substance: syrup, gravy, soup. □ *Do you want some of this wonderful goozlum on your ice cream?* □ *Just keep putting that goozlum on my mashed potatoes.*

gopher AND **gofer** [ˈgofɚ] **1.** *n.* someone who goes for things and brings them back. (From *go for.*) □ *You got a gopher who can go get some coffee?* □ *Send the gofer out for cigarettes.* **2.** *n.* a dupe; a pawn; an underling. □ *The guy's just a gopher. He has no say in anything.* □ *I'll send a gopher over to pick up the papers.*

gorilla juice *n.* steroids. (Bodybuilding. Steroids build muscle tissue rapidly.) □ *Andy really wanted to get hold of some gorilla juice, but his parents said no.* □ *Do all those muscle-bound creatures take gorilla juice?*

gork [gork] **1.** *n.* a fool; a dupe. □ *Merton acts like such a gork sometimes.* □ *The gorks are taking over the world!* **2.** AND

GORK *phr.* an alleged hospital chart notation of the diagnosis "God only really knows." □ *I see old Mr. Kelly is in again with a hundred complaints. His chart says GORK.* □ *He's down with gork again.* **3.** *tr.* to give a patient sedation. □ *Dr. Wilson says to gork the patient in 226.* □ *He'll quiet down after we gork him.*

gorked (out) [gorkt...] *mod.* heavily sedated; knocked out. □ *Once the patient was gorked, he was more cooperative.* □ *The guy in 226 is totally gorked out now.*

gotcha ['gɑtʃə] **1.** *phr.* "I got you!"; "I've caught you!" (Usually **Gotcha!**) □ *I gotcha, and you can't get away.* □ *Ha, ha! Gotcha! Come here, you little dickens.* **2.** *n.* an arrest. (Underworld.) □ *The cop reached out, grasped Reggie's shoulder, and made the gotcha.* □ *It was a fair gotcha. Reggie was nabbed, and he went along quietly.* **3.** *phr.* "I understand you." □ *Gotcha! Thanks for telling me.* □ *Seven pounds, four ounces? Gotcha! I'll tell everybody.*

gourd [gord] *n.* the head. □ *I raised up and got a nasty blow on the gourd.* □ *My gourd aches something awful.*

go West *in.* to die. □ *Ever since Uncle Ben went West, things have been peaceful around here.* □ *When I go West, I want flowers, hired mourners, and an enormous performance of Mozart's "Requiem."*

go zonkers *in.* to go slightly crazy. □ *What a day! I almost went zonkers.* □ *I went a little zonkers there for a minute.*

grabbers *n.* the hands. □ *Keep your grabbers to yourself.* □ *Wash your grubby little grabbers before coming to the table.*

grade-grubber **1.** *n.* an earnest, hard-working student. (In the way a pig roots or grubs around for food.) □ *Merton is a grade-grubber and a real hard worker.* □ *If there are too many grade-grubbers in a class, it will really throw off the grading scale.* **2.** *n.* a student who flatters the teacher in hopes of a higher grade. □ *Toward the end of a semester, my office is filled with grade-*

grubbers. □ *A few grade-grubbers help assure old professors that the world is not really changing at all.*

grand AND **G.**   *n.* one thousand dollars. □ *That car probably cost about 20 grand.* □ *Four G.s for that thing?*

grape(s)   *n.* champagne; wine. □ *These grapes are great!* □ *No more of the grapes for me. It tickles my nose.*

grapes of wrath   *n.* wine. (A play on the title of a John Steinbeck novel.) □ *Fred had taken a little too much of the grapes of wrath.* □ *How about another dose of the grapes of wrath?*

grass   **1.** *n.* marijuana. □ *These kids manage to find their grass somewhere.* □ *Almost everybody knows that grass means marijuana.* **2.** *n.* lettuce; salad greens. □ *I could use a little more grass in my diet.* □ *Do you want some dressing on your grass?*

grave-dancer   *n.* someone who profits from someone else's misfortune. (From the phrase *dance on someone's grave.*) □ *I don't want to seem like a grave-dancer, but his defeat places me in line for a promotion.* □ *The guy's a grave-dancer. Anything to get ahead.*

gravel-pounder   *n.* an infantry soldier. (Military.) □ *Do you really want to join the Army and be a gravel-pounder?* □ *The life of a gravel-pounder is not for me.*

gravy   *n.* extra or easy money; easy profit. □ *Virtually every cent that came in was pure gravy—no expenses and no materials costs at all.* □ *After I pay expenses, the rest is pure gravy.*

gravy train   *n.* a job that brings in a steady supply of easy money or *gravy.* □ *This kind of job is a real gravy train.* □ *The gravy train is just not for me.*

grease   *n.* protection money; bribery money. □ *Walter was in charge of making sure that enough grease was spread around city* hall. □ *See that the commissioner of the park district gets a little grease to help us get the contract.*

greaser ['grizɚ OR 'grisɚ] *n.* a rough and aggressive male, usually with long greased-down hair. □ *Who's the greaser who just swaggered in?* □ *Donna has been going out with a real greaser.*

green AND **green folding, green stuff** *n.* money; paper money. □ *How much green you got on you?* □ *I have so much green stuff, I don't know what to do with it.*

green folding See the previous entry.

greenie ['grini] *n.* a bottle of Heineken (brand) beer. (It comes in a green bottle.) □ *Tom ordered a greenie and had it put on his tab.* □ *Can I have a couple of greenies over here, please?*

green stuff See *green*.

greldge [grɛldʒ] **1.** *n.* something nasty or *yucky*. □ *What is this greldge on my shoe?* □ *That's not any special greldge, that's just plain mud.* **2.** *exclam.* "Nuts!"; "Darn!" (Usually **Greldge!**) □ *Oh, greldge! I'm late!* □ *This is the last straw! Greldge!*

grit *n.* courage; nerve. □ *It takes a lot of grit to do something like that.* □ *Well, Tod has lots of grit. He can do it.*

gritch [grɪtʃ] **1.** *in.* to complain. (A blend of *gripe* and *bitch*.) □ *Stop gritching all the time.* □ *Are you still gritching about that?* **2.** *n.* a complainer; a griper. □ *You are getting to be such a gritch.* □ *Don't be such a gritch!*

groaty See *grody*.

grod(dess) ['grɑd(əs)] *n.* an especially sloppy man or woman. (Patterned on *god* and *goddess*.) □ *Hello, grods and groddesses, what's new?* □ *She is the groddess of scraggly ends.*

grody AND **groaty** ['grodi] *mod.* disgusting. (From *grotesque.* See *grotty.*) □ *What a grody view of the street from this window.* □ *These shoes are getting sort of groaty. I guess I'll throw them out.*

grody to the max ['grodi tu ðə 'mæks] *mod.* totally disgusting. (California. From *grotesque.* See also *grody.*) □ *Oo, this is grody to the max!* □ *This pizza is, like, grody to the max!*

gronk [grɔŋk] *n.* a nasty substance, such as dirt that collects between the toes. □ *I don't want to hear any more at all about your gronk.* □ *What is this gronk here?*

gronk (out) *in.* to *conk out;* to crash, as with a car or a computer. □ *My car gronked out on the way to work this morning.* □ *The program gronks every time I start to run it.*

groove *n.* something pleasant or *cool.* □ *This day has been a real groove.* □ *Man, what a groove!*

grooved [gruvd] *mod.* pleased. □ *I am so grooved. I'll just kick back and meditate.* □ *You sure look grooved. What's been happening in your life?*

groove on someone or something *in.* to show interest in someone or something; to relate to someone or something. □ *Fred was beginning to groove on new-age music when he met Phil.* □ *Sam is really grooving on Mary.*

grooving *mod.* enjoying life; being *cool* and *laid back.* □ *Look at those guys grooving in front of the television set.* □ *They were just sitting there grooving.*

groovy 1. *mod. cool;* pleasant. □ *Man, this music is groovy.* □ *What a groovy day!* 2. *mod.* out of date; passe. (California.) □ *Your clothes are so groovy. They barf me out.* □ *Oh, how groovy!*

gross [gros] *mod.* crude; vulgar; disgusting. (Slang only when overused. See also *So gross!*) □ *This food is gross!* □ *What a gross thing to even suggest.*

gross-out **1.** *n.* something disgusting. □ *This whole day has been a total gross-out.* □ *That horror movie was a real gross-out.* **2.** *mod.* disgusting; *gross.* □ *What a gross-out day this has been!* □ *Well, it looks like another gross-out movie.*

gross someone out AND **gross out someone** *tr.* to disgust someone. □ *Those horrible pictures just gross me out.* □ *Jim's story totally grossed out Sally.*

grotty ['grɑdi] *mod.* highly undesirable. (Originally British. From grotesque. See *grody.*) □ *Let's not see another grotty movie tonight.* □ *What is this grotty stuff they serve here?* □ *It's not grotty!*

grub [grəb] **1.** *n.* food. □ *Hey, this grub's pretty good.* □ *What time's grub?* **2.** *in.* to eat (a meal). (Black.) □ *When do we grub?* □ *Let's grub and get going.* **3.** *n.* an earnest student. (Collegiate. See also *grade-grubber.*) □ *Merton is not exactly a grub. He gets good grades without trying.* □ *The test was so hard, even the grubs did poorly.*

grubbers See the following entry.

grubbies AND **grub(ber)s** ['grəbiz AND 'grəb(ɚ)z] *n.* worn-out clothing; clothing one wears for the occasional dirty job. □ *I have to go home, put some grubbies on, and paint the house.* □ *There I was, running around in my grubs when the senator stops by to say hello!*

grubby ['grəbi] *mod.* unclean; untidy; unshaven. □ *Tod looks sort of grubby today. What's wrong?* □ *Who's that grubby guy?* □ *I feel grubby, and I want a shower.*

grubs See *grubbies.*

grunch See the following entry.

grunge AND **grunch** [grəndʒ AND grəntʃ] **1.** *n.* any nasty substance; dirt; *gunk*. □ *There's some gritty grunge on the kitchen floor.* □ *What's that grunch on your tie?* **2.** *n.* an ugly or nasty person; a repellent person. □ *Alice thinks that Carl is a grunge.* □ *Some grunch came by and dropped off this strange package for you.*

grungy ['grəndʒi] *mod.* dirty and smelly; *yucky*. □ *Get your grungy feet off the table!* □ *My feet are not grungy!* □ *What is this grungy stuff on the closet floor?*

gubbish *n.* nonsense; useless information. (Computers. A combination of *garbage* and *rubbish*.) □ *There's nothing but gubbish on my printout.* □ *I can't make any sense out of this gubbish.*

guber AND **goober** ['gubɚ] *n.* a facial pimple. (See also *goob*.) □ *Wow, look at that giant guber on my nose.* □ *How does anybody get rid of goobers?*

guck [gək] *n.* a thick, sticky substance; *yuck*. □ *What is this guck on the bottom of my shoe?* □ *The doctor painted some nasty guck on my throat and told me not to swallow for a while.*

gucky ['gəki] *mod.* thick and sticky; *yucky*. □ *This is a gucky day. Look at the sky.* □ *Yes, it is gucky.* □ *There is a lot of gucky oil and grease on the garage floor.*

gump [gəmp] *n.* a fool; an oaf. □ *Who's the gump in the yellow slacks?* □ *Don't act like such a gump!*

gunk [gəŋk] *n.* any nasty, messy stuff. □ *What is this gunk on the counter?* □ *Get this gunk up off the floor before it dries.*

gunner *n.* an earnest student. (Collegiate.) □ *Merton is a gunner, all right.* □ *The gunners in my algebra class always get the A's.*

gusto ['gəsto] **1.** *n.* beer. (Black.) □ *Can you stop at the filling station and get some gusto?* □ *How about another tube of gusto?* **2.** *in.* to drink beer. (Black.) □ *Don't you ever do anything but gusto?* □ *Let's go out and gusto all night!*

gut [gət] **1.** *n.* the belly; the intestines. □ *What a gut that guy has.* □ *Tom poked Bill right in the gut.* **2.** *mod.* basic; fundamental. □ *This is a gut issue, and we have to deal with it now.* □ *We are not dealing with what I would call one of the gut matters of the day.* **3.** *mod.* easy. (Said of a course in school.) □ *That's a gut course. Nothing to it.* □ *I won't take any more gut economics courses. Even those are hard.* **4.** *n.* an easy course in school. □ *That course is a gut.* □ *If it's a gut, it's for me.*

guts [gəts] **1.** *n.* courage; bravado. □ *Man, she's got guts!* □ *It takes guts to do something like that.* **2.** *n.* the belly; the intestines. □ *Ted poked Frank right in the guts.* □ *I've got some kind of pain in the guts.* **3.** *n.* the inner workings of anything. □ *There's something wrong in the guts of this clock.* □ *My tape recorder needs all new guts.* **4.** *n.* the essence of something. □ *Let's discuss the real guts of this issue.* □ *The guts of your proposal are really easy to understand.*

gweeb [gwib] *n.* a studious student. (Collegiate. A variant of dweeb.) □ *I'm in a physics class full of gweebs.* □ *Merton is a gweeb, all right, but he's a good guy.*

H

hacked ['hækt] *mod.* worn-out; ready to quit. □ *What a day! I'm hacked.* □ *We were all hacked at the end of the climb.*

hacked (off) *mod.* angry; annoyed. □ *Wally was really hacked off about the accident.* □ *Oh, Wally is always hacked about something.*

hacker **1.** *n.* a taxi driver. □ *That hacker nearly ran into the back of my car!* □ *You wonder how some of these hackers keep their licenses.* **2.** *n.* a sloppy or inefficient computer programmer. □ *This program was written by a real hacker. It's a mess, but it works.* □ *I may be a hacker, but I get the job done.* **3.** *n.* a generally unsuccessful person. □ *Poor Tod is just a hacker. He'll never go any place.* □ *Hackers keep trying, but they never succeed.*

had See *taken*.

hairy *mod.* hazardous; difficult. □ *That was a hairy experience!* □ *Wow, that's hairy!* □ *What a hairy ride!*

halvsies ['hævziz] *mod.* with each person paying half. □ *Let's do it halvsies.* □ *Let's make it halvsies, and I pay for the parking, too.*

hamburger *n.* a stupid and worthless person—meat. □ *The guy is just hamburger. You can't teach him anything.* □ *There is a lot of hamburger around here. Who hired them?*

hammer   *n.* the accelerator of a vehicle. □ *She pressed down the hammer, and off they went.* □ *The hammer went straight to the floor.*

hang a huey   ['hæŋ ə 'hjui] *tr.* to turn left. □ *Hang a huey at the next corner.* □ *Right here! Hang a huey!*

hang a left   *tr.* to turn left. □ *He hung a left at the wrong corner.* □ *Hey, here! Hang a left here!*

hang a louie   ['hæŋ ə 'lui] *tr.* to turn left. □ *You have to hang a louie at the stop sign.* □ *Go another block and hang a louie.*

hang a ralph   ['hæŋ ə 'rælf] *tr.* to turn right. □ *He skied down the easy slope and hung a ralph near a fir tree.* □ *Don't hang a ralph until you get past the traffic light.*

hang a right   *tr.* to turn right. □ *Hang a right about here.* □ *I told him to hang a right at the next corner, but he went on.*

hang five AND **hang ten**   *tr.* to stand toward the front of a surfboard or diving board and hang the toes of one or both feet over the edge. (Teens and collegiate.) □ *The coach told her to hang ten and not to look down.* □ *Get out there and hang five. You can swim. Nothing can go wrong.*

hang it up   *tr.* to quit something. □ *I finally had enough and decided to hang it up.* □ *Oh, hang it up! It's hopeless.*

hang loose AND **stay loose**   *in.* to relax and stay cool. □ *Just hang loose, man. Everything'll be all right.* □ *Stay loose, chum. See ya later.*

hang ten   See *hang five.*

hang tough (on something)   *in.* to stick to one's position (on something). □ *I decided I'd hang tough on it. I tend to give in too easy.* □ *Yes, just hang tough.*

hang up 1. *n.* a problem or concern; an obsession. (Usually **hang-up**.) □ *She's got some serious hang-ups about cats.* □ *I don't have any hang ups at all. Well, almost none.* 2. *in.* to say no; to cancel out of something. □ *I hung up. That's not for me anyway.* □ *If you don't want to do it, just hang up. I'll understand.*

hard coin *n.* lots of money. (See *coin*.) □ *A car like that takes hard coin.* □ *Old Freddie is earning some hard coin these days.*

hard up 1. *mod.* alcohol intoxicated. □ *After a couple of six-packs, Wally found himself a little hard up.* □ *The whole gang was hard up by midnight.* 2. *mod.* in need of drugs or alcohol. □ *Gert was hard up and needed a fix.* □ *The old hobo was hard up for a drink.* 3. *mod.* desperate for companionship. □ *Freddie said he was hard up and needed a date.* □ *Mary must be hard up to date a jerk like that.*

hardware 1. *n.* a weapon; a gun. (Underworld and Western.) □ *I think I see your hardware showing.* □ *Lefty keeps his hardware under his mattress.* 2. *n.* computer parts, as opposed to computer programs. □ *What kind of hardware are you running this program on?* □ *The software is okay, so it must be the hardware that's off.*

harsh toke 1. *n.* an irritating puff of a marijuana cigarette. (Drugs.) □ *Wow, that was a harsh toke. Yuck!* □ *Pat got a harsh toke and coughed a lot.* 2. *n.* anything or anyone unpleasant. (From sense 1.) □ *Sally can sure be a harsh toke when she wants.* □ *This meeting has been a real harsh toke.*

have a buzz on *tr.* to be tipsy or alcohol intoxicated. (*Have got* can replace *have*.) □ *Tod has a buzz on and is giggling a lot.* □ *Both of them had a buzz on by the end of the celebration.*

have a spaz [...spæz] *tr.* to get angry or hysterical. (Teens and collegiate.) □ *If my dad hears about this, he'll have a spaz.* □ *The teacher had a spaz when I came in so late.*

have good vibes [...vɑɪbz] *tr.* to have good feelings (about someone or something). (*Have got* can replace *have*.) □ *I've got good vibes about Alice.* □ *I know everything will go all right. I have good vibes.*

have it all together *tr.* to be mentally and physically organized; to be of sound mind. (*Have got* can replace *have*.) □ *I don't have it all together today.* □ *Try me again later when I have it all together.*

head (See the entry that follows and *airhead, bonehead, bone-headed, budhead, conehead, goophead, Go soak your head!, helium head, keep one's head right, pointy-head, rotorhead, skinhead, talking head.*) **1.** *n.* a headache. □ *Man, do I have a head. You got any aspirin?* □ *Music that loud gives me a head.* **2.** *n.* a hangover. (Always with *a*.) □ *Boy, do I have a head this morning.* □ *How do you get rid of a head so you can go to work?* **3.** *n.* a toilet; a restroom. (Originally nautical. Usually with *the*.) □ *Where's the head around here?* □ *Ralph is in the head. He'll be back in a minute.*

headache **1.** *n.* an annoying person or thing. □ *Here comes that Kelly Johnson. He's a real headache.* □ *Cars can be such a head-ache.* **2.** *n.* liquor. □ *Pour me some more of that headache, will you?* □ *Give the man some more headache.*

heart *tr.* to love someone or something. (Teens.) □ *Oh, I just, like, heart your letter.* □ *She's hearting him more every day.*

heave [hiv] *in.* to empty one's stomach; to vomit. □ *He heaved and heaved and sounded like he was dying.* □ *I think I have to go heave.*

heavy **1.** *n.* a villain. (Especially in movies, etc.) □ *He is well known for playing heavies in the movies.* □ *Do I always have to be the heavy?* **2.** *mod.* important; profound; serious. □ *This is a very heavy matter.* □ *This matter is too heavy.* □ *I have some heavy things to talk over with you, Sam.* **3.** *mod.* really fine. □

Man, this is some heavy chocolate cake! □ *This stuff is really heavy!* □ *This is a real heavy thing you're doing for me.*

heavy artillery   *n.* powerful or persuasive persons or things. (See examples.) □ *Finally, the mayor brought out the heavy artillery and quieted things down.* □ *The heavy artillery seemed to know how to handle matters.*

heavy bread AND **heavy money**   *n.* a great deal of money. □ *Man, that car cost some heavy bread.* □ *It takes heavy money to run a household like this.*

heavy into someone or something   *mod.* much concerned with someone or something; obsessed with someone or something. (Black.) □ *Freddie was heavy into auto racing and always went to the races.* □ *Sam is heavy into Mary.*

heavy money   See *heavy bread.*

heavy scene   *n.* a serious state of affairs; an emotionally charged situation. □ *Man, that meeting was really a heavy scene.* □ *Another heavy scene like that and I quit.*

helium head   ['hiliəm 'hɛd] *n.* a fool; an *airhead.* □ *Well, what's that helium head done now?* □ *You can be such a helium head without even trying.*

hep   [hɛp] *mod.* aware; informed. □ *The chick is simply not hep.* □ *Fred is one of the most hep guys you're going to run into.*

herped up   *mod.* infected with the *herpes simplex* virus. □ *Why do all the boys treat me like I was herped up or something?* □ *They say all those frat guys are herped up.*

herpie   ['hɚpi] *n.* a person infected with the *herpes simplex* virus. □ *Oo, somebody said he's a herpie!* □ *Stay away from that chick. She's a herpie.*

hick(e)y ['hɪki] **1.** *n.* a love bite; a mark on the skin caused by biting or sucking. (See also *monkey bite*.) □ *He's mad at her because she gave him a hicky.* □ *She wore a high collar to cover up a hickey.* **2.** *n.* a pimple, especially if infected. □ *There is a hickey on my nose!* □ *Wouldn't you know I'd get a hickey like this right when I have to have my picture taken!*

hides *n.* drums. (See also *skins*.) □ *Andy can really bang those hides.* □ *They say his hides are worth about 4,000 clams.*

high **1.** *mod.* alcohol or drug intoxicated. □ *Wally is a little high for so early in the evening.* □ *They went out for the evening to get high, and for no other reason.* **2.** *n.* a state of euphoria caused by drugs or alcohol. □ *His life is nothing but one high after another.* □ *Her only goal is a high.*

high five **1.** *n.* a greeting where the palm of the hand is raised and slapped against another person's palm similarly raised. (Compare to *low five*.) □ *They exchanged a high five and went on with the show.* □ *How about a high five, man?* **2.** *tr. & in.* to greet someone as described in sense 1. □ *They high fived and went off together.* □ *Ted high fived Sam, and they stopped to talk.*

hip **1.** *mod.* informed; aware. (See also *hep*.) □ *The guy is just not hip. He's a nerd.* □ *Get hip, Tom!* **2.** *tr.* to tell someone; to inform someone. □ *Hey, man, hip me to what's going on!* □ *What's happening? Take a minute and hip me!*

hip-shooter *n.* someone who talks without thinking; someone who speaks very frankly. (Like a person who shoots a gun "from the hip.") □ *He's just a loudmouth hip-shooter. Pay no attention.* □ *The press secretary was a hyper and a hip-shooter. She won't last long.*

hipster ['hɪpstɚ] *n.* a youth of the 1950s, characterized by an interest in jazz and *cool* things. □ *Can you imagine your father as a hipster?* □ *Were the hipsters the ones with the big shoulder pads?*

history *n.* someone or something in the past. □ *Dave? Oh, he's just history. I never go out with him anymore.* □ *Susan is just history. We're through.* □ *Don't make a move! If this gun goes off, you're history.*

hit 1. *n.* a success; something that meets with approval. (Often with *with*.) □ *The play was a hit.* □ *The fudge with nuts in it was a great hit at the sale.* **2.** *n.* a drink of liquor; a dose of a drug. (See also *bop*.) □ *He had a hit of sauce and went out to finish his work.* □ *She popped a hit by the water cooler.*

hit the books AND **pound the books** *tr.* to study hard. □ *I spent the weekend pounding the books.* □ *I gotta go home and hit the books.*

hit the bricks AND **hit the pavement 1.** *tr.* to start walking; to go into the streets. □ *I have a long way to go. I'd better hit the bricks.* □ *Go on! Hit the pavement! Get going!* **2.** *tr.* to go out on strike. □ *The workers hit the pavement on Friday and haven't been back on the job since.* □ *Agree to our demands, or we hit the bricks.*

hit the fan *tr.* to become publicly known; to become a scandal. (From the phrase "when the shit hit the fan.") □ *I wasn't even in the country when it hit the fan.* □ *It hit the fan, and within ten minutes the press had spread it all over the world.*

hit the pavement See *hit the bricks*.

hodad(dy) ['hodæd(di)] *n.* an obnoxious person; a repellent person. (California.) □ *Ted is a total hodad.* □ *Who's the hodaddy in the plaid pants?*

hog 1. AND **hog cadillac** *n.* a large car; a souped-up car. (See also *road hog*.) □ *How do you like my new hog?* □ *That hog cadillac needs new shocks.* **2.** *n.* a police officer; a *pig*. □ *The hogs are on to you.* □ *Who called the hogs?*

hog cadillac See the previous entry.

ho-jo('s) ['hodʒo(z)] *n.* a Howard Johnson's restaurant or hotel. (Collegiate. Often with *the.*) □ *Let's hit ho-jo's for some grub.* □ *We're going to meet the others at the ho-jo.*

hole up *in.* to hide (somewhere). □ *Lefty wanted to hole up somewhere till things cooled down.* □ *I just want to hole up until the whole matter is settled.*

Hollywood **1.** *mod.* having phony glitter. □ *Who is this Hollywood dame who just came in?* □ *This whole thing is just too Hollywood.* **2.** *n.* a gaudily dressed person in sunglasses. (Also a term of address.) □ *Hey, Hollywood! What's cooking?* □ *Ask Hollywood over there to take off his shades and make himself known.*

honcho ['hɑntʃo] **1.** *n.* the headman; the boss. (Usable for either sex.) □ *The marketing honcho couldn't say when the product would be on the shelves.* □ *The top honcho at the water department was no help at all.* **2.** *tr.* to manage or boss something. □ *Who's supposed to honcho this affair?* □ *I'll honcho it until Larry gets here.*

honey ['həni] *n.* beer. (See also *honey wagon*.) □ *Let's stop at the liquor store and get some honey.* □ *You want another can of honey?*

honey cart See the following entry.

honey wagon **1.** AND **honey cart** *n.* any vehicle used for or designed for carrying excrement: a farm manure wagon; a tank truck used to pump out septic tanks; a tank truck used to pump out airplane toilets; a portable latrine truck used in movie making. □ *I drove a honey wagon in Hollywood for a year. How's that for glamour?* □ *The honey cart was stalled with a flat tire in front of the plane.* **2.** *n.* a beer truck. □ *What time does the honey wagon bring in new supplies?* □ *I drove a honey cart in the city for a while.*

honk 1. *n.* a drinking spree; a *toot.* □ *Jed's last honk lasted nearly a week.* □ *The guys went off on the honk to end all honks.* **2.** *n.* a white male; a *honk(e)y.* (Black. Not necessarily derogatory.) □ *Who's the honk who keeps driving by?* □ *There are mainly honks where I work.*

honked AND **honkers** *mod.* alcohol intoxicated. □ *Wally was too honked to stand up.* □ *Man, is that guy honkers!*

honk(e)y AND **honkie** ['hɔŋki] **1.** *n.* a Caucasian. (Black. Not necessarily derogatory. Probably from *hunky.*) □ *The honkies are taking over this neighborhood.* □ *Some honky was around asking for you.* **2.** *mod.* in the manner of a Caucasian; white-like. (Black.) □ *Where'd you get that honky car?* □ *That's honky music. I want to hear soul.*

hook 1. *tr.* to cheat someone. □ *Watch the clerk in that store. He might try to hook you.* □ *They hooked me on the car deal.* **2.** *tr.* to steal something. □ *Lefty hooked a couple of candy bars just for the hell of it.* □ *What did they hook last night?* **3.** *tr.* to addict someone (to something). (Not necessarily drugs.) □ *The constant use of bicarb hooked him to the stuff.* □ *The pot hooked him.*

hooker *n.* a prostitute. □ *There were some hookers standing right on that corner.* □ *Clare dresses like a hooker.*

hoops *n.* the game of basketball. □ *You wanna go play some hoops?* □ *Welcome to another evening of college hoops, brought to you by the Nova Motor Company.*

hoot 1. *in.* to laugh loudly. □ *The audience screamed and hooted with their appreciation.* □ *They howled and hooted. I know they just loved it.* **2.** *n.* a joke; something laughable. □ *The whole business was a terrific hoot.* □ *The skit was a hoot, and everyone enjoyed it.* **3.** *in.* to boo at someone's performance. □ *The audience hooted until the performer fled the stage in disgrace.* □ *They hooted for a few minutes after she left the stage.*

hooted *mod.* alcohol intoxicated. □ *Jed got himself good and hooted.* □ *Ted is too hooted to drive.*

hooter *n.* a nose; a big nose. □ *I sort of wish my hooter wasn't so big.* □ *He blew his hooter and went back to his reading.*

hop **1.** AND **hops** *n.* beer. □ *Pretty good hops, Tom. This a new brand?* □ *How about some hop with your hamburger?* **2.** *tr.* to get aboard a plane or train. □ *I'll hop a plane and be there in a couple of hours.* □ *Hop a train or anything, but get here as soon as you can.*

horn **1.** *n.* the nose. □ *He scratched his horn with his pencil and opened his mouth to speak.* □ *He had the biggest horn I have ever seen on man or beast.* **2.** *n.* the telephone. □ *Get Mrs. Wilson on the horn, please.* □ *She's on the horn now. What'll I tell her?*

horny *mod.* sexually aroused. (Caution with topic.) □ *Tom said he was horny.* □ *Who is that horny jerk?* □ *All the guys in that fraternity are horny.*

horse hockey **1.** *n.* horse dung. □ *I try to get horse hockey for my garden.* □ *You don't see horse hockey in the streets anymore.* **2.** *n.* nonsense. □ *I've heard enough of your horse hockey.* □ *The guy specializes in producing horse hockey for the gossip columns.*

horses *n.* horsepower, as in an engine. □ *How many horses does this thing have?* □ *Isn't 400 horses a lot for just one car?*

hoser ['hozɚ] **1.** *n.* a good guy or buddy. □ *You're a real hoser, Ted.* □ *Old Fred is a good hoser. He'll help.* **2.** *n.* a cheater or deceiver. □ *Stop acting like a hoser and tell me the truth!* □ *You dirty lying hoser!*

hot **1.** *mod.* of great renown; doing quite well for the time being. □ *The opera tenor was hot, and even the lowbrows would pay to hear him.* □ *The dancer was hot and was offered movie roles and* *all sorts of things.* **2.** *mod.* sexy; sexually aroused. □ *Man, is that chick hot!* □ *She's not my idea of hot.* □ *Wow, who was that hot hunk you were with?*

hot item **1.** *n.* an item that sells well. □ *This little thing is a hot item this season.* □ *Now here's a hot item that everybody is looking for.* **2.** *n.* a romantically serious couple. □ *Sam and Mary are quite a hot item lately.* □ *A hot item like Bill and Clare isn't likely to show up for the party.*

hot number **1.** *n.* an exciting piece of music. □ *Now here's a hot number by the Wanderers.* □ *Another hot number after this message.* **2.** *n.* an attractive or sexy person, typically a (young) woman. □ *She's quite a hot number.* □ *Who's that hot number I saw you with last night?*

(hot) skinny *n.* inside information. (See also *poop*.) □ *What's the skinny on the tower clock? Is it broken?* □ *I've got the hot skinny on Mary and her boyfriend.*

howl **1.** *n.* something funny. □ *What a howl the surprise party turned out to be when the guest of honor didn't show up.* □ *The gag was a real howl.* **2.** *in.* to laugh very hard. □ *Everybody howled at my mistake.* □ *John howled when the joke was told.*

howler *n.* a big, but funny mistake; an embarrassing error. □ *Who is responsible for this howler on the Wilson account?* □ *That howler cost us plenty.*

huffy *mod.* angry; haughty. □ *Now, don't get huffy. I said I was sorry, didn't I?* □ *Who's the huffy old lady?* □ *She was so huffy about it.*

hughie ['hjui] *in.* to empty one's stomach; to vomit. (See also *cry hughie*.) □ *I gotta go hughie.* □ *Oo, who hughied?*

humongous [hju'mɑŋgəs] *mod.* huge. □ *She lives in a humongous house on the hill.* □ *Wally has a humongous nose.* □ *That nose is not humongous.*

hump (along) *in.* to move along in a hurry. □ *I guess I'd better hump along over there.* □ *Come on, move it! Hump to the main office and be fast about it!*

hump it (to somewhere) *tr.* to move rapidly (to somewhere). □ *I have to hump it over to Kate's place right now.* □ *You'll have to hump it to get there in time.*

hung **1.** *mod.* hungover. □ *John is really hung this morning.* □ *I'm miserable when I'm hung.* **2.** *mod.* annoyed. □ *Fred is hung and looking for somebody to take it out on.* □ *How can you get so hung about practically nothing?*

hungries *n.* hunger. (Always with *the*.) □ *Jimmy's crying because he's got the hungries.* □ *I get the hungries about this time every day.*

hungry **1.** *mod.* eager to make money. □ *He doesn't sell enough because he's not hungry enough.* □ *When he gets hungry for wealth, he'll get busy.* **2.** *mod.* ambitious. □ *He gets ahead because he's hungry.* □ *We like to hire the hungry ones.*

hurl *in.* to empty one's stomach; to vomit. (Like the *throw* in *throw up*.) □ *I think I gotta go hurl.* □ *Who's in the john hurling so loud?*

hurt **1.** *mod.* very ugly; damaged and ugly. (Black. Similar to *hurting*.) □ *Man, are you hurt!* □ *That poor girl is really bad hurt.* **2.** *mod.* drug intoxicated. (Black.) □ *Gert was really hurt and nodding and drooling.* □ *One hit of that dope and he was really hurt.*

hurting *mod.* very ugly; "in pain" from being ugly. (Similar to *hurt*.) □ *That dog of yours is something to behold. It's really hurting.* □ *Man, is she hurting!*

husky ['həski] *n.* a strong man; a thug. □ *Tell your husky to lay off, Reggie.* □ *A couple of huskies helped me get my car unstuck.*

hustle ['həsl] **1.** *in.* to move rapidly; to hurry. □ *Come on, hustle, you guys.* □ *It's late. I've got to hustle.* **2.** *n.* hurried movement; confusion. □ *All the hustle and confusion made it hard to concentrate.* □ *I can't work when there is all this hustle around me.* **3.** *n.* a scheme to make money; a special technique for making money. (Underworld. This includes drug dealing, prostitution, and other vice activities.) □ *Each of these punks has a hustle—a specialty in crime.* □ *We all know what Carl's hustle is.* **4.** *in.* to use one's special technique for making money. □ *He's out there on the streets hustling all the time.* □ *I gotta go hustle. I need some bread.*

hustler ['həslɚ] **1.** *n.* a gambler in a pool hall. □ *Wasn't he the guy who played the hustler in that famous movie?* □ *He made a lot of money as a hustler.* **2.** *n.* a swindler. □ *The chick is a real hustler. I wouldn't trust her at all.* □ *The hustler conned me out of a month's pay.* **3.** *n.* a prostitute. □ *Gert almost became a hustler to pay for a habit.* □ *A lot of hustlers are addicted to heroin.*

hyped (up) **1.** *mod.* excited; stimulated. □ *They were all hyped up before the game.* □ *She said she had to get hyped before the tennis match.* **2.** *mod.* contrived; heavily promoted; falsely advertised. □ *I just won't pay good money to see these hyped-up movies.* □ *If it has to be hyped so much, it probably isn't very good.*

hyper ['haɪpɚ] **1.** *mod.* excited; overreacting. □ *I'm a little hyper because of the doctor's report.* □ *Here's another hyper patient.* □ *Now, now, don't get hyper.* **2.** *n.* a person who praises or promotes someone or something. □ *She's a hyper, and she doesn't always tell things the way they are.* □ *As a hyper, she is a whiz.* **3.** *n.* a person who is always overly excited or hyperactive. □ *Pat is such a hyper. Just can't seem to relax.* □ *My dad is a hyper.*

I

I am so sure! *exclam.* "I am right!" (California.) □ *You are way rad! I am so sure!* □ *This is too much. I am so sure!*

iced *mod.* settled once and for all; done easily. (Essentially "frozen.") □ *I've got it iced. Nothing to it.* □ *The whole business is iced. Don't fret.*

ick [ɪk] **1.** *n.* any nasty substance. □ *What is this ick on my shoe?* □ *That's not ick; it's good clean mud.* **2.** *exclam.* "Nasty!" (Usually **Ick!**) □ *Oh, ick! What now?* □ *Ick! I'm late!* **3.** *n.* a disliked person. □ *Tell that ick to leave. He's polluting the place.* □ *Oh, Tod, don't be such an ick!*

icky [ˈɪki] *mod.* distasteful; nasty. □ *What is this icky old stuff?* □ *This is icky.* □ *This was an icky day.*

I.D. **1.** *n.* some kind of identification card. □ *Can you show me an I.D.?* □ *I don't have any I.D. on me.* **2.** *tr.* to check someone for a valid identification card. □ *They I.D.ed us at the door.* □ *I hate being I.D.ed.*

idiot oil *n.* alcohol. □ *She drinks too much of that idiot oil.* □ *Idiot oil can wreck you as much as smack does.*

(I) love it! *exclam.* "That is wonderful!" (A catchphrase.) □ *It's wonderful, Ted. I love it!* □ *Love it! More, more!* □ *You're so clever! Love it! Love it!*

I'm out of here. AND **I'm outa here.** *sent.* "I am leaving this minute." □ *In three minutes I'm outa here.* □ *I'm out of here. Bye.*

in **1.** *mod.* current; fashionable. □ *This kind of thing is in now.* □ *What's in around here in the way of clothing?* **2.** *mod.* private. □ *Is this in information?* □ *If it's in or something, I'm sure they won't spread it around.* **3.** *n.* someone in a special position; someone who is serving in an elective office. □ *Well, now that I am an in, there's going to be some changes.* □ *When Ralph is one of the ins, he'll throw the crooks out.*

in a bad way See *in bad shape.*

in a snit *mod.* in a fit of anger or irritation. □ *Don't get in a snit. It was an accident.* □ *Mary is in a snit because they didn't ask her to come to the shindig.*

in a twit *mod.* upset; frantic. □ *She's all in a twit because she lost her keys.* □ *Tod was in a twit and was quite rude to us.*

in bad shape AND **in a bad way** **1.** *mod.* injured or debilitated in any manner. □ *Fred had a little accident, and he's in bad shape.* □ *Tom needs exercise. He's in bad shape.* **2.** *mod.* pregnant. □ *Molly's in bad shape again, I hear.* □ *Yup, she's in bad shape all right—about four months in bad shape.*

in deep **1.** *mod.* deeply involved (with someone or something). □ *Mary and Sam are in deep.* □ *Carl is in deep with the mob.* **2.** *mod.* deeply in debt. (Often with *with* or *to.*) □ *Reggie is in deep with his bookie.* □ *I'm in deep to the department store.*

ink slinger *n.* a professional writer; a newspaper reporter. □ *The ink slingers have been at the candidates again.* □ *The problem is that there are too many ink slingers around.*

in play **1.** *mod.* being played. (Said of a ball in a game.) □ *The ball's in play, so you made the wrong move.* □ *No, it wasn't in play, you twit!* **2.** *mod.* having to do with a company (or its stock) that is a candidate for acquisition by another company. (Financial markets.) □ *The company was in play, but nobody was buying it.* □ *The deal stocks that are in play right now offer excellent buying opportunities.*

intense *mod.* serious; *heavy*. □ *That man is so intense!* □ *This is an intense matter.* □ *Oh, wow! Now that's what I call intense!*

in the bag **1.** *mod.* achieved; settled. □ *It's in the bag—as good as done.* □ *The election is in the bag unless the voters find out about my past.* **2.** See **bagged**.

in there *mod.* sincere; likable. □ *Martha is really in there. Everybody likes her.* □ *I like a guy who's in there—who thinks about other people.*

in the suds *mod.* alcohol intoxicated. □ *Fred is in the suds and can't see.* □ *When Bob is in the suds, he's mean.*

in the tube **1.** *mod.* in the tube of a large wave. (Surfing.) □ *Tod is in the tube and looks great.* □ *On a day like today, I want to be out there in the tube.* **2.** *mod.* at risk. □ *He's in the tube now, but things should straighten out soon.* □ *If you find yourself in the tube in this matter, just give me a ring.*

iron **1.** *n.* a gun; a revolver. (Underworld.) □ *Walter never carries iron unless he's going to use it.* □ *What kind of iron do you carry?* **2.** *n.* computer hardware. (See also *big iron.*) □ *What kind of iron are you people running over there?* □ *This is good old compatible iron.*

I've got to fly. AND **I('ve) gotta fly.** *sent.* "I have to leave right now." □ *Time's up. I've got to fly.* □ *I've gotta fly. See you later.*

ivories ['ɑɪvriz] **1.** *n.* the teeth. □ *I gotta go brush my ivories.* □ *Look at those nice white ivories!* **2.** *n.* piano keys. (From the time when piano keys were made from real elephant ivory.) □ *She can really bang those ivories.* □ *I'd say she has mastered the ivories.*

J

jack 1. *n.* money. □ *I don't have the jack for a deal like that.* □ *How much jack will it take?* **2.** *n.* tobacco for rolling cigarettes. □ *You got some jack I can bum?* □ *I don't use jack at all.*

jackal *n.* a low and devious person. □ *You are nothing but a slimy jackal!* □ *What does that jackal want here?*

jack around *in.* to waste time; to mess around. □ *Stop jacking around and get busy.* □ *The gang was jacking around and broke your window.*

jacked (out) *mod.* angry; annoyed. □ *Boy, was that old guy jacked out at you.* □ *Yup, he was jacked all right.*

jacked up 1. *mod.* excited. □ *Don was really jacked up about the election.* □ *The gang was jacked up and ready to party.* **2.** *mod.* arrested. (Underworld.) □ *What time did Reggie get himself jacked up?* □ *He was jacked up at midnight on the dot.* **3.** *mod.* upset; *stressed.* □ *I was really jacked up by the bad news.* □ *Don't get jacked up. It'll work out.*

jack someone around AND **jack around someone** *tr.* to hassle someone; to harass someone. (Compare to *jerk someone around*.) □ *The I.R.S. is jacking my brother around.* □ *The boss was jacking around Gert, so she just walked out.*

jack someone or something up AND **jack up someone or something 1.** *tr.* [with *someone*] to motivate someone; to stimulate someone to do something. □ *I'll jack him up and try to*

get some action out of him. □ *What does it take to jack you up?*
2. *tr.* [with *something*] to raise the price of something. □ *They kept jacking the price up with various charges, so I walked.* □ *How can they jack up the published price?*

jag **1.** *n.* a Jaguar automobile. □ *What I really want is a jag.* □ *How much will a jag set me back?* **2.** *n.* a drinking bout; a prolonged state of alcohol or drug intoxication. □ *Is he off on another jag, or is this the same one?* □ *One more jag will kill her. Try to keep her away from the stuff.* **3.** *n.* a prolonged state of emotional excess. □ *I've been on a jag and can't get my work done.* □ *She's off on a jag again.*

jam **1.** *n.* a problem; trouble. □ *I hear you're in a bad jam.* □ *Well, it's not a bad jam.* **2.** *in.* [for musicians] to play together, improvising. □ *They jammed until the neighbors complained.* □ *Come over and let's jam, okay?* **3.** *tr. & in.* to force a basketball into the basket; to *slam dunk* a basketball. □ *He tried to jam it, but blew it.* □ *Andy broke the goal by trying to jam.* **4.** *n.* an act of forcing a basketball into the basket; a *slam dunk.* □ *The jam didn't work, and Fred's team got the ball.* □ *One more jam for Wilbur!*

jammed ['dʒæmd] **1.** *mod.* arrested. (Underworld.) □ *Reggie got jammed for speeding.* □ *When did he get jammed?* **2.** *mod.* alcohol intoxicated. □ *I'm a little jammed, but I think I can still drive.* □ *They were jammed by midnight.*

jammed up **1.** AND **jammed** *mod.* in trouble. □ *He got himself jammed up with the law.* □ *I'm sort of jammed and need some help.* **2.** *mod.* glutted; full of food or drink. □ *I'm jammed up. I can't eat another bite.* □ *After dinner, I am so jammed up that I need a nap.*

jamming *mod.* excellent. □ *This music is really jamming.* □ *What a jamming class session.*

jaw **1.** *n.* a chat. □ *Come over for a jaw this weekend.* □ *I could use a good jaw with my old friend.* **2.** *in.* to chat. □ *Stop jawing* *and get to work.* □ *Come over, and we can jaw for a while.* **3.** See the following entry.

jaw(bone) *tr.* to try to persuade someone verbally; to apply verbal pressure to someone. □ *They tried to jawbone me into doing it.* □ *Don't jaw me. I won't do it.*

jazzed (up) **1.** *mod.* alert; having a positive state of mind. □ *I am jazzed up and ready to face life.* □ *Those guys were jazzed and ready for the game.* **2.** *mod.* alcohol or drug intoxicated. □ *Dave was a bit jazzed up, but not terribly.* □ *Gert was jazzed out of her mind.* **3.** *mod.* enhanced; with something added; having been made more enticing. □ *The third act was jazzed up with a little skin.* □ *It was jazzed enough to have the police chief around asking questions.*

jazz someone or something up AND **jazz up someone or something** *tr.* to make someone or something more exciting or sexy; to make someone or something appeal more to contemporary and youthful tastes. □ *Let's jazz this up a little bit.* □ *They jazzed up the old girl till she looked like a teenager.* □ *Don't jazz up the first number too much.*

jazzy ['dʒæzi] *mod.* stimulating; appealing. □ *That's a jazzy sweater you got.* □ *He's a real jazzy guy.*

jel [dʒɛl] *n.* a stupid person with gelatin where brains ought to be. □ *The guy's a jel. Forget him.* □ *Oh, Wallace, don't act like such a jel.*

jerk *n.* a stupid or worthless person. (For both males and females.) □ *What a loony jerk!* □ *You are such a classic jerk!*

jerk someone around AND **jerk around someone** *tr.* to hassle someone; to waste someone's time. □ *Stop jerking me around and give me my money back.* □ *They sure like to jerk around people in that music shop.*

jillion ['dʒɪljən] *n.* an enormous, indefinite number. □ *I've got a jillion things to tell you.* □ *This car cost me about a jillion bucks.*

jive [dʒaɪv] **1.** *n.* back talk. □ *Cut the jive, man!* □ *Don't you give me any of that jive!* **2.** *n.* lies; deception; nonsense. □ *No more of your jive. Talk straight or don't talk.* □ *I've listened to your jive for years. You'll never change.* **3.** *mod.* deceptive; insincere. □ *Don't give me all those jive excuses.* □ *I listened to her little jive speech and then fired her.*

jive-ass *mod.* foolish. (Black. Caution with **ass**.) □ *You can tell that jive-ass jerk to forget it.* □ *Don't pay any attention to that jive-ass jerk.*

jive talk *n.* slang; contemporary fad words. □ *I like to hear jive talk. It's like trying to work a puzzle.* □ *He stands by the window with a pad of paper and takes down the jive talk he hears.*

jive turkey *n.* a stupid person. □ *What jive turkey made this mess?* □ *Get that jive turkey out of here!*

jock **1.** *n.* an athlete. (See also **strap**. See **jockstrap**. Now of either sex.) □ *The jocks are all at practice now.* □ *She's dating a jock who has to be home by 10.* **2.** *n.* an athletic supporter (garment). □ *Somebody dropped a jock in the hall.* □ *Whose jock is that out there on Molly's clothesline?*

[jockey] See *bench jockey, desk jockey, disk jockey.*

jockstrap **1.** AND **jockstrapper** *n.* an athlete. (From the name of the supporting garment worn by male athletes.) □ *The jockstrappers are all at practice now.* □ *Here comes one of the best jockstrappers on the team.* **2.** *in.* to work as a professional athlete. □ *I jockstrapped for a few years and then lost my interest in it.* □ *I made a lot of money jockstrapping.*

jockstrapper See the previous entry.

Joe Six-pack *n.* the average guy who sits around drinking beer by the six-pack. □ *Joe Six-pack likes that kind of television program.* □ *All Joe Six-pack wants is a good game on T.V.*

john **1.** *n.* a toilet; a bathroom. □ *Somebody's in the john.* □ *Is there another john around here?* **2.** *n.* a man. □ *Some john was around asking for you.* □ *This john came up and asked if I had seen the girl in a picture he had.* **3.** *n.* a prostitute's customer. □ *She led the john into an alley, where Lefty robbed him.* □ *The john looked a little embarrassed.*

joint **1.** *n.* a tavern. □ *Lefty has his own joint over on 12th.* □ *I wanted to open a joint, but I don't have the cash.* **2.** *n.* a low-class establishment. □ *Let's get out of this crummy joint.* □ *This joint bores me.* **3.** *n.* a marijuana cigarette. □ *He always has a joint with him.* □ *The joint wasn't enough to carry him very long.* **4.** *n.* a jail; a prison. □ *Lefty just got out of the joint.* □ *He learned a lot in the joint that he was anxious to try out.*

joke *tr.* to tease someone; to make fun of someone. □ *Everybody was joking my roommate because of her accent.* □ *Don't joke me, man. I do the best I can.*

jones **1.** *n.* a thing. (Black.) □ *There's a big turf jones down on the corner.* □ *This get-rich-quick jones will land you in the joint, Lefty.* **2.** *n.* a penis. (Black. Caution with topic.) □ *Zip up, man. You want your jones getting out?* □ *Cut out all this talk about joneses!*

joy juice *n.* liquor; beer. □ *Joy juice makes Ted sad.* □ *Can I pour some more of this joy juice?*

jug **1.** *n.* jail. (Usually with *the.*) □ *Take it easy. I don't want to end up in the jug.* □ *A couple of days in the jug would do you fine.* **2.** *n.* a jug of liquor. □ *Where's my jug? I need a swig.* □ *Pass her the jug, Sam.* **3.** AND **jug up** *in.* to drink heavily. □ *Let's jug up and have a good time.* □ *We jugged till about noon and then went to sleep.*

juice **1.** *n.* liquor; wine. □ *Let's go get some juice and get stewed.* □ *You got any juice in your room?* **2.** *in.* to drink heavily. □ *Both of them were really juicing.* □ *Stop juicing and listen to me.* **3.** *n.* electricity. □ *The juice has been off since dawn.* □ *Turn on the juice, and let's see if it runs.* **4.** *n.* energy; power; political influence. □ *The boss has the juice with the board to make the necessary changes.* □ *Dave left the president's staff because he just didn't have the juice to be useful.*

juice house *n.* a liquor store. (Black.) □ *Would you stop by the juice house for some foam?* □ *The juice house was held up last night.*

juice something back AND **juice back something** *tr.* to drink alcohol. □ *He's been juicing it back since noon.* □ *Juice back your drink, and let's go.*

jump start **1.** *n.* the act of starting a car by getting power—through jumper cables—from another car. □ *I got a jump start from a friend.* □ *Who can give me a jump start?* **2.** *tr.* to start a car by getting power from another car. □ *I jump started her car for her.* □ *I can't jump start your car. My battery is low.*

jump (street) *n.* the beginning; the start (of something). (Prisons and streets.) □ *I knew from jump that you were going to be trouble.* □ *Way back at jump street, I spotted you as a troublemaker.*

junk **1.** *n.* liquor; inferior liquor. □ *Pour this junk down the drain and get me something good.* □ *After a while the derelicts grow to prefer junk.* **2.** *tr.* to dispose of something, such as a piece of equipment. □ *Junk this thing. It's broken.* □ *I can't junk it. It's the only one I have.*

junkie AND **junky** [ˈdʒəŋki] **1.** *n.* a drug dealer. □ *Carl is a junkie.* □ *Junkies should be put into the jug.* **2.** *n.* a drug user; an addict. □ *The junkies can be helped, you know.* □ *Junkies have to steal to support their habits.*

just off the boat   *mod.* to be freshly immigrated and perhaps gullible and naive. □ *I'm not just off the boat. I know what's going on.* □ *He may act like he's just off the boat, but he's all right.*

K

K. [ke] *n.* a thousand (of anything, such as dollars, bytes, etc.) □ *This car is worth at least 20 K.* □ *I have 640 K. memory in my computer.*

Keep in touch. *sent.* "Good-bye." (Sometimes a sarcastic way of saying good-bye to someone one doesn't care about.) □ *Nice talking to you. Keep in touch.* □ *Sorry, we can't use you today. Keep in touch.*

keep one's cool *tr.* to remain calm and in control. (Compare to *blow one's cool*.) □ *Relax, man! Just keep your cool.* □ *It's hard to keep your cool when you've been cheated.*

keep one's head right *tr.* to maintain control of oneself. (Black.) □ *Chill, man, chill. You've got to keep your head right.* □ *I can keep my head right. I'm mellow.*

keester AND **keyster, kiester** ['kistɚ] **1.** *n.* a chest; a suitcase. □ *The old lady was hauling the most enormous keester.* □ *The keester was full of cash.* **2.** *n.* the buttocks; the anus. □ *Get your keester over here!* □ *He fell flat on his keester.*

keg *in.* to pay attention. □ *You're not kegging. I'll try it again.* □ *Keep kegging, you guys! This is important.*

kegger 1. *n.* a party where beer is served from a keg. (Teens and collegiate.) □ *Tiffany is having a kegger, and a few of her intimates are invited.* □ *Isn't there a kegger somewhere tonight?* **2.** AND **keggers** *n.* a keg of beer. (Collegiate.) □ *We need an-*

other kegger. It's only nine o'clock. □ *We came here because somebody said there was keggers.*

keg party *n.* a party where liquor, especially beer, is served. □ *There is a free keg party at Freddy's.* □ *The keg party ended early owing to the arrival of uninvited cops.*

kick **1.** *n.* a charge or good feeling (from something); pleasure or enjoyment from something. □ *That song really gives me a kick. I love it!* □ *What a kick that gives me!* **2.** *n.* a complaint. □ *What's the kick, man?* □ *You got another kick, troublemaker?* **3.** *in.* to complain. □ *Why are you always kicking?* □ *Ernie kicks about everything.*

kick around See under *knock around.*

kick back **1.** *in.* to relax (and enjoy something). □ *Now you just kick back and enjoy this.* □ *I like to kick back and listen to a few tunes.* **2.** *n.* money received in return for a favor. (Usually **kickback.**) □ *The kickback the cop got wasn't enough, as it turned out.* □ *You really don't believe that the cops take kickbacks!*

kicker *n.* a clever but stinging remark; a sharp criticism. □ *I waited for the kicker, and finally it came.* □ *The kicker really made me mad.*

kickin' ['kɪkn̩] *mod.* wild; super; excellent. □ *Your rally was really kickin'.* □ *I don't know where you get your clothes, but that jacket's kickin'.*

kick off *in.* to die. □ *We've been waiting for years for that cat to kick off.* □ *The old girl finally kicked off.*

kicks *n.* cleats or shoes. (Collegiate. See also *kick.*) □ *Don't you dare wear those kicks in here!* □ *Take your kicks off before coming in.*

kick some ass (around) *tr.* to take over and start giving orders. (Caution with *ass.*) □ *Do I have to come over there and kick* some ass around? □ *Reggie is just the one to kick some ass over there.*

kicky ['kɪki] *mod.* exciting and energetic. □ *Man, what a kicky idea!* □ *She is a real kicky gal.*

killer 1. *n.* a very funny joke. □ *That last one was a killer!* □ *She told a killer about a red-nosed juicer.* 2. *n.* something extraordinary. □ *That jacket is a real killer!* □ *That car is a killer. I like it!* 3. *mod.* extraordinary. □ *What a killer jacket you're wearing!* □ *This is a killer hamburger all right.*

kilobucks *n.* a tremendous sum of money. (See also *megabucks*.) □ *These boondoggles waste kilobucks!* □ *How many kilobucks does a set of wheels like that cost?*

kink 1. *n.* a strange person; a *kinky* person. □ *The guy's a kink. Watch out for him.* □ *There are kinks all over this place.* 2. *n.* a sexually deviant person. □ *He was a kink, and I broke up with him.* □ *The kinks congregate two streets over.*

kinky 1. *mod.* having to do with someone or something strange or weird. □ *The guy is so kinky that everyone avoids him.* □ *Who is that kinky dame in the net stockings?* 2. *mod.* having to do with unconventional sexual acts or people who perform them. □ *She seems to have a morbid interest in kinky stuff.* □ *He showed her a picture of some kind of kinky sex thing.*

kipe *tr.* to steal something. □ *Where did you kipe this thing?* □ *The punk kiped a newspaper just for the heck of it.*

kiper ['kaɪpɚ] *n.* a thief; someone who steals. □ *The punk is a two-bit kiper and needs to be taught a lesson.* □ *You dirty little kiper. Give it back!*

[kiss] See the four entries that follow and *French kiss, fish-kiss, soul kiss.*

kiss off 1. ['kɪs ɔf] *n.* the dismissal of someone or something. (Usually **kiss-off**.) ☐ *The kiss-off was when I lost the Wilson contract.* ☐ *Tod got the kiss off and is now looking for a new job.* **2.** *n.* death. (Usually **kiss-off**.) ☐ *When the time comes for the kiss-off, I hope I'm asleep.* ☐ *The kiss-off came wrapped in lead, and it was instant.* **3.** ['kɪs 'ɔf] *in.* to die. ☐ *The cat is going to have to kiss off one of these days soon.* ☐ *The cat kissed off after 18 years of joy and devotion.*

kiss the porcelain god *tr.* to empty one's stomach; to vomit. ☐ *He fled the room to kiss the porcelain god, I guess.* ☐ *Who's in there kissing the porcelain god?*

kiss up to someone *in.* to flatter someone; to make over someone. ☐ *I'm not going to kiss up to anybody to get what's rightfully mine.* ☐ *If I have to kiss up to her, I guess I will.*

kissyface ['kɪsifes] **1.** *n.* kissing. ☐ *There was a lot of kissyface going on in the backseat.* ☐ *They're mostly involved with kissyface at this age.* **2.** *mod.* feeling the need to kiss and be kissed. ☐ *I feel all kissyface.* ☐ *They were both sort of kissyface, so they left.*

kite!, Go fly a See *Go chase yourself!*

klotz See *klutz.*

klu(d)ge [klədʒ OR kludʒ] **1.** *n.* a patch or a fix in a computer program or circuit. ☐ *This is a messy kludge, but it will do the job.* ☐ *Kluges that are invisible don't bother anybody.* **2.** *tr.* to patch or fix a computer program circuit. ☐ *I only have time to kludge this problem.* ☐ *The kid kluged a program for us in an hour.*

kludgy ['klədʒi OR 'kludʒi] *mod.* having to do with an inefficient or sloppily written computer program. ☐ *This program is too kludgy to be acceptable.* ☐ *Who wrote this kludgy mess?* ☐ *I don't care if it's kludgy. Does it work?*

klutz AND **klotz** [kləts AND klɑts] *n.* a stupid and clumsy person. □ *Don't be a klutz!* □ *Some klotz put mustard in the stew.*

klutzy ['klətsi] *mod.* foolish; stupid. □ *That was really a klutzy thing to do.* □ *You are so klutzy!* □ *Whose klutzy idea was this?*

knock *tr.* to criticize someone or something. □ *Don't knock it if you haven't tried it.* □ *The papers are knocking my favorite candidate again.*

knock around 1. *in.* to waste time. □ *Stop knocking around and get to work!* □ *I need a couple of days a week just for knocking around.* 2. AND **kick around.** *in.* to wander around; to loiter. □ *I think I'll kick around a few months before looking for another job.* □ *We're just kicking around and keeping out of trouble.*

knock down something AND **knock something down** 1. *tr.* to drink a portion of liquor. □ *He knocked down a bottle of beer and called for another.* □ *Here, knock this down and let's go.* 2. *tr.* to earn a certain amount of money. □ *She must knock down about 40 thou a year.* □ *I'm lucky to knock down 20 thousand.*

knocked out 1. *mod.* exhausted. □ *We were all knocked out at the end of the day.* □ *I'm knocked out after just a little bit of work.* 2. *mod.* overwhelmed. □ *We were just knocked out when we heard your news.* □ *Were we surprised? We were knocked out —elated!* 3. *mod.* alcohol or drug intoxicated. □ *They were all knocked out by midnight.* □ *Gary was knocked out when we dropped by, so we tried to sober him up.*

knocked up 1. *mod.* battered; beaten. □ *Sally was a little knocked up by the accident.* □ *This book is a little knocked up, so I'll lower the price.* 2. *mod.* alcohol intoxicated. □ *Bill was knocked up and didn't want to drive.* □ *Wow, was that guy knocked up!* 3. *mod.* pregnant. □ *Molly got knocked up again.* □ *Isn't she knocked up most of the time?*

knock one over AND **knock over one, knock one back, knock back one** *tr.* to take a drink of liquor. □ *He knocked one over right away and demanded another.* □ *He knocked back one and belched grossly.*

knockout **1.** *n.* something that is quite stunning. □ *Your new car is a knockout.* □ *Isn't her dress a knockout?* **2.** *n.* a good-looking man or woman. □ *Your date is a real knockout.* □ *Who is that knockout I saw you with last weekend?* **3.** *mod.* very exciting. □ *It was a real knockout evening.* □ *What a knockout idea!*

knock someone some skin *tr.* to shake hands with someone. □ *Hey, man, knock me some skin!* □ *Tod knocked Sam some skin, and they left the building together.*

knock someone up AND **knock up someone** *tr.* to make a woman pregnant. (Crude.) □ *They say it was Reggie who knocked her up.* □ *He did not knock up Molly. I did.*

know from something *in.* to know about something. □ *Do you know from timers, I mean how timers work?* □ *I don't know from babies! Don't ask me about feeding them!*

know where one is coming from *tr.* to understand someone's motivation; to understand and relate to someone's position. □ *I know where you're coming from. I've been there.* □ *We all know where he's coming from. That's why we are so worried.*

knuckle-dragger *n.* a strong, ape-like man. □ *Reggie is the boss's favorite knuckle-dragger.* □ *Call off your knuckle-draggers. I'll pay you whatever you want.*

knuckle sandwich *n.* a blow struck in the teeth or mouth. □ *How would you like a knuckle sandwich?* □ *He threatened to give me a knuckle sandwich.*

kong [kɔŋ] *n.* strong whiskey; illicit whiskey. (Black. From the movie ape King Kong.) □ *How about a big swallow of that kong?* □ *Here, have some kong.*

konk See *conk*.

kook [kuk] *n.* a strange person. □ *She seems like a kook, but she is just grand, really.* □ *Tod's a kook, but I love him.*

kookish ['kukıʃ] *mod.* strange; eccentric. □ *There's a lot of kookish things going on around here.* □ *He is just too kookish.* □ *Who is the kookish one over there with the purple shades?*

L

L7 ['ɛl 'sɛvn̩] **1.** *n.* a **square**. □ *That guy is an L7.* □ *Who is that L7 in the wingtip shoes?* **2.** *mod.* dull; **square**. □ *This guy was real, like, you know, L7.* □ *Who is the most L7 person you know?*

labonza [lə'banzə] **1.** *n.* the buttocks. □ *Good grief, what a gross labonza!* □ *She fell flat on her labonza.* **2.** *n.* the pit of the stomach. □ *That kind of beautiful singing really gets you right in the labonza.* □ *She experienced the kind of gut-wrenching anger that starts in your labonza and cuts through right to the tip of your noggin.* **3.** *n.* the belly. □ *I feel the effects of last night's celebration in my wallet and in my labonza.* □ *Look at the labonza on that creep! He's gonna deliver triplets.*

laid-back **1.** *mod.* calm and relaxed. □ *Reggie is not what I would call laid-back.* □ *You are really one laid-back guy!* **2.** *mod.* alcohol or drug intoxicated. □ *He's a little laid-back and can't come to the phone.* □ *How can those guys work when they are laid-back by noon?*

laid out **1.** *mod.* alcohol or drug intoxicated. □ *Man, you got yourself laid out!* □ *I'm too laid out to go to work today.* **2.** *mod.* well dressed. (Black.) □ *Look at those silks! Man, are you laid out!* □ *She is all laid out in her Sunday best.*

lake!, Go jump in the See *Go chase yourself!*

lame AND **laine, lane** **1.** *mod.* inept; inadequate. □ *That guy's so lame, it's pitiful.* □ *This mark is about as laine as they come.*

2. *n.* a *square* person. (Streets. Underworld.) □ *Let's see if that lame over there has anything we want in his pockets.* □ *He won't drink anything at all. He is such a lame!* **3.** *n.* an inept person. □ *The guy turned out to be a lame, and we had to fire him.* □ *Maybe the lane can work in the front office answering phones or something.*

lamps *n.* the eyes. □ *His lamps are closed. He's asleep or dead.* □ *Look at them blue lamps that dame's got.*

lard *n.* the police. (Streets. Derogatory. See also *bacon, pig, pork*.) □ *Here comes the lard!* □ *If the lard catches you violating your parole, you're through.*

lats [læts] *n.* the *latissimus dorsi*; the muscles of the back. (Bodybuilding.) □ *Your lats are coming along fine. Now let's start working on your delts.* □ *Nice lats on that guy.*

launch (one's lunch) *tr. & in.* to empty one's stomach; to vomit. □ *When I saw that mess, I almost launched my lunch.* □ *Watch out! She's going to launch!*

lay a guilt trip on someone See under *lay a (heavy) trip on someone.*

lay a (heavy) trip on someone **1.** *tr.* to criticize someone. □ *There's no need to lay a trip on me. I agree with you.* □ *When he finally does get there, I'm going to lay a heavy trip on him like he'll never forget.* **2.** *tr.* to confuse or astonish someone. □ *After he laid a heavy trip on me about how the company is almost broke, I cleaned out my desk and left.* □ *After Mary laid a trip on John about her other self, he sat down and stared at his feet.* **3.** AND **lay a guilt trip on someone** *tr.* to attempt to make someone feel very guilty. □ *Why do you have to lay a guilt trip on me? Why don't you go to a shrink?* □ *Of course, she just had to lay a trip on him about being bossy, self-centered, and aloof.*

lay some sweet lines on someone AND **put some sweet lines on someone** *tr.* to speak kindly to someone; to flatter someone. □ *I just laid some sweet lines on her, and she let me use her car.* □ *If you put some sweet lines on him, maybe he won't ground you.*

leeky store ['liki stor] *n.* a liquor store. (Black. From *liquor.*) □ *Get me some grapes at the leeky store.* □ *The leeky store is closed till noon.*

lettuce *n.* money. □ *Put your lettuce on the table; then we'll talk.* □ *How much lettuce do you have left?*

lid *n.* an eyelid. □ *Her lids began to close, and the professor raised his voice to a roar.* □ *Pop your lids open! It's morning!*

lid, blow one's See *blow a fuse.*

light *n.* an eye. (Usually plural.) □ *You want I should poke your lights out?* □ *Open your lights and watch for the turnoff sign.*

line *n.* a story or argument; a story intended to seduce someone. (See also *lines.*) □ *I've heard that line before.* □ *Don't feed me that line. Do you think I was born yesterday?*

lines *n.* words; conversation. (Black. See *line.*) □ *I like your lines, but I don't have the time.* □ *We tossed some lines back and forth for a while and then split.*

lip **1.** *tr. & in.* to kiss someone intimately. □ *The two of them were in the corner, lipping intently.* □ *Hey, honeycakes, I really want to lip you.* **2.** *n.* a lawyer. □ *So I brought in my lip, and he got me off the rap.* □ *How much do you pay your lip?* **3.** *n.* back talk; impudent talk. □ *Don't give me any more of your lip!* □ *I've had enough of her lip.*

L.I.Q. *n.* a liquor store. (Black. Also an acronym.) □ *Let's stop at the L.I.Q. and get some berries.* □ *I got a headache already. I don't need anything from any L.I.Q. to make it worse.*

liquid laugh   *n.* vomit. □ *If you drink much more, you're gonna come out with a liquid laugh.* □ *There's some liquid laugh on your shoe.*

loady AND **loadie**   ['lodi] *n.* a drinker or drug user. (Teens and collegiate.) □ *I hear that Wally is a loady. Is that true?* □ *These loadies are all very difficult to deal with.*

long bread AND **long green**   *n.* money. (Black.) □ *Man, that must have cost you some long bread!* □ *Look at the long green you get for doing the job!*

long green   See the previous entry.

loose cannon   *n.* a loudmouth; a braggart. □ *As it turned out, he's not just a loose cannon. He makes sense.* □ *Some loose cannon in the State Department has been feeding the press all sorts of crap as a diversion.*

lorg   [lorg] *n.* a stupid person. □ *Why is Frank such a lorg? Can't he get with it?* □ *Tell that lorg to find his own chair.*

lose it   **1.** *tr.* to empty one's stomach; to vomit. (Collegiate.) □ *Oh, God! I think I'm going to lose it!* □ *Go lose it in the bushes.* **2.** *tr.* to get angry; to lose one's temper. □ *It was too much for him. Ted lost it.* □ *I sat there calmly, biting my lip to keep from losing it.*

lose one's doughnuts   See *blow one's doughnuts.*

lose one's lunch   See *blow (one's) lunch.*

loser   ['luzɚ] *n.* an inept person; an undesirable or annoying person. □ *Dave is a real loser.* □ *Only losers wear clothes like that.*

love bombs   *n.* affirmations of affection. □ *These two were dropping love bombs on each other, even though they hate each other's guts.* □ *What a phony bunch of kooks. They were throwing love bombs all over the place!*

love handles *n.* a roll of fat around the waist. □ *I wish I could get rid of these love handles.* □ *Are you troubled with a spare tire or love handles? Here is a product that has helped thousands and will help you!*

low five *n.* the slapping of hands at waist level as a greeting. (Compare to *high five*.) □ *They turned to each other, throwing a quick low five as they passed.* □ *The two eight-year-olds tried to give each other a low five, but they both hurt their hands.*

lowlife **1.** *n.* a low person; a repellent person. □ *This lowlife smells like bacon.* □ *Hey, lowlife, keep out of my way.* **2.** *mod.* mean; belligerent. (Black.) □ *Don't be so lowlife, man!* □ *We don't need any lowlife characters around here.*

low rent **1.** *n.* a low person; someone without grace or spirit. (Also a rude term of address.) □ *Look, low rent, where is what you owe me?* □ *This low rent here thinks he can push Reggie around, huh?* **2.** *mod.* cheap; unfashionable. □ *This place is strictly low rent.* □ *Why don't you go live with some of your low rent friends?*

lube *n.* butter. □ *Pass the lube, will ya, huh?* □ *We're outa lube.*

luck out *in.* to be fortunate; to strike it lucky. □ *I really lucked out when I ordered the duck. It's excellent.* □ *I didn't luck out at all. I rarely make the right choice.*

[lunch] See *blow (one's) lunch, launch (one's) lunch, lose one's lunch, toss one's lunch.*

M

mace someone's face [mes...] *tr.* to do something drastic to someone, such as spraying mace in the face. (Chemical Mace™ is a brand of tear gas sold in pressurized cans for personal protection.) □ *Do you want me to mace your face? Then shut up!* □ *I look at him, and suddenly I just want to mace his face or something.*

mac out *in.* to overeat, especially the type of food served at McDonald's fast food restaurants. (From the Big Mac™ sandwich. See also *blimp out, pig out, pork out, scarf out.*) □ *I've been in Europe for a month, and I just want to get home and mac out.* □ *I mac out every weekend. It's like going to church.*

maggot 1. *n.* a cigarette. □ *Can I bum a maggot off of you?* □ *Get your own maggots.* **2.** *n.* a low and wretched person; a vile person. □ *You maggot! Take your hands off me!* □ *Only a maggot would do something like that.*

magic bullet See *silver bullet.*

major *mod.* excellent. (Collegiate.) □ *This rally is, like, major!* □ *Wally is one of the most major beach guys!*

Make a lap! *exclam.* to sit down. □ *Hey, make a lap and get out of the way!* □ *Pull up a chair and make a lap!*

Make my day! *exclam.* "Go ahead, do what you are going to do, and I will be very happy to do what I have to do!" (A catchphrase said typically by a movie police officer who has a gun pointed at a criminal. The police officer wants the criminal to do something that will justify pulling the trigger, which the police officer will do with pleasure. Used in real life in any context, and especially in sarcasm.) □ *Move a muscle! Go for your gun! Go ahead, make my day!* □ *Make my day. Just try it.*

make waves *tr.* to cause difficulty. (Often in the negative.) □ *Just relax. Don't make waves.* □ *If you make waves too much around here, you won't last long.*

make with the something *in.* to make something visible; to use something. □ *Come on, make with the cash.* □ *I want to know. Come on, make with the answers!*

mallet *n.* a police officer. (Black.) □ *Sam was struck by a mallet this noon.* □ *Some mallet is going around asking questions about you.*

[man] See *con man, dead man, face man, fuzz man.*

map **1.** *n.* one's face. □ *There was fear and hatred all over his map.* □ *With a map like that, she could really go somewhere.* **2.** *n.* sheet music. (Jazz musicians. See also *chart.*) □ *Check my map, and see where you come in.* □ *I left the map at home. Can I look at yours?*

massive *mod.* excellent. (California.) □ *The bash at Tiffany's was, like, massive!* □ *That was a totally massive party, Tiff.*

maw [mɔ] *tr. & in.* to kiss and pet; to smooch. (Probably from *maul.*) □ *Come on, don't maw me. You've been watching too many movies—or too few.* □ *Let's go out somewhere and maw.*

max *n.* the maximum. (See also *to the max.*) □ *Is this the max I can have?* □ *I want the max. I'm hungry.*

maxed out **1.** *mod.* exhausted; tired. □ *I am just maxed out. I haven't been getting enough sleep.* □ *I had to stop work because I almost maxed out on the keyboard.* **2.** *mod.* alcohol intoxicated. □ *Sam was maxed out and seemed happy enough to sit under the table and whimper.* □ *I hadn't seen Marlowe so maxed out in years. He was nearly paralyzed.*

mazulla See the following entry.

mazuma AND **mazulla** [mə'zumə AND mə'zulə] *n.* money. (From Hebrew *mezu* via Yiddish.) □ *How much mazuma do you want for this?* □ *She's got more mazuma than she knows what to do with.*

McD's AND **McDuck's** *n.* McDonald's, the franchised fast-food restaurant. (Teens and collegiate. The *duck* is a play on the Walt Disney character Donald Duck.) □ *Can you take McD's tonight, or do you want some slow food?* □ *I can always handle Mc-Duck's.*

McDuck's See the previous entry.

mean 1. *mod.* having to do with someone or something that is very good. □ *This music is mean, man, mean. What a great sound!* □ *This is the meanest wine I ever drank.* 2. *mod.* having to do with an excellent example of the art of doing something well habitually. (Always with *a* as in the examples.) □ *John plays the piano quite well. Fred says that John plays a mean piano.* □ *You may say that your mother bakes delicious pies, but all my friends say she bakes a mean pie.* □ *Tom says that his father plays a mean game of golf.*

mean-green *n.* money. □ *How much of that mean-green do you need?* □ *Can I borrow a little mean-green till payday?*

mega ['mɛgə] *mod.* large. □ *Some mega beast boogied down to the front of the auditorium and started screaming.* □ *You see I have this, like, mega problem, ya know.*

megabucks ['mɛgəbəks] *n.* a lot of money. (See also *kilobucks*.) □ *A stereo that size must cost megabucks.* □ *Mr. Wilson has megabucks in pharmaceutical stocks.*

megadork ['mɛgədork] *n*. a very stupid person. (See *dork*.) □ *What a wimpy megadork!* □ *Tiffany, you are, like, such a megadork!*

mellow **1.** *mod*. relaxed; untroubled; *laid back*. □ *Being mellow is my only goal in life.* □ *She is the mellowest fox I know.* **2.** *mod*. slightly alcohol or drug intoxicated. □ *I got mellow and stopped drinking right there.* □ *I'm only mellow, but you drive anyway.*

mellow out **1.** *in*. to calm down; to get less angry. □ *When you mellow out, maybe we can talk.* □ *Come on, man, mellow out!* **2.** *in*. to become generally more relaxed; to grow less contentious. □ *Gary was nearly 40 before he started to mellow out a little and take life less seriously.* □ *After his illness, he mellowed out and seemed more glad to be alive.*

meltdown *n*. a total collapse of anything. (From the term used to describe the self-destruction of a nuclear reactor.) □ *There seems to have been a meltdown in the computer center, and all our records were lost.* □ *The meltdown in the financial markets was caused by a combination of things.*

melvin ['mɛlvən] *n*. a studious or unattractive male. (Teens and collegiate.) □ *Gary is such a melvin!* □ *Do you think I would go out with that melvin?*

mess **1.** *n*. a hopeless, stupid person. □ *Harry has turned into a mess.* □ *The guy's a mess!* **2.** *n*. dung. (Usually with *a*.) □ *There is a dog mess on the lawn again this morning.* □ *There's a mess in Jimmy's diapers, Mom.*

mess someone's face up AND **mess up someone's face** *tr*. to beat someone around the face. □ *You want me to mess up your face, or do you want to come along quietly?* □ *I had to mess his face up a little, boss, but he's been real cooperative since then.*

Mickey D's *n.* McDonald's fast-food restaurant. (Teens and collegiate.) □ *Let's hit Mickey D's for chow this noon.* □ *We're going to Mickey D's for dinner, too.*

mickey mouse **1.** *n.* nonsense; something trivial. (From the Walt Disney character by the same name.) □ *This is just a lot of mickey mouse.* □ *This mickey mouse is wasting my time.* **2.** *mod.* trivial; time wasting; lousy. □ *I want out of this mickey mouse place.* □ *No more mickey mouse questions if I agree to stay?* **3.** *n.* a police officer. (Streets.) □ *Mickey mouse is hanging around asking about you.* □ *Tell mickey mouse he knows where to find me.*

miffed ['mɪft] *mod.* slighted; offended. □ *She seemed sort of miffed when I told her.* □ *Don't get so miffed. It was only a joke.*

mink *n.* a woman. (Black.) □ *I see your mink has some new silks, man.* □ *Take this home to your mink. She'll like it.*

mitt *n.* a hand. □ *Get your mitts off my glass.* □ *The kid's got mitts on him like a gorilla.*

moby ['mobi] **1.** *mod.* enormous; unwieldy. (Like Herman Melville's great white whale, *Moby Dick*.) □ *This is a very moby old car.* □ *Why does he let himself get so moby?* **2.** *n.* a "megabyte," a measurement of computer memory size. (A megabyte is whale-sized compared to a kilobyte.) □ *My fixed disks give me a capacity of over 75 mobies.* □ *My new computer has one moby of random access memory.*

mondo ['mɑndo] *mod.* totally. (California.) □ *You are, like, mondo gross!* □ *This place is like, so, like, mondo beige.*

monkey bite *n.* a kiss that leaves a blotch or mark. (See also **hickey**.) □ *Who gave you that monkey bite?* □ *Do you have some makeup that'll cover this monkey bite?*

monolithic [mɑnəˈlɪθɪk] *mod.* heavily drug intoxicated. (A play on *stoned*.) □ *She's not just stoned, she's monolithic!* □ *I was monolithic—dead drunk.*

moon **1.** *n.* the buttocks. □ *He rubbed a plump moon where he had been kicked, but said no more.* □ *She fell square on her moon and slowly broke into a smile.* **2.** *tr. & in.* to show (someone) one's nude posterior through a window (usually of an automobile). (Compare to *gaucho*.) □ *When the plane flew over Cuba, this guy named Victor actually mooned a Russian M.I.G. that flew by.* □ *The kids were mooning, and they got arrested for indecent exposure.*

mope [mop] **1.** *n.* a tired and ineffectual person. □ *I can't afford to pay mopes around here. Get to work or get out!* □ *I feel like such a mope today.* **2.** AND **mope around** *in.* to move around slowly and sadly. □ *I feel like moping and nothing else.* □ *He just mopes around all day and won't eat anything.*

mope around See under *mope*.

motor-mouth See *ratchet-mouth*.

[mouth] See the two entries that follow and *big mouth, motor-mouth, ratchet-mouth, run off at the mouth*.

mouth-breather *n.* a stupid-acting person. □ *I always end up with a mouth-breather on a blind date.* □ *Who's the mouth-breather with Fred?*

mouthwash *n.* liquor; a drink of liquor. □ *I could use a shot of that mouthwash.* □ *You could use a little mouthwash after that long trip, I bet.*

move on someone *in.* to attempt to pick up someone; to attempt to seduce someone. (Collegiate.) □ *Don't try to move on my date, old chum.* □ *Harry is trying to move on Tiffany. They deserve each another.*

movies   *n.* a case of diarrhea. □ *A case of the movies kept me going all night.* □ *I can't go too far from the little boys' room. I got the movies.*

M.T.   *n.* an empty bottle. □ *Put your M.T.s in the garbage.* □ *Here's another M.T. for your collection.*

munchkin   ['mənt∫kən] *n.* a small or insignificant person. □ *You're not going to let that munchkin push you around, are you?* □ *Who is the munchkin holding the clipboard?*

munch out   *in.* to eat ravenously. (See also *pig out*.) □ *I had to munch out after the party. I can't imagine why.* □ *I can munch out for no reason at all.*

mung   **1.** AND **MUNG** [məŋ] *n.* something that is "mashed until no good"; anything nasty or gooey. □ *Get this mung off my plate.* □ *This mung looks like barf.* **2.** *tr.* to ruin something. □ *You munged my car!* □ *Look at it! You munged it!*

mung something up AND **mung up something**   *tr.* to mess something up. □ *Don't mung it up this time.* □ *The team munged up the play, and the coach blasted them but good.*

mungy   ['məŋi] *mod.* gloppy; messy. □ *Get that mungy stuff off my plate!* □ *The spaghetti was cold and mungy by the time it was served.*

mush   **1.** *n.* nonsense. □ *What mush! Come on, talk straight!* □ *That's just mush. Don't believe it.* **2.** *n.* romance; lovemaking; kissing. □ *I can't stand movies with lots of mush in them.* □ *When an actor looks at an actress like that, you just know that there's gonna be some mush.* **3.** *n.* one's face. (Crude.) □ *Put some paint on your mush, and let's get going.* □ *With a mush like that, you ought to be in pictures. Maybe another King Kong remake.*

musical beds *n.* acts of sexual promiscuity; sleeping with many people. (From the name of the game "musical chairs.") □ *Mary has been playing musical beds for about a year.* □ *She thinks that playing musical beds is the way to get ahead.*

N

nada [ˈnɑdɑ] *n.* nothing; none. (Spanish.) □ *I asked him, but he didn't say nada.* □ *The score was nada to nada.*

narked [nɑrkt] *mod.* annoyed. (Usually with *at* or *with*.) □ *He's really narked at us.* □ *She is narked with you and your car.*

narky [ˈnɑrki] *n.* a narcotic drug. □ *They caught him with a lot of narky in his pockets.* □ *The mugger wanted money to buy some narky.*

narly See *gnarly*.

nause someone out *tr.* to nauseate someone. □ *That horrible smell really nauses me out.* □ *Things like that nause me out, too.*

nay *mod.* ugly; unfavorable. (From *nasty*.) □ *She is really nay.* □ *What a nay thing to say.*

neat **1.** *mod.* great; cool; fine. □ *What a neat idea!* □ *That was not a very neat thing to do.* **2.** *exclam.* "Wow!" (Usually **Neat!**) □ *Neat! I'm glad you came.* □ *Five of them! Neat!*

necessary *n.* money; an income. (Always with *the*.) □ *I can always use more of the necessary.* □ *I gotta have more of the necessary, man.*

negative **1.** *n.* any drawback or bad thing about someone or something. □ *There are too many negatives associated with your plan.* □ *I know another negative you didn't mention.* **2.** *n.* a bad experience. □ *Carl had one negative after another.* □ *That day was a real negative.*

nerd AND **nurd** [nɚd] *n.* a dull and bookish person, usually a male. □ *Fred can be such a nerd!* □ *That whole gang of boys is just a bunch of nurds.*

nerd mobile *n.* a full-sized, uninteresting car; a family car. □ *My father always buys some kind of stupid nerd mobile.* □ *There is nothing but nerd mobiles on our block.*

nerd pack *n.* a plastic sheath for holding pens in a pocket, protecting the cloth from ink. (This is the classic symbol of a bookish nerd.) □ *A lot of engineers have nerd packs.* □ *A real nerd wears a nerd pack in the pocket of a dirty shirt.*

nerts See *nurts.*

nick **1.** *tr.* to arrest someone. □ *The cops nicked Paul outside his house.* □ *They are going to nick Joe, too.* **2.** *tr.* to steal something. □ *The thugs nicked a couple of apples from the fruit stand.* □ *Don't ever nick anything! Do you hear me?* **3.** *tr.* to get or take something. □ *Would you please nick me a slice of bread?* □ *Tom nicked a copy of the test for Sam, who also needed one.*

nip **1.** *n.* a small, quick drink of liquor. □ *Here, have a nip of this stuff.* □ *One nip is enough. That is powerful!* **2.** *tr.* to steal something. □ *The thief nipped my purse.* □ *The punk kid nipped two candy bars from the drugstore.*

nix [nɪks] **1.** *interj.* "no." (All senses from German *nichts.*) □ *The man said nix, and he means nix.* □ *Nix, I won't do it.* **2.** *exclam.* "No!"; "Stop it!"; "I disagree!" (Usually **Nix!**) □ *Nix! I won't do it.* □ *"Nix," said Paul. "I can't permit that."* **3.** *n.* nothing. □ *What did I get for all my trouble? Nix!* □ *I got nix for a tip. And after I was so helpful!* **4.** *tr.* to put a stop to something; to say no to something; to ban something. □ *The boss nixed my plan.* □ *I wanted to say a certain word in my speech, but the management nixed it.*

noid *n.* a "paranoid" person. □ *Some of those noids write hilarious letters to the editor.* □ *Who's the noid screaming about Big Brother?*

noodge See *nudge.*

no stress *interj.* "no problem"; "no bother." □ *Don't worry, man, no stress.* □ *Relax. No stress. It doesn't bother me at all.*

no sweat *interj.* "no problem"; "Don't worry; it is no problem." □ *It's no big deal. No sweat.* □ *No sweat, don't fret about it.*

notch *tr.* to count up something; to add up or score something. □ *Well, it looks like we notched another victory.* □ *The crooks notched one more theft before they were caught.*

No way! *exclam.* "No!" □ *Me join the Army? No way!* □ *She can't do that. No way!*

nowhere *mod.* bad; no good; dull. □ *This place is really nowhere. Let's go.* □ *I want to get out of this nowhere party.*

nudge AND **noodge** [nʊdʒ AND nʊdʒ] **1.** *n.* someone who nags. □ *Sally can be such a nudge!* □ *I really can't stand a noodge.* **2.** *in.* to nag. □ *Don't noodge all the time.* □ *Stop always noodging.* **3.** *tr.* to nag someone. □ *Stop nudging me about that.* □ *I'll noodge him a little to remind him.*

nuke **1.** *n.* a nuclear weapon. □ *Are there nukes aboard that ship?* □ *The military establishment is working on a number of new nukes.* **2.** *tr.* to destroy someone or something. (As with a nuclear weapon.) □ *Your cat ran through my garden and totally nuked my flowers!* □ *I'm going to nuke that cat the next time I see it.* **3.** to cook something with a microwave oven. □ *I'm going to go home and nuke me a nice meal.* □ *Nuke this steak awhile to thaw it.*

nurd See *nerd.*

nurts AND **nerts** [nɚts] *n.* nonsense. □ *Don't talk that kind of nurts to me!* □ *Oh, that's just nerts. I don't believe a word of it.*

nut **1.** *n.* an odd or strange person; a crazy person. □ *Who is that nut over there in the corner?* □ *Some nut is going to try to fly from the top of one building to another.* **2.** *n.* [someone's] head. □ *A brick fell and hit him on the nut.* □ *The baseball came in fast. "Clonk!" Right on the nut!* **3.** *n.* an enthusiast (about something). □ *Paul is a nut about chocolate cake.* □ *Mary is a party nut.*

nuts **1.** *mod.* crazy. □ *You're nuts if you think I care.* □ *That whole idea is just nuts!* **2.** *exclam.* "No!"; "I don't believe you!"; "I don't care!" (Usually **Nuts!**) □ *Nuts! You don't know what you are talking about.* □ *Oh, nuts! I forgot my wallet.*

nut up *in.* to go crazy; to go nuts. □ *I've got to have a vacation soon, or I'm going to nut up.* □ *Poor Sue nutted up and had to take it easy for a few months.*

O

occifer See *ossifer.*

off artist See *rip-off artist.*

oink [ɔɪŋk] *n.* a police officer. (A play on *pig.*) □ *There is an oink following us on a motorcycle.* □ *Here come the oinks!*

O.K. AND **okay** **1.** *interj.* "accepted." (This may be originally from a jocular "oll kerrect," but no one really knows its origin.) □ *O.K., I'll do it.* □ *You want me to lend you $100? Okay.* □ *So, he said, like, "okay," and, like, I go "okay." So we both go "Okay." Okay?* **2.** *mod.* acceptable. □ *Fred is an O.K. guy.* □ *This cake is okay, but not what I would call first rate.* **3.** *mod.* acceptably. □ *She ran okay—nothing spectacular.* □ *They usually do it okay.* **4.** *n.* [someone's] acceptance. □ *I won't give the final okay until I see the plans.* □ *We got her O.K. and went on with the job.*

O-sign *n.* the rounded, open mouth of a dead person. (A semijocular usage. Hospitals. See also *Q-sign.*) □ *The guy in room 226 is giving the O-sign.* □ *That's the third O-sign we've got since noon.*

ossifer AND **occifer** ['ɑsəfɚ] *n.* a police officer. (Also an ill-advised term of address.) □ *Look here, ossifer, I was just having a little fun.* □ *Ask the occifer there if he wants to step outside and discuss it.*

P

pad *n.* a place to live; one's room or dwelling. □ *Why don't you come over to my pad for a while?* □ *This is a nice pad you've got here.*

pad out *in.* to go to bed or to sleep. (See *pad*.) □ *Man, if I don't pad out by midnight, I'm a zombie.* □ *Why don't you people go home so I can pad out?*

pain in the ass AND **pain in the butt, pain in the rear** *n.* a very annoying thing or person. (Crude. An elaboration of *pain*. Caution with *ass*. *Butt* is less offensive. *Rear* is euphemistic.) □ *That guy is a real pain in the ass.* □ *Things like that give me a pain in the butt.* □ *You are nothing but a pain in the rear.*

pain in the neck *n.* a difficult or annoying thing or person. (Compare to *pain in the ass*.) □ *This tax form is a pain in the neck.* □ *My boss is a pain in the neck.*

panic *n.* a very funny or exciting person or thing. □ *John's party was a real panic.* □ *Paul is a panic. He tells a joke a minute.*

paper-pusher **1.** *n.* a bureaucrat; a clerk in the military services; any office worker. (See also *pencil-pusher*.) □ *If those paper-pushers can't get their work done on time, make them stay late.* □ *I don't want to talk to some paper-pusher, I want to talk to the boss.* **2.** *n.* someone who passes bad checks. □ *The bank teller spotted a well-known paper-pusher and called the cops.* □ *The old lady was charged as a paper-pusher and sent to jail.*

pard *n.* partner. (From *pardner* [partner]. Also a term of address.) □ *Come on, pard, let's go find some action.* □ *This is my old pard, Clarence.*

(parental) units *n.* parents. (Teens. Also a term of address.) □ *I don't think my parental units will let me stay out that late.* □ *Hey, units! I need to talk to you about something really important.*

park it (somewhere) *tr.* to sit down somewhere; to sit down and get out of the way. □ *Hey, park it! You're in the way.* □ *Carl, park it over there in the corner. Stop pacing around. You make me nervous.*

party *in.* to celebrate; to spend a lot of time at drinking or drugging or other "party" activities. (See also *rally.*) □ *She did nothing but party at school.* □ *Come on! Let's party!*

party animal *n.* someone who loves parties. □ *My boyfriend and I are real party animals. Let's party!* □ *If you weren't such a party animal, you'd have more time for studying.*

party-hearty *in.* to have a great time; to celebrate. (Originally teenage. The past tense is variable.) □ *Let's get some stuff and party-hearty.* □ *The whole class decided to celebrate and party-hearty.* □ *They partied-hearty for a long time.*

pass go *tr.* to complete a difficult or dangerous task successfully. (From "pass go and collect $200" in the game Monopoly™.) □ *Man, I tried to get there on time, but I just couldn't pass go.* □ *You had better pass go with this job, or you've had it.*

pasting *n.* a beating; a defeat in a game. □ *Our team took quite a pasting last weekend.* □ *I gave him a pasting.*

paw 1. *n.* someone's hand. (Jocular.) □ *Get your paws off me!* □ *That dog bit my paw.* 2. *tr.* to feel someone or handle someone sexually. □ *If you paw me again, I'll slap you!* □ *I can't stand men who paw you to pieces.*

peanuts *n.* practically no money at all. □ *They want me to do everything, but they only pay peanuts.* □ *The cost is just peanuts compared to what you get for the money.*

pec(k)s AND **pects** [pɛks AND pɛkts] *n.* the pectoral muscles. (From weight-lifting and bodybuilding.) □ *Look at the pecks on that guy!* □ *With pects like that he needs a bra.*

peepers *n.* the eyes. □ *Come on, use your peepers. Take a good look.* □ *My peepers are tired.*

pencil-pusher *n.* a bureaucrat; a clerk; an office worker. (See also *paper-pusher*.) □ *Look here, you lousy pencil-pusher, I want to talk to your boss!* □ *City Hall is filled with a bunch of overpaid pencil-pushers.*

penny *n.* a police officer. (A play on *copper*. See the note at *cop*.) □ *The penny over on the corner told the boys to get moving.* □ *We better get going before the pennies get here.*

Period! *exclam.* "...and that's final!" (A way of indicating that there will be no more discussion or negotiation.) □ *I don't want to hear any more about it! Period!* □ *My final offer is $30. Period!*

petrified *mod.* alcohol intoxicated. (Literally, turned into stone. Another way of saying *stoned*.) □ *She's not drunk; she's petrified.* □ *He drank beer till he was petrified.*

P.G. *mod.* "pregnant." □ *Do you think Sally's P.G.?* □ *I think I'm P.G. You know, pregnant.*

phfft [ffft] **1.** *mod.* done for; dead. (See also *piffed*.) □ *There is my cat, and zoom comes a car. My cat is phfft.* □ *Yup. Deader than a doornail. Phfft!* **2.** *mod.* alcohol intoxicated. □ *You won't wake him up for hours yet. He's phfft.* □ *Three beers and she's phfft, for sure.*

phooey AND **fooey**   **1.** *n.* nonsense. □ *Your story is just a lot of phooey.* □ *I've heard enough fooey. Let's get out of here.* **2.** *exclam.* an expression of disgust, disagreement, or resignation. (Usually **Phooey!** or **Fooey!** Used typically when something smells or tastes bad.) □ *Who died in here? Phooey!* □ *This is the worst food I ever ate. Fooey!*

phutz AND **futz**   [fəts] *tr.* to rob, swindle, or cheat someone. □ *Don't futz me! Tell the truth!* □ *The muggers phutzed his wallet and watch.*

pickled   *mod.* alcohol intoxicated. (Very common.) □ *She's usually pickled by noon.* □ *It only takes a few drinks to get him pickled.*

piddle (around)   *in.* to waste time; to work aimlessly or inefficiently. □ *Stop piddling around! Get to work!* □ *Can't you get serious and stop piddling?*

piece of cake   **1.** *n.* something easy to do. □ *No problem. When you know what you're doing, it's a piece of cake.* □ *Glad to help. It was a piece of cake.* **2.** *exclam.* "It's a piece of cake!"; "It's easy!" (Usually **Piece of cake!**) □ *No problem, piece of cake!* □ *Rescuing drowning cats is my specialty. Piece of cake!*

piffed   [pɪft] **1.** AND **pifted**   ['pɪftəd] *tr.* killed. (Past tense only. See also *phfft*.) □ *He piffed his goldfish by mistake.* □ *The speeding car pifted the cat yesterday.* **2.** AND **pifted**   ['pɪftəd] *mod.* dead. □ *What will I do with a pifted cat?* □ *He's as piffed as they come.*

pifted   See under *piffed*.

pig   **1.** *n.* someone who eats too much; a glutton. (All senses are usually derogatory.) □ *Stop being a pig! Save some for other people.* □ *I try to cut down on calories, but whenever I see red meat I make a pig of myself.* **2.** *n.* an ugly and fat woman. □ *Clare is a pig. Why doesn't she lose a ton or two?* □ *Every girl in that sorority is a pig.* **3.** *n.* a dirty or slovenly person. (Also a rude term of address.) □ *Carl is a pig. I don't think he bathes enough.* □ *Jimmy, change your clothes. Look at that mud, you little pig!* **4.** *n.* an officer; a police officer or a military officer. (Derogatory. Used mostly for a police officer. Widely known since the 1960s.) □ *The pigs are coming to bust up the fight.* □ *The pigs are driving around busting innocent people like me.*

pig out *in.* to overeat; to overindulge in food or drink. (Compare to *blimp out, mac out, pork out, scarf out.*) □ *I always pig out on Fridays.* □ *I can't help myself when I see ice cream. I have to pig out.*

pin 1. *n.* someone's leg. (Usually plural.) □ *My pins are a little wobbly.* □ *Stand up on your pins and speak your mind.* **2.** *n.* an important criminal leader. □ *The pin sent me. He says you're to come with me.* □ *The mob's getting careless. The cops think they caught the pin this time.*

pinch 1. *n.* a small amount of a powdered substance, such as salt, snuff, a spice, etc. (Not slang.) □ *He put a pinch under his lips and walked up to home plate.* □ *Do you have any oregano? I need a pinch.* **2.** *tr.* to arrest someone. □ *The cops pinched her in front of her house.* □ *The police captain pinched her for passing bad checks.* **3.** *n.* the arresting of someone. □ *They made the pinch in front of her house.* □ *The pinch was for forgery.*

pinstriper *n.* a businessman or woman wearing a pinstriped suit. (Compare to *suit, vest.*) □ *Who's the pinstriper driving the big black car?* □ *Wall Street is nothing but wall-to-wall pinstripers.*

pip *n.* a pimple; a *zit.* □ *Good grief, I've got ear-to-ear pips!* □ *Do you ever outgrow pips?*

pipe *n.* an easy course in school. □ *Take this course. It's a pipe.* □ *I don't want a full load of pipes. I want to learn something.*

piss (Caution with *piss* in both senses.) **1.** to urinate. □ *He went out to piss.* □ *Your stupid dog pissed on my pants leg!* **2.** urine. □ *There's piss on the floor!* □ *You got piss on your pants leg.*

pissed **1.** *mod.* alcohol intoxicated. (Caution with *pissed*.) □ *He was really pissed.* □ *He was so pissed he could hardly stand up.* **2.** See the following entry.

pissed (off) *mod.* angry. (Crude. Caution with *piss*. Compare to *piss someone off*.) □ *I was so pissed off I could have screamed.* □ *He's come back, and he's sure pissed.*

piss someone off AND **piss off someone** *tr.* to make someone angry. (Crude. Caution with *piss*.) □ *She really pissed me off!* □ *That's enough to piss off anybody.* (More at *pissed (off)*.)

pitch a bitch *tr.* to make a complaint. (Crude.) □ *You really love to pitch a bitch, don't you? What makes you happy?* □ *Complain, complain! You could pitch a bitch all day long.*

pits **1.** *n.* the armpits. (Usually crude.) □ *Man, you have a problem in your pits.* □ *Who's got the smelly pits in here?* **2.** *n.* anything really bad. (Always with *the*.) □ *Life is the pits.* □ *This whole day was the pits from beginning to end.* **3.** *n.* the depths of despair. (Always with *the*. Often with *in* as in the example.) □ *It's always the pits with him.* □ *She's depressed and in the pits.*

pit stop **1.** *n.* a pause in a journey (usually by car) to urinate. (From the name of a service stop in automobile racing.) □ *I think we'll pull in at the next rest area. I need a pit stop.* □ *Poor Carl needs a pit stop every 30 miles.* **2.** *n.* an underarm deodorant. (Because it *stops* arm*pit* odor.) □ *Man, do you need some pit stop!* □ *Can I borrow your pit stop? I need it bad.*

plastered *mod.* alcohol intoxicated. □ *She's really plastered.* □ *She's so plastered she can't see.*

plastic *mod.* phony; false. □ *She wears too much makeup and looks totally plastic.* □ *I'm tired of living in such a plastic society.*

play **1.** *n.* a strategy; a plan of action. □ *That was a bad play, Bill. We lost the account.* □ *Here's a play that worked for us last* *year at this time.* **2.** *n.* an attractive investment; a way to make some money in the financial markets. □ *I just heard about a good play in the options market.* □ *Not talking it over with your friends first was a bad play.* □ *Buying bonds at a discount is an interesting play.*

played (out) **1.** *mod.* having to do with a portion of marijuana (in a cigarette or a pipe) that has had all of the effective substance smoked out of it. □ *This stuff is played. Get rid of it.* □ *You gave me pot that was played out!* **2.** *mod.* worn-out; exhausted; no longer effective. □ *This scenario is played out. It no longer makes sense.* □ *I'm played. I have no new ideas.*

player *n.* someone who plays around, especially sexually. □ *He's a player, and I'm just a country girl who wanted to go dancing.* □ *I don't want a player. I want a good solid homemaker type.*

play, in See *in play.*

play it cool **1.** *tr.* to do something while not revealing insecurities or incompetence. (See *cool.*) □ *Play it cool, man. Look like you belong there.* □ *If the boss walks in, just play it cool.* **2.** *tr.* to hold one's temper. □ *Come on now. Let it pass. Play it cool.* □ *Don't let them get you mad. Play it cool.*

play the dozens AND **shoot the dozens** *tr.* to trade insulting remarks concerning relatives with another person. (Chiefly black. See also *(dirty) dozens.*) □ *They're out playing the dozens.* □ *Stop shooting the dozens and go do your homework.*

plootered ['pludɚd] *mod.* alcohol intoxicated. □ *We went out and got totally plootered.* □ *How can anyone get so plootered on a bottle of wine?*

plop **1.** *n.* the sound of dropping something soft and bulky, such as a hunk of meat. □ *When the roast fell on the floor, it made a nasty plop.* □ *When I heard the plop, I looked up and saw our dinner on the floor.* **2.** *tr.* to put or place something (somewhere). □ *I don't mind cooking a turkey. You only have to plop it in the* *oven and forget about it.* □ *I plopped my books on the table and went straight to my room.* **3.** *tr.* to sit oneself down somewhere; to place one's buttocks somewhere. (The *it* in the examples is the buttocks.) □ *Come in, Fred. Just plop it anywhere you see a chair. This place is a mess.* □ *Just plop it down right there, and we'll have our little talk.*

pluck AND **plug** *n.* wine; cheap wine. (Originally black.) □ *Where can I get some plug?* □ *You spilled plug all over my car seat.*

plug **1.** *n.* a bite-sized, pressed mass of chewing tobacco. □ *He put a plug in his cheek and walked away.* □ *Hey, gimme a piece of that plug!* **2.** *n.* a drink of beer. □ *Let me have a plug out of that bottle.* □ *I just want a plug, not the whole thing.* **3.** *n.* a free advertisement or a commercial boost from someone for a product. □ *I managed to get a plug on the Mike Michael show.* □ *How about a free plug during your introduction?*

plug See *pluck.*

poindexter ['pɔɪndɛkstɚ] *n.* a bookish person; a well-mannered good student, usually male. □ *Charles is a poindexter, but he's a good guy.* □ *I'm no poindexter. In fact, my grades are pretty low.*

pointy-head *n.* a studious thinker; an intellectual. (Compare to conehead.) □ *The pointy-heads seem to be living in a world of their own.* □ *Why do pointy-heads spend so much time arguing about nothing?*

poky **1.** *n.* jail; a jail cell. □ *She spent a day in the poky.* □ *Have you ever been in the poky?* **2.** *mod.* slow; lagging and inefficient. □ *Hurry up! Don't be so poky.* □ *What a poky old horse.*

polluted *mod.* alcohol or drug intoxicated. □ *Those guys are really polluted.* □ *Madam, you are polluted!*

pond scum *n.* a mean and wretched person; a worthless male. (Collegiate. An elaboration of *scum*, less crude than *scumbag*.

Also a rude term of address.) □ *Tell that pond scum to beat it.* □ *Get your hands off me, pond scum!*

poop 1. *n.* information; the detailed knowledge of something. (See also *(hot) skinny.*) □ *What's the poop on the broken glass in the hall?* □ *Tell me all the poop.* 2. *n.* fecal matter. (Caution with topic.) □ *Don't step in the poop.* □ *There's poop on the sidewalk.* 3. *in.* to defecate. □ *Your dog pooped on my lawn.* □ *I tried to chase the cat away while it was pooping.*

pooped (out) 1. *mod.* exhausted; worn-out. (Said of a person or an animal.) □ *I'm really pooped out.* □ *The horse looked sort of pooped in the final stretch.* 2. *mod.* alcohol intoxicated. □ *How much of that stuff does it take to get pooped?* □ *He's been drinking all night and is totally pooped out.*

poop out *in.* to quit; to wear out and stop. □ *He pooped out after about an hour.* □ *I think I'm going to poop out pretty soon.* (More at *pooped (out).*)

poop sheet *n.* a sheet containing information. □ *Where is the poop sheet on today's meeting?* □ *You can't tell one from the other without a poop sheet.*

pop 1. *tr.* to hit or strike someone. □ *Please don't pop me again.* □ *She popped him lightly on the shoulder.* 2. *mod.* popular. □ *This style is very pop.* □ *I don't care for pop stuff.* 3. *n.* popular music. □ *I like most pop, but not if it's too loud.* □ *Pop is the only music I like.* 4. *n.* a time; a try, apiece. (Always with *a.*) □ *Twenty dollars a pop is too much.* □ *I love records, but not at $15.98 a pop.*

pop for something *in.* to pay for a treat (for someone). (See *spring for something.*) □ *Let's have some ice cream. I'll pop for it.* □ *It's about time you popped for coffee.*

pop off 1. *in.* to make an unnecessary remark; to interrupt with a remark; to sound off. □ *Please don't pop off all the time.* □ *Bob keeps popping off when he should be listening.* 2. *in.* to lose one's temper. (Compare to *pop one's cork*.) □ *Now, don't pop off. Keep cool.* □ *I don't know why she popped off at me. All I did was say hello.* **3.** *in.* to die. □ *My uncle popped off last week.* □ *I hope I'm asleep when I pop off.*

pop one's cork *tr.* to release one's anger; have an angry outburst. □ *I'm just about to pop my cork.* □ *She tried to hold it back, but suddenly she popped her cork.*

popped **1.** *mod.* arrested. (Similar to "busted." See *bust*.) □ *Tom got popped for speeding.* □ *He was popped for hardly anything at all.* **2.** *mod.* alcohol or drug intoxicated. □ *She looks glassy-eyed because she's popped.* □ *They went out last night and got good and popped.*

popper **1.** *n.* a handgun. (Underworld. From the sound of a gunshot.) □ *He carries a popper under his coat.* □ *It's illegal to carry a popper in this state.* **2.** *n.* a can of beer (in a pop-top can.) □ *Hey, toss me a popper, Fred!* □ *You ready for another popper, Tom?*

[porcelain] See *bow to the porcelain altar, drive the porcelain bus, kiss the porcelain god, pray to the porcelain god, ride the porcelain bus, worship the porcelain god.*

pork *n.* the police in general; a *pig*. (Underworld.) □ *Keep an eye out for the pork.* □ *The pork hauled all of them to the station.*

pork out *in.* to overindulge in food and drink. (A play on *pig out*.) □ *Whenever I see french fries, I know I'm going to pork out.* □ *We porked out on pizza.*

porky *mod.* fat; obese; pig-like. □ *You are beginning to look a little porky.* □ *See that porky man over there?*

pot **1.** *n.* a toilet. (Usually with *the*.) □ *Jimmy's on the pot, Mommy.* □ *Where's the pot around here?* **2.** *n.* cannabis; marijuana. (Originally drugs, now widely known.) □ *She had pot on* *her when she was arrested.* □ *The cops found pot growing next to city hall.*

potato *n.* the head. □ *I got a nasty bump on my potato.* □ *Put your hat on your potato, and let's get out of here.*

pound a beer AND **pound some beers** *tr.* to drink a beer. □ *On a hot day like this, I want to go home and pound a beer.* □ *Let's go down to the tavern and pound some beers.*

pound one's ear *tr.* to sleep. □ *I've got to spend more time pounding my ear.* □ *She went home to pound her ear an hour or two before work.*

pounds *n.* dollars; money. (Black.) □ *How many pounds does this thing cost?* □ *I don't have any pounds on me.*

pound the books See *hit the books.*

power tool *n.* a student who studies most of the time. (An elaboration of *tool.*) □ *Willard is a power tool if there ever was one. Studies most of the night.* □ *All the power tools always get the best grades.*

prayerbones *n.* the knees. □ *Okay, down on your prayerbones.* □ *He pushed one of his prayerbones into my gut.*

pray to the porcelain god *in.* to empty one's stomach; to vomit. (Refers to being on one's knees (praying) in front of a porcelain toilet bowl.) □ *Boy, was I sick. I was praying to the porcelain god for two hours.* □ *I think I'd better go home and pray to the porcelain god.*

pricey *mod.* expensive. □ *This stuff is too pricey.* □ *That's a pretty pricey car.* □ *Do you have anything less pricey?*

pro **1.** *n.* a "professional" (at anything); someone as good as a professional. □ *I'm a pro at photography.* □ *When it comes to typing, he's a pro.* **2.** *mod.* professional. □ *I hope to play pro*

ball next year. □ *This is not what I'd call a pro performance.*
3. *n.* a prostitute. □ *Do you think she's a pro or just overly friendly?* □ *This pro comes up to me and acts like she's met me before.*

prod 1. *n.* a reminder. □ *She gave me a little prod about the report that is due Monday.* □ *Call me up and give me a little prod so I won't forget.* **2.** *tr.* to remind someone (about something). □ *Call me up and prod me just before the due date.* □ *Stop prodding me about these minor matters.*

prosty AND **prostie** *n.* a prostitute. □ *The cops haul in about 40 prosties a night from that one neighborhood alone.* □ *This one prosty was high on something and started screaming.*

psyched (out) *mod.* excited; overwhelmed; thrilled. □ *She's really psyched out.* □ *That's great. I'm really psyched!* □ *What a psyched-out way to talk!*

psyched (up) *mod.* completely mentally ready (for something). □ *I'm really psyched for this test.* □ *The team isn't psyched up enough to do a good job.*

psycho *n.* a psychopathic person; a crazy person. □ *Get that psycho out of here!* □ *Pat is turning into a real psycho.*

psych out *in.* to have a nervous or emotional trauma; to go mad for a brief time. (Compare to *freak (out)*.) □ *Another day like this one and I'll psych out for sure.* □ *He looked at the bill and psyched out.*

psych someone out AND **psych out someone** *tr.* to try to figure out what someone is likely to do. □ *The batter tried to psych out the pitcher, but it didn't work.* □ *Don't try to psych me out.*

psych someone up AND **psych up someone** *tr.* to get someone excited or mentally prepared for something. □ *The coach psyched up the team for the game.* □ *I psyched myself up to sing in front of all those people.* (More at *psyched (up)*.)

ptomaine-domain AND **ptomaine-palace** ['tomen...] *n.* any institutional dining facility; a mess hall; a cafeteria. □ *I can't stand the food at the ptomaine-domain.* □ *Time to go over to the ptomaine-palace and eat—if you can call it that.*

puggled **1.** *mod.* exhausted; bewildered. □ *I have had a long day, and I'm really puggled.* □ *Who is that puggled old man?* **2.** *mod.* alcohol intoxicated. □ *When he started pouring his drink down his collar, I knew he was puggled.* □ *The whole gang got puggled last night.*

puke [pjuk] **1.** *in.* to empty one's stomach; to vomit. □ *I think I am going to puke.* □ *Carl went home and puked for an hour.* **2.** *n.* vomit. □ *There's puke on the floor!* □ *Good grief, Tom. Is that puke on your shoe, or what?* **3.** *n.* a disgusting person. □ *I can't stand that puke!* □ *Make that puke get out of here, or I will scream!*

pukes *n.* the feeling of nausea; the feeling of impending vomiting. (Especially with *have, get.* Always with *the.*) □ *Oh my God, I've got the pukes.* □ *I hate having the pukes.*

pukey AND **pukoid** *mod.* disgusting; repellent. □ *Who is that pukey-looking guy?* □ *Gosh, it's pukoid!* □ *What a pukey day!*

pukoid See the previous entry.

pull **1.** *n.* a drink; a drink from a flask. □ *He took another pull and kept on talking.* □ *Can I have a pull?* **2.** *tr.* to take a drink or a mouthful of liquor from a bottle or other container. □ *He pulled a slug from the bottle.* □ *She pulled a mouthful and then spat it out.*

pull jive *tr.* to drink liquor. (See *jive.* Black.) □ *Let's go pull jive for a while.* □ *Don't you ever do anything but pull jive?*

pummelled *mod.* alcohol intoxicated. (Collegiate.) □ *Can you imagine getting pummelled on peppermint schnapps?* □ *They get pummelled every Friday night.*

pump 1. *tr.* to press someone for an answer or information. □ *Pump him until he talks.* □ *Don't pump me! I will tell you nothing!* 2. *n.* the heart. (See also **ticker**.) □ *He has the pump of a 40-year-old.* □ *My pump's getting sort of weak.* 3. *n.* a pumped-up muscle. (Bodybuilding.) □ *Look at the size of that pump.* □ *He's tired and can't quite make a pump.*

pumped (up) *mod.* excited; physically and mentally ready. (Sports.) □ *The team is really pumped up for Friday's game.* □ *She really plays well when she's pumped!*

pump ship 1. *tr.* to urinate. (Crude. From an expression meaning to pump the bilge water from a ship.) □ *He stopped and pumped ship right in the alley.* □ *I'll be with you after I pump ship.* 2. *tr.* to empty one's stomach; to vomit. (Crude. Less well-known than the previous sense.) □ *After I pumped ship, I felt better.* □ *Oh, man! I think I gotta pump ship!*

pump something up AND **pump up something** *tr.* to flex and tense a muscle until it is expanded to its fullest size, as with thighs and forearms. (Bodybuilding.) □ *She pumped up her thighs and struck a pose.* □ *He really can pump up his pecs.*

punk 1. AND **punk kid** *n.* an inexperienced boy or youth. (Derogatory. Also a term of address.) □ *Ask that punk to come over here.* □ *Look here, punk, I need some help.* 2. *n.* a petty (male) hoodlum; a (male) juvenile delinquent. □ *We know how to deal with punks like you.* □ *The jails are packed with crooks who were just punks a few years ago.* 3. *mod.* poor; dull and inferior. □ *The party turned punk, and we left.* □ *This is pretty punk food.*

punker *n.* a punk rocker; a young person who dresses in the style of punk rockers or has the wild hairstyles. □ *It's not safe to walk on the street with all those weird punkers out there.* □ *The punkers don't even have a sense of rhythm.*

punk kid See under *punk*.

punk out **1.** *in.* to chicken out. □ *He was supposed to ask her out, but he punked out at the last minute.* □ *Come on! Stick with it! Don't punk out!* **2.** *in.* to become a punker. □ *If I punked out, my parents would probably clobber me.* □ *If my kids ever punked out and looked like that, I think I'd clobber them.*

puppy **1.** *n.* a wimpy person; a softie. □ *That silly puppy is still waiting outside your door.* □ *Oh, Paul, you're such a puppy!* **2.** *n.* a thing; a piece or part of something. □ *Put this little puppy right here.* □ *Where is that puppy?*

[pusher] See *cookie-pusher, paper-pusher, pencil-pusher.*

push money *n.* extra money paid to a salesperson to aggressively sell certain merchandise. (See also *spiff.*) □ *The manufacturer supplied a little push money that even the store manager didn't know about.* □ *I got about $300 last month in push money for selling some low-grade sweaters.*

push off AND **shove off** *in.* to leave. (As if one were pushing away from a dock.) □ *Well, it looks like it's time to push off.* □ *It's time to go. Let's shove off.*

puss [pʊs] *n.* the face. □ *I ought to poke you right in the puss!* □ *Look at the puss on that guy! What an ugly face!*

put a con on someone *tr.* to attempt to deceive someone; to attempt to swindle someone. (Underworld.) □ *Don't try to put a con on me, Buster! I've been around too long.* □ *I wouldn't try to put a con on you. I'm not that dumb.*

put-on *n.* a deception; an entertaining deception. □ *Of course, it was a joke. It was a really good put-on.* □ *Don't take it seriously. It's just a put-on.*

putrid *mod.* alcohol intoxicated. (See also *rotten.*) □ *That guy is stinking drunk. Putrid, in fact.* □ *They went out last night and got putrid.*

put some sweet lines on someone See *lay some sweet lines on someone.*

put something on the street *tr.* to make something known publicly; to tell everyone one's troubles. □ *Man, can't you keep a secret? Don't put everything on the street.* □ *She gets a little problem, and she puts it on the street right away!*

put the chill on someone AND **put the freeze on someone** *tr.* to ignore someone. □ *She was pretty snooty till we all put the chill on her.* □ *Let's put the freeze on Ted until he starts acting better.*

put the freeze on someone See the previous entry.

put the moves on someone *tr.* to attempt to seduce someone. (With *any* in the negative.) □ *At least he didn't try to put any moves on me.* □ *If somebody doesn't try to put the moves on her, she thinks she's a failure.*

put the pedal to the metal *tr.* to press a car's accelerator to the floor. □ *Let's go, man. Put the pedal to the metal.* □ *Put the pedal to the metal, and we're out of here.*

put to it *mod.* in trouble or difficulty; hard up (for something such as money). (As if one's back were put to the wall.) □ *Sorry, I can't lend you anything. I'm a bit put to it this month.* □ *What a day. I'm really put to it.*

putz [pəts] **1.** *n.* a penis. (Yiddish. Caution with *putz* and topic.) □ *Tell him to cover his putz and run and grab a towel.* □ *He told some joke about a putz, but nobody laughed.* **2.** *n.* a stupid person, typically a male; a *schmuck.* (Yiddish. Also a rude term of address.) □ *And this stupid putz just stood there smiling.* □ *Tell that putz to leave his card with the secretary.*

putz around [pəts...] *in.* to fiddle around; to mess around. (See the previous entry.) □ *Stop putzing around and get to work.* □ *Those guys spend most of their time just putzing around.*

Q

Q-sign *n.* the rounded, open mouth of a dead person with the tongue hanging out like the tail of a capital Q. (A semi-jocular usage. Hospitals. See also *O-sign*.) □ *The old lady in the corner room is giving the Q-sign.* □ *I can't handle another Q-sign today.*

quaff a brew ['kwɑf ə 'bru] *tr.* to drink a beer. (See *brew*.) □ *I went down to the bar to quaff a brew.* □ *Let's go somewhere and quaff a brew.*

quan See under *quant*.

quant **1.** AND **quan** *n.* quantitative analysis. (Scientific and collegiate.) □ *I didn't study enough for my quant test.* □ *I flunked quan twice.* **2.** *n.* a technician who works in financial market analysis. □ *He was a quant on Wall Street for two years.* □ *The quants have been warning us about the danger for a month.*

quarterback *tr.* to manage, lead, or direct someone or something. □ *Who is going to quarterback this organization after you go?* □ *I quarterbacked the whole company for more years than I care to remember.*

Qué pasa? [ke 'pɑsə] *interrog.* "Hello, what's going on?" (Spanish.) □ *Hey, man! Qué pasa?* □ *What's happening? Qué pasa?*

quick-and-dirty *mod.* rapidly and carelessly done. □ *I'm selling this car, so all I want is a quick-and-dirty repair job.* □ *They only do quick-and-dirty work at that shop.*

quick buck AND **fast buck**   *n.* a quickly or easily earned profit. □ *I'm always on the lookout to make a fast buck.* □ *I need to make a quick buck without much effort.*

quick fix   **1.** *n.* a quick and probably none too permanent or satisfactory solution to a problem. □ *The quick fix isn't good enough in this case.* □ *He's a master of the quick fix.* **2.** *mod.* having to do with a temporary or unsatisfactory solution or repair. (Usually **quick-fix**.) □ *Frank is a master of the quick-fix solution.* □ *This is no time for quick-fix efforts.*

quick one AND **quickie**   *n.* a quick drink of booze; a single beer consumed rapidly. □ *I could use a quick one about now.* □ *I only have time for a quickie.*

R

rack *n.* a bed. □ *I need some more time in the rack.* □ *You don't get to see the rack very much in the army.*

rack duty See *rack time.*

racked (up) *mod.* alcohol or drug intoxicated. □ *They drank till they were good and racked.* □ *Man, are you racked. What did you drink? A gallon?* □ *They all got racked up last weekend.*

racket **1.** *n.* noise. □ *Cut out that racket! Shut up!* □ *Who's making all that racket?* **2.** *n.* a deception; a scam. □ *He operated a racket that robbed old ladies of their savings.* □ *This is not a service station; it's a real racket!* **3.** *n.* any job. □ *I've been in this racket for 20 years and never made any money.* □ *I'm a stockbroker. What's your racket?*

rack (out) *in.* to go to sleep or to bed. □ *What time do you rack out?* □ *I've got to rack out or drop from exhaustion.* □ *If I don't rack by midnight, I'm dead the next day.*

rack something up AND **rack up something** **1.** *tr.* to accumulate something; to collect or acquire something. □ *We racked up a lot of money in the stock market.* □ *They all racked up a lot of profits.* □ *We racked up 20 points in the game last Saturday.* **2.** *tr.* to wreck something. □ *Fred racked up his new car.* □ *He racked up his arm in the football game.*

rack time AND **rack duty**   *n.* time spent in bed. (Military.) □ *I need more rack time than I'm getting.* □ *I was on rack duty for my entire leave.*

rad   [ræd] **1.** *n.* a radical person. (California.) □ *He's such a rad! For sure!* □ *My brother is a rad, but he's a good guy.* **2.** *mod.* great; wonderful; excellent. (California. From *radical.*) □ *Oh my God, that's, like, really rad!* □ *What a rad swimsuit!*

radical   *mod.* great; excellent. (California.) □ *It's so, like, radical!* □ *My boyfriend, he's, like, so radical!*

rag   **1.** *n.* a newspaper. □ *I'm tired of reading this rag day after day. Can't we get a different paper?* □ *What a rag! It's only good for putting in the bottom of bird cages!* **2.** *n.* ugly or badly styled clothing; an ugly garment. (Usually plural.) □ *I can't wear that rag!* □ *I need some new clothes. I can't go around wearing rags like these.* □ *I wouldn't be seen in last season's rags.* **3.** *n.* any clothing, even the best. (Always plural.) □ *Man, I got some new rags that will knock your eyes out!* □ *You got soda pop all over my new rags!*

rag out   *in.* to dress up. □ *I like to rag out and go to parties.* □ *I hate to rag out. I like comfortable clothes.*

railroad tracks   *n.* dental braces. □ *I can't smile because of these railroad tracks.* □ *My railroad tracks cost nearly $1,200.*

rainbow   *n.* a bowlegged person, typically a male. (Also a rude term of address.) □ *Hey, rainbow! Are you a cowboy?* □ *Ask that rainbow if he has to have special trousers made.*

rain on someone or something   See the following entry.

rain on someone's parade AND **rain on someone or something**   *in.* to spoil something for someone. □ *I hate to rain on your parade, but your plans are all wrong.* □ *She really rained on our parade.* □ *Did anyone rain on the meeting?*

rake in something AND **rake something in**   *tr.* to take in a lot of something, usually money. □ *Our candidate will rake in votes by the thousand.* □ *They were raking in money by the bushel.*

rally   ['ræli] **1.** *n.* a party or get-together of some kind. □ *There's a rally over at Tom's tonight.* □ *The rally was a flop. Everyone left early.* **2.** *in.* to hold a party of some kind; to *party*. (Collegiate.) □ *Let's rally tonight about midnight.* □ *They rallied until dawn.*

ralph AND **rolf**   [rælf AND rɔlf] *in.* to empty one's stomach; to vomit. (Teens and collegiate.) □ *She went home and ralphed for an hour.* □ *I think I'm going to rolf.*

ralph something up AND **ralph up something**   (Teens and collegiate.) *tr.* to vomit (something). □ *He ralphed up his dinner.* □ *The doctor gave him some stuff that made him ralph it up.*

rambo   ['ræmbo] *tr.* to (figuratively) annihilate someone or something. (Collegiate. From the powerful film character Rambo.) □ *The students ramboed the cafeteria, and the cops were called.* □ *Please don't rambo the other team. Just win the game.*

rammy   ['ræmi] *mod.* sexually excited or aroused. (Refers to the ram, a symbol of arousal.) □ *Fred was looking a little rammy, so I excused myself and left.* □ *Your rammy boyfriend is on the telephone.*

ramrod   *tr.* to lead something; to act as the driving force behind something. □ *Who is going to ramrod this project?* □ *Don't ramrod us into something we don't really want.*

rank   *tr.* to give someone a hard time; to annoy someone. □ *Stop ranking me!* □ *The dean was ranking the boys for pulling the prank.* □ *When he finished with the boys, he started ranking their parents.*

rank someone (out) AND **rank out someone** *tr.* to annoy or chastise someone. (Compare to *rank*.) □ *He really ranks me out. What a pest!* □ *I ranked out the whole gang, but good!*

rap **1.** *in.* to talk or chat about something. □ *Something wrong? Let's rap about it.* □ *The kids sat down and rapped for an hour or so.* **2.** *n.* a conversation; a chat. □ *How about a rap?* □ *Let's have a rap sometime.* **3.** *n.* sweet talk; seductive talk; *line*. □ *I like your rap, but that's all I like about you.* □ *Don't lay that rap on me! You're not my type.* **4.** *n.* a criminal charge; the blame for something. (Underworld.) □ *I won't take the rap for something you did.* □ *The cops tried to make the rap stick, but they didn't have enough evidence.*

rap session *n.* an informal conversation session. □ *The kids settled down for a long rap session.* □ *The rap session was interrupted by a fire drill.*

(rap) sheet *n.* a criminal record listing all recorded criminal charges. (See *rap*.) □ *This guy has a rap sheet a mile long.* □ *The sergeant asked if there was a sheet on the prisoner.*

raspberry ['ræzberi] *n.* the Bronx cheer; a rude noise made by vibrating the lips with air blown between them. □ *The entire audience gave the performer the raspberry.* □ *The performer gave them a raspberry right back.*

rasty ['ræsti] *mod.* having to do with a harsh-looking young woman. (Collegiate.) □ *Who is that rasty dame I saw you with?* □ *That dark lipstick makes you look a little rasty.*

rat **1.** *n.* a wretched-acting person. (Also a term of address.) □ *You dirty rat, you!* □ *Stop acting like a dirty rat!* **2.** See *rat (on someone)*.

rat around *in.* to waste time loafing around; to loiter. (Collegiate.) □ *I didn't do anything but rat around all summer.* □ *If kids don't have jobs, they just rat around.*

ratchet-mouth AND **motor-mouth** *n.* someone who talks incessantly. (Also a term of address.) □ *Tell that ratchet-mouth to shut up!* □ *Hey, motor-mouth, quiet!*

rat fink *n.* an informer. (Also a term of address. See *rat*.) □ *That guy is nothing but a rat fink. A dirty squealer!* □ *Fred told the teacher about the plot, and everybody called him a rat fink for the next two years.*

rathole **1.** *n.* a run-down place. □ *I refuse to live in this rathole any longer.* □ *Why don't you clean up this rathole?* **2.** *n.* a bottomless pit; an endless cause for the expenditure of money. (Typically with *throw...down* as in the examples.) □ *Why do they keep throwing money down that rathole?* □ *That rathole will absorb as much money as they can supply.* □ *The transportation system is beyond help. Giving it more subsidies is just throwing money down a rathole.*

rat (on someone) *in.* to inform (on someone). □ *Bill said he was going to rat on that punk.* □ *If you rat on me, I'll get you!* □ *Who ratted?*

rat out *in.* to quit; to quit (on someone or something). □ *It's too late to rat out.* □ *He tried to rat out at the last minute.*

rattled **1.** *mod.* confused; bewildered. □ *He tends to get a little rattled at minor things.* □ *Try not to get her rattled.* **2.** *mod.* tipsy; alcohol intoxicated. □ *After an hour of drinking, Bill was more than a little rattled.* □ *Being rattled from beer, I stopped drinking beer and began on the rum.*

rattling *mod.* excellent. (Collegiate. Compare to *rocking*.) □ *Her party was really rattling.* □ *What a rattling place to live!*

raw **1.** *mod.* harsh and cold, especially weather. □ *What a raw day!* □ *The weather was cold and raw.* **2.** *mod.* inexperienced; brand new. □ *The raw recruit did as well as could be expected.* □ *She'll get better. She's just a little raw.* **3.** *mod.* vulgar; crude. □ *I've had enough of your raw humor.* □ *That joke was a little raw.*

rays *n.* sunshine. (Collegiate. See also *catch some rays.*) □ *I'm going to go out and get some rays today.* □ *I've had too many rays. I'm cooked.*

razz [ræz] *tr.* to tease someone. □ *Please stop razzing me.* □ *I was just razzing you. I didn't mean any harm.*

real gone *mod.* really cool; mellow and pleasant. □ *Man, this music is real gone.* □ *That's a real gone drummer.* □ *You are something—real gone.*

ream someone out AND **ream out someone** *tr.* to scold someone severely. □ *The teacher really reamed him out.* □ *The coach reamed out the whole team.*

rear (end) *n.* the tail end; the buttocks. (Euphemistic.) □ *She fell right on her rear.* □ *The dog bit her in the rear end.*

rear-ender AND **back-ender** *n.* an automobile wreck where one car runs into the back of another. (Compare to *fender-bender.*) □ *It wasn't a bad accident, just a rear-ender.* □ *My neck was hurt in a back-ender.*

rear, pain in the See *pain in the ass.*

red hot **1.** *mod.* important; in great demand. □ *This is a red hot item. Everybody wants one.* □ *The stock market is a red hot issue right now.* **2.** *n.* a hot dog (sausage). □ *"Get your red hots right here!" shouted the vendor.* □ *In Chicago they eat red hots with catsup. Imagine!*

regs *n.* regulations. □ *Follow the regs or pay the penalty.* □ *There is a list of regs posted on the back of your door.*

rent(al)s *n.* one's parents. (Teens. See *(parental) units.* Also a term of address.) □ *I'll have to ask my rents.* □ *Hey, rentals, let's go out for dinner.*

rentals See the preceding entry.

rep [rɛp] **1.** *n.* a representative, usually a sales representative. □ *Please ask your rep to stop by my office.* □ *Our rep will be in your area tomorrow.* **2.** *n.* someone's reputation. □ *I hope this doesn't ruin my rep.* □ *I've got my own rep to think about.* **3.** *n.* repertory theater. □ *He spent a year in rep on the East Coast.* □ *Rep is the best place to get experience, but not to make connections.*

repo ['ripo] **1.** *n.* a repossessed car. □ *It's a repo, and I got it cheap.* □ *I'd rather have a plain used car than a repo.* **2.** *tr.* to repossess a car. □ *Some guy came around and tried to repo my car.* □ *She's good at repoing family cars.*

ret [rɛt] *n.* a tobacco cigarette. (Collegiate. A front clipping.) □ *You got a ret I can bum?* □ *Give my buddy a ret, will ya?*

retread ['ritrɛd] *n.* a burned-out person; a made-over person. □ *Chuck is just a retread. He's through.* □ *I need somebody fresh and alive, not some tired retread.*

ride shotgun *tr.* to accompany and guard someone or something. (A term from the days of stagecoaches and their armed guards.) □ *I have to take the beer over to the party. Why don't you come along and ride shotgun?* □ *Who's going to ride shotgun with Bill?*

ride the porcelain bus See *drive the big bus.*

rif [rɪf] **1.** *tr.* to dismiss an employee. (From the euphemism *reduction in force.*) □ *They're going to rif John tomorrow.* □ *Who'll they rif next?* **2.** *n.* a firing; a dismissal. □ *Who got the rif today?* □ *There's a rif in your future.*

riff [rɪf] **1.** *n.* a short, repeated line of music played by a particular performer. □ *Jim just sat there and forgot his riff.* □ *Listen to this riff, Tom.* **2.** *n.* a digression while speaking. (From the previous sense.) □ *Excuse the little riff, but I had to mention it.* □ *If she didn't make so many riffs while she spoke, we could understand her better.*

riffed [rɪft] **1.** *mod.* alcohol or drug intoxicated. □ *That guy is really riffed!* □ *I can't keep getting riffed every night like this.* **2.** AND **rift** *mod.* fired; released from employment. (From *R.I.F.*, "reduction in force.") □ *Poor Walter got riffed Friday.* □ *Most of the sales force was riffed last week.*

rift See under *riffed*.

righteous ['raɪtʃəs] *mod.* good; of good quality. (Originally black.) □ *She is a righteous mama.* □ *This stuff is really righteous!*

right guy *n.* a good guy; a straight guy. □ *Tom is a right guy. No trouble with him.* □ *I'm glad you're a right guy. I can trust you.*

rinky-dink ['rɪŋki'dɪŋk] *mod.* cheap; inferior; broken down. □ *I sold my rinky-dink old car yesterday.* □ *What a rinky-dink job! I quit!*

riot ['raɪət] *n.* someone or something entertaining or funny. □ *Tom was a riot last night.* □ *Her joke was a real riot.*

rip **1.** *n.* a drinking bout. □ *All four of them went out on a rip.* □ *Fred had another rip last night. He's rotten now.* **2.** *n.* the loot from a *rip-off*. □ *I want my share of the rip, now!* □ *Give him some of the rip and tell him to beat it.* **3.** *n.* a theft; a *rip-off*. □ *The crooks pulled a rip on Fourth Street last night.* □ *That was the third rip there this week.*

rip-off **1.** *n.* a theft; a deception; an exploitation. (See *rip*.) □ *This sandwich is a rip-off!* □ *What a rip-off! I want my money back.* **2.** *mod.* having to do with theft and deception. □ *I consider myself to be rip-off champion of North America.* □ *All I hear is rip-off stories. Isn't anybody honest?*

rip-off artist AND **off artist** *n.* a con artist. □ *Fred is such an off artist.* □ *Beware of the rip-off artist who runs that shop.*

rip on someone *in.* to give someone a hard time; to annoy someone. □ *Fred was ripping on me, and I heard about it.* □ *Stop ripping on my friend!*

rip someone or something off AND **rip off someone or something** **1.** *tr.* [with *someone*] to assault, kill, beat, rob, rape, or cheat someone. (Note the *for* in the example.) □ *They ripped me off, but they didn't hurt me.* □ *Man, they ripped me off for three hundred dollars.* **2.** *tr.* [with *something*] to steal something. □ *The crooks ripped off the hubcaps of my car.* □ *They ripped them all off.*

rivets ['rɪvəts] *n.* dollars; money. (From *copper* rivets.) □ *You got enough rivets on you for a snack?* □ *Who can come up with that many rivets?*

roach-coach *n.* a truck or van from which snacks and sandwiches are sold. □ *Let's go get a sandwich at the roach-coach.* □ *Here comes the roach-coach! Let go spend some coin!*

road apple *n.* a lump of horse excrement. (Compare to *alley apple*.) □ *Don't step on the road apples.* □ *There must be horses around here. I see road apples.*

road hog *n.* someone who takes too much space on a road or highway; someone who tries to run other people off the road. □ *Get over! Road hog!* □ *A road hog nearly ran me off the road.*

roadie AND **roady** ['rodi] **1.** AND **roadster** ['rodstɚ] *n.* a young person who helps rock groups set up for performances. □ *I want to be a roadie when I grow up.* □ *I was a roadster for a while, but I didn't like it.* **2.** AND **roadster** *in.* to help rock groups set up. □ *Let's go downtown and roadie tonight. The Red Drips are in town.* □ *I hate to roady. It's, like, work!* **3.** *mod.* eager to travel; eager to get on the road. □ *I get a little roady when the weather gets warm.* □ *We'd better get going. Your father looks a little roadie.*

roadster See under *roadie*.

roast **1.** *tr.* to put on an entertaining program where the guest of honor is teased and insulted. □ *They roasted Dave when he retired.* □ *If they roast me at the dinner, I'll cry.* **2.** *n.* an entertaining program where the guest of honor is insulted all in fun. □ *It was a wonderful roast. The guest of honor was pleased with the quality of the insults.* □ *It was a little too polite for a real roast.*

rock **1.** AND **rock candy** *n.* *crack*, a crystallized form of cocaine. (See also *rocks*.) □ *Some call it rock, and some call it crack.* □ *Rock is pretty expensive.* **2.** *n.* a crystallized form of heroin used for smoking. □ *Carl is hooked on rock—the kind that you smoke.* □ *Powder is everywhere, but you can hardly find any rock these days.* **3.** *n.* a diamond or other gemstone. □ *Look at the size of that rock in her ring.* □ *How many rocks are there decorating the edges of your watch?*

rock candy See under *rock*.

rocking *mod.* excellent. (Collegiate.) □ *Man, what a rocking party!* □ *This set is really rocking.* □ *We had a rocking time!*

rocks **1.** *n.* ice cubes. (See also *rock*.) □ *No rocks, please. I like my drink warm.* □ *Can I have a few rocks in my drink, please?* **2.** *n.* money; a dollar. □ *How many rocks do you want for that?* □ *Twenty rocks for that?*

rolf See *ralph*.

rotorhead *n.* a helicopter pilot or member of a helicopter crew. (Military. Also a term of address.) □ *Radio those rotorheads and tell them to get back to the base, now!* □ *Hey, rotorhead, where's your eggbeater?*

rotsee ['rɑtsi] *n.* "R.O.T.C.," the Reserve Officers Training Corps. □ *I joined rotsee to help pay my way through school.* □ *How long have you been in the rotsee program?*

rotten **1.** *mod.* smelly; disgusting. (Not slang.) □ *What is that rotten smell?* □ *Something rotten is under that board.* **2.** *mod.*

alcohol intoxicated. (From the previous sense. See also *putrid*.) □ *It takes a case of beer to get Wilbur rotten.* □ *When he gets rotten, he's sort of dangerous.* **3.** *mod.* poor or bad. (From the first sense.) □ *We have nothing but one rotten problem after another.* □ *This is the most rotten mess I've ever been in.*

rough time *n.* a hard time; a bad time. □ *I didn't mean to give you such a rough time. I'm sorry.* □ *What a rough time we had getting the car started!*

round tripper *n.* a home run in baseball. □ *Ted is responsible for four round trippers in Saturday's game.* □ *He hit a round tripper in the fourth inning.*

roundup *n.* a collection or summary of news items, such as a weather roundup, news roundup, etc. □ *Tune in at noon for a roundup of the day's news.* □ *Now for a weather roundup.*

rubber sock *n.* a timid person; a passive and compliant person. □ *What a rubber sock. She's afraid of her own shadow.* □ *Come on! Stand up for your rights. Don't be such a rubber sock!*

rubbish *n.* nonsense. (Also an exclamation.) □ *I'm tired of listening to your rubbish.* □ *Rubbish! That's the stupidest thing I've ever heard.*

rug *n.* a wig or toupee. (See also *divot*.) □ *Is that guy wearing a rug, or does his scalp really slide from side to side?* □ *I wear just a little rug to cover up a shiny spot.*

rug rat *n.* a child. (Also a term of address.) □ *You got any rug rats at your house?* □ *Hey, you cute little rug rat, come over here.*

rule *in.* to dominate; to be the best. (Slang only in certain contexts. Typical in graffiti. See examples.) □ *The Rockets rule!* □ *Pizza rules around here.*

run **1.** *n.* a session or period of time spent doing something; a period of time when something happens. □ *The market had a good run today.* □ *We all have enjoyed a good run of luck.* **2.** *tr.* to transport contraband, alcohol, or drugs. □ *Carl used to run booze during prohibition.* □ *The soldiers were caught running guns.* **3.** *n.* an act of transporting contraband. □ *Four soldiers were killed during a run.* □ *In their final run the cocaine smugglers made over four million dollars.*

run down some lines **1.** *in.* to converse (with someone). □ *I was running down some lines with Fred when the bell rang.* □ *Hey, man, let's run down some lines.* **2.** *in.* to try to seduce someone; to go through a talk leading to seduction. (See *run one's rhymes.*) □ *Go run down some lines with someone else.* □ *I was just standing there running down some lines with Mary when those guys broke in.*

run it down *tr.* to tell the whole story; to tell the truth. □ *Come on! What happened? Run it down for me!* □ *I don't care what happened. Run it down. I can take it.*

run off *in.* to have diarrhea. □ *Jimmy has been running off since midnight.* □ *At least he's not running off now.*

run off at the mouth *in.* to talk too much; to have "diarrhea of the mouth." □ *I wish you would stop running off at the mouth.* □ *Tom runs off at the mouth too much. I wish he would temper his remarks.*

run one's rhymes *tr.* to say what you have to say; to give one's speech or make one's plea. (Collegiate.) □ *Go run your rhymes with somebody else!* □ *I told him to run his rhymes elsewhere.*

run out of gas *in.* to lose momentum or interest. □ *His program is running out of gas.* □ *I hope I don't run out of gas before I finish what I set out to do.*

runs   *n.* diarrhea. (Always with *the*.) □ *That stuff we ate gave me the runs.* □ *I can't believe those cute little hamburgers could give anybody the runs.*

rush   **1.** *n.* a quick print of a day's shooting of a film. (Film making. Usually plural.) □ *After today's shooting, we'll watch yesterday's rushes.* □ *Take these rushes right over to Mr. Hitchcock's office.* **2.** *n.* a period of time when fraternities and sororities are permitted to pursue new members. (Collegiate.) □ *When does rush start this year?* □ *I've got to be at school in time for rush.* **3.** *tr.* [for a fraternity or sorority member] to try to persuade someone to join. □ *The frat tried to rush me, but I'm too busy.* □ *They can't rush anyone except during rush week.* **4.** *tr.* to court or date someone, usually a woman. (From the previous sense.) □ *Tom's trying to rush Betty, but she's not interested.* □ *He spent some time trying to rush her, but had to give up.*

ruth   [ruθ] **1.** *n.* a women's restroom. (Compare to *john*.) □ *Where's the ruth?* □ *Point me toward the ruth!* **2.** *in.* to empty one's stomach; to vomit. (See also *cry ruth*.) □ *I gotta go ruth!* □ *I just can't stand to ruth.*

S

sack 1. *n.* a bed. □ *I was so tired I could hardly find my sack.* □ *Somebody put a spider in my sack.* 2. *tr.* to dismiss someone from employment; to fire someone. □ *The boss sacked the whole office staff last week.* □ *If I do that again, they'll sack me.* 3. *n.* a dismissal. (Always with *the.*) □ *The boss gave them all the sack.* □ *The sack is what I am afraid of.* 4. *tr.* to tackle someone in football. □ *I tried to sack him, but he was too fast.* □ *Sack that guy or else!* 5. *n.* the completion of a tackle in football. □ *Andy made the sack on the 10-yard line.* □ *Who failed to make the sack?*

sack out *in.* to go to bed or go to sleep. □ *It's time for me to sack out.* □ *Let's sack out early tonight.*

savage *mod.* excellent. (Collegiate.) □ *This is really a savage piece of music.* □ *Man, Fred is a totally savage guy.* □ *Wow, is he savage!*

scag See *skag.*

scam [skæm] 1. *n.* a swindle; a *hustle.* (See also *What's the scam?*) □ *I lost a fortune in that railroad scam.* □ *What a scam! I'm calling the cops.* 2. *tr.* to swindle someone; to deceive someone. □ *They were scammed by a sweet-talking southern lady who took all their money.* □ *She scammed them for every cent they had.* 3. *in.* to seek out and pick up young women, said of males. (Collegiate.) □ *Bob was out scamming last night and ran into Clare.* □ *Those guys are always scamming around.* 4. *in.* to copulate. (Caution with topic.) □ *All you ever want to do is* *scam.* □ *I think those people over there are scamming.* **5.** *in.* to fool around and waste time. □ *Quite scamming and get busy.* □ *You'd get better grades if you didn't scam so much.*

scammer ['skæmɚ] **1.** *n.* a swindler; a *hustler.* □ *Carl is a scammer if I ever saw one.* □ *There are a couple of scammers on the street corner. Watch out.* **2.** *n.* a lecher; a fast worker with the opposite sex. □ *Bob thinks he's a great scammer, but he's just a wimp.* □ *Do scammers have a great future? What's for an encore?*

scank See *skank.*

scarf 1. *tr.* to eat something. □ *Andy scarfed the whole pie.* □ *Are you going to scarf the whole thing?* **2.** *in.* to eat. □ *I'll be with you as soon as I scarf.* □ *I gotta go scarf now.* **3.** *n.* food. □ *I want some good scarf. This stuff stinks.* □ *No more of that fried scarf for me.*

scarf out *in.* to overeat. (See also *blimp out, pig out, pork out, mac out.*) □ *I scarf out every weekend.* □ *My brother scarfs out every day—around the clock!*

scarf something down AND **scarf down something** *tr.* to eat something, perhaps in a hurry; to swallow something, perhaps in a hurry. □ *Are you going to scarf this whole thing down?* □ *Here, scarf down this sandwich.*

schiz(z) out [skɪz...] *in.* to freak out; to lose mental control. □ *What a day! I nearly schizzed out.* □ *I schizzed out during the test. Got an F.*

s(c)hlep [ʃlɛp] **1.** *tr.* to drag or carry someone or something. (From German *schleppen* via Yiddish.) □ *Am I supposed to schlep this whole thing all the way back to the store?* □ *I am tired of shlepping kids from one thing to another.* **2.** *n.* a journey; a distance to travel or carry something. □ *It takes about 20 minutes to make the schlep from here to there.* □ *That's a 10-mile schlep, and I won't go by myself.* **3.** *n.* a stupid person; a bothersome person. (Literally, a *drag*.) □ *What a schlep! The guy's a real pain.* □ *Ask that shlep to wait in the hall until I am free. I'll sneak out the back way.*

s(c)hlepper [ˈʃlɛpɚ] *n.* an annoying person who always wants a bargain or a favor. (See *schlep*.) □ *Why am I surrounded by people who want something from me? Is this a schlepper colony or what?* □ *Tell the shleppers that they'll get their money after I close the sale on my wife and kids.*

s(c)hmooze AND **schmoose** [ʃmuz] **1.** *in.* to chat or gossip. (From Hebrew *schmuos* via Yiddish.) □ *You were schmoozing when you should have been listening.* □ *We were schmoozing before quitting time, and then the boss walked by.* **2.** *n.* a session of chatting or conversing. □ *Come over, and let's have a schmooze before you go.* □ *A good schmoose is what you need.*

schmoozer *n.* someone who chats or converses well. □ *Clare can't sing a note, but what a schmoozer!* □ *Two old schmoozers sat muttering to one another all afternoon by the duck pond.*

schmuck [ʃmək] **1.** *n.* a jerk; a repellent male. (Also a rude term of address. Yiddish.) □ *Who is that stupid schmuck over there?* □ *Ask that schmuck how long he will be on the phone.* **2.** *n.* a penis. (Yiddish. Caution with topic.) □ *If I hear that joke about a camel's schmuck one more time, I'm going to scream.* □ *There are probably better names than schmuck for what you are talking about.*

scoff [skɔf] **1.** *tr. & in.* to eat (something). (Compare to *scarf*.) □ *He's upstairs scoffing in his room.* □ *She scoffed three hamburgers and a large order of fries.* **2.** *n.* food. □ *This scoff is gross!* □ *I want some good old American scoff.*

scope someone AND **scope on someone** *tr.* to visually evaluate a member of the opposite sex. □ *He scoped every girl who came in the door.* □ *He wouldn't like it if somebody scoped on him. Or would he?*

scope someone out AND **scope out someone** *tr.* to look someone over; to check someone out. □ *Dave was scoping out all the girls.* □ *Nobody was scoping Dave out, though.*

score **1.** *in.* to succeed. □ *I knew if I kept trying I could score.* □ *It takes hard work and luck to score.* **2.** *tr. & in.* to obtain something; to obtain drugs or sex. (Very close to sense 1.) □ *Carl spent an hour trying to score some pot.* □ *Fred is always trying to score with women.* **3.** *n.* the result of a scoring: drugs, loot, winnings. □ *Where's the score? How much did you get?* □ *The crooks dropped the score as they made their getaway.*

scraggy ['skrægi] *mod.* bony. □ *That dame is too scraggy for me.* □ *Who is that scraggy dame?* □ *I lost weight till I was scraggy as a hungry bear.*

scratch **1.** *n.* money. □ *I just don't have the scratch.* □ *How much scratch does it take to buy a car like this one?* **2.** *tr.* to eliminate something from a list; to cancel something. □ *Scratch Fred. He can't make the party.* □ *We decided to scratch the idea of a new car. The old one will have to do.* **3.** *mod.* impromptu; temporary. □ *We started a scratch game of basketball, but most of the girls had to leave at dinnertime.* □ *This is just a scratch tape. After you use it for your computer program, someone else will write something over it.*

screw around *in.* to waste time. □ *Stop screwing around and get busy.* □ *John's always screwing around and never does anything on time.*

screw someone over AND **screw over someone** *tr.* to give someone a very bad time; to scold someone severely. □ *Those guys really screwed you over. What started it?* □ *Let's get those kids in here and screw over every one of them. This stuff can't continue.*

screw up **1.** *in.* to mess up. □ *I hope I don't screw up this time.* □ *The waiter screwed up again.* **2.** *n.* a mess; a blunder; utter confusion. (Usually **screw-up**.) □ *This is the chef's screw-up, not mine.* □ *One more screw up like that and you're fired.*

scrog [skrɔg] *tr. & in.* to have sex; to copulate (with someone). (Caution with topic.) □ *You know what! I think those people over in the corner are scrogging!* □ *The movie showed scene after scene of this woman scrogging some guy.*

scrub *tr.* to cancel something. □ *We had to scrub the whole plan because of the weather.* □ *The manager scrubbed the party because people wouldn't cooperate.*

scruff(y) ['skrəf(i)] *mod.* sloppy; unkempt. □ *Her boyfriend is a little scruffy, but he's got money!* □ *Why don't you clean up this scruff car? It's—like—grody!*

scrump [skrəmp] *tr. & in.* to copulate (with someone). (Caution with topic.) □ *You know what! I think those people over by the garage are scrumping!* □ *The movie showed a scene of some woman scrumping her lover.*

scrunge [skrənd3] *n.* nastiness; gunk. □ *What is this scrunge on my shoe?* □ *When you find some scrunge on your shoe or something, never try to find out what it is. Just wipe it off.*

scrungy ['skrənd3i] **1.** *mod.* filthy. □ *This place is too scrungy for me. I'm outa here.* □ *What a scrungy guy. Put him somewhere to soak for a day or two.* **2.** *mod.* inferior; bad. □ *I don't need scrungy merchandise like this. I'm going elsewhere.* □ *You have a very scrungy outlook on life.* □ *Life is scrungy.*

scum [skəm] *n.* a wretched person. (Also a rude and provocative term of address. See also *pond scum*.) □ *Who is that scum? Who does she think she is?* □ *Look, you scum, I'm gonna fix you once and for all!*

scumbag *n.* a mean and wretched person, usually a male. (Also a rude term of address. The term is also a nickname for a condom.) □ *That scumbag is going to get caught some day.* □ *All those* *guys are scumbags. I don't want to have anything to do with any of them.*

scurvy [ˈskɚvi] *mod.* repulsive; *gross.* (Collegiate.) □ *Who is that scurvy guy who just came in?* □ *That class is scurvy. You'll wish you hadn't taken it.*

scuz(z) [skəz] **1.** *n.* filth. □ *What is this scuzz all over the floor?* □ *There is some scuzz on your shoe.* **2.** *n.* a nasty person; an undesirable person; a scraggly person. □ *And this scuzz comes up to me and asks me to dance, and I'm like, "What?"* □ *I told the scuz, like, I was feeling sick, so I couldn't dance with anybody.*

scuzzbag *n.* a despicable person. (Also a rude term of address.) □ *Who is that scuzzbag who just came in?* □ *Look, scuzzbag, we don't want your kind around here.*

scuzzo *n.* a repellent person. □ *There's the scuzzo who thinks I like him.* □ *How do you get rid of a scuzzo like that?*

scuzz someone out AND **scuzz out someone** *tr.* to nauseate someone. □ *He had this unreal face that almost scuzzed me out!* □ *It's not nice to scuzz out people like that, especially when you hardly know them.*

scuzzy [ˈskəzi] *mod.* repellent; unkempt. □ *His clothes are always so scuzzy. He probably keeps them in a pile in his room.* □ *Whose scuzzy car is that in the driveway?*

seeyabye [ˈsijəˈbaɪ] *interj.* "bye." (California.) □ *Oh, that's, like, so, like, rad. Okay, seeyabye.* □ *Gotta go now. Seeyabye.*

sell a wolf ticket AND **sell wolf tickets** *tr.* to boast, bluff, or lie. (Originally black.) □ *Freddie is out selling wolf tickets again.* □ *Are you trying to sell me a wolf ticket?*

serious *mod.* good; profound; excellent. (See *heavy.*) □ *He plays some serious guitar.* □ *Man, these tunes are, like, serious.*

set **1.** *n.* a period of time that a band plays without a break; a 30-minute jam session. □ *I'll talk to you after this set.* □ *We do two sets and then take a 20-minute break.* **2.** *n.* a party. □ *Your set was a totally major bash!* □ *Let's throw a set tonight and invite some chicks.*

sexy **1.** *mod.* having great sex appeal. □ *What a sexy chick!* □ *He's not what I would call sexy, but I suppose it's a matter of taste.* **2.** *mod.* neat; exciting. □ *That's a sexy set of wheels.* □ *You play really sexy music.* □ *Your idea is real sexy.*

shades *n.* dark glasses. (See *sunshades*.) □ *Where are my shades? The sun is too bright.* □ *The guy stood there—wearing shades and carrying a violin case. Marlowe grimaced.*

shag (off) *in.* to depart. □ *I gotta shag. It's late.* □ *Go on! Shag off!* □ *I gotta shag. Somebody's calling my name.*

shank **1.** *n.* a knife. □ *The mugger pulled a shank on the victim.* □ *The cops found the shank in the bushes.* **2.** *in.* to dance. □ *They were busy shankin' and didn't hear the gunshots.* □ *We were all shanking to a great band.*

shank it *tr.* to use one's legs to get somewhere; to walk. □ *My car needs fixing so I had to shank it to work today.* □ *I like to shank it every now and then.*

sharp **1.** *mod.* clever; intelligent. □ *She's a real sharp chick! Got lots of savvy.* □ *She's sharp enough to see right through everything you say.* **2.** *mod.* good-looking; well-dressed. □ *You really look sharp today.* □ *That's a sharp set of wheels you got there.*

sheen [ʃin] *n.* a car. (From *machine*.) □ *You have one fine sheen there.* □ *I have to get my sheen's oil changed today.*

sheet, (rap) See *(rap) sheet. See also poop sheet.*

shekels [ˈʃɛkl̩z] *n.* dollars; money. □ *You got a few shekels you can spare?* □ *These things cost plenty of shekels.*

shellac [ʃəˈlæk] *tr.* to beat someone; to outscore someone. □ *We're gonna shellack those bums Friday night.* □ *We'll be shellacking every team in the league this year.*

shellacked **1.** *mod.* beaten; outscored. □ *They were shellacked, and they knew it.* □ *The team got shellacked in last week's game.* **2.** *mod.* alcohol intoxicated; overcome by booze. □ *Ernie was so shellacked he couldn't see.* □ *How did he get so shellacked? I didn't see him drink anything.*

shellacking *n.* a beating. □ *We gave them a shellacking they'll never forget.* □ *Our team took a real shellacking.*

shit (Caution with *shit* in all senses.) **1.** *n.* dung. □ *Don't step in that shit there.* □ *There's dog shit in my yard!* **2.** *n.* something poor in quality; junk. □ *This stuff is shit. Show me something better.* □ *What do you keep all this shit around here for?* **3.** *n.* nonsense; *bullshit.* □ *Don't give me that shit! I know you're lying.* □ *I'm tired of your shit!* **4.** *n.* drugs in general; heroin; marijuana. □ *Lay off the shit, Harry! You're gonna end up hooked.* □ *So Marty scores a bag of shit—I mean skag—you know, H.—and we get out the stuff to shoot.* **5.** *tr.* to deceive someone; to lie to someone. □ *Stop shittin' me, you bastard!* □ *You wouldn't shit me, would you?* **6.** *n.* a despicable person. (Crude. Also a rude and provocative term of address.) □ *Tell that stupid shit to get out of here, or I'll bust him one.* □ *What a shit you are!*

shitsky [ˈʃɪtski] **1.** *n.* dung. (Caution with *shit.*) □ *There's some shitsky on your shoe.* □ *Some rude dog has left a little pile of grade-A shitsky on the sidewalk.* **2.** *n.* a despicable person. (Provocative. Caution with *shit.*) □ *The stupid shitsky is back on skag again.* □ *With a shitsky like that on your side, who needs enemies?*

shlep See *s(c)hlep.*

shlepper See *s(c)hlepper.*

shmen [ʃmɛn] *n.* freshmen. □ *A couple of shmen wandered by—looking sort of lost.* □ *The shmen are having a party all to themselves this Friday.*

shoot one's breakfast See the following entry.

shoot one's cookies AND **shoot one's breakfast, shoot one's supper** *tr.* to empty one's stomach; to vomit. □ *I think I'm gonna shoot my cookies.* □ *I shot my supper, and I was glad to get rid of it.*

shoot one's supper See the previous entry.

shoot the bull AND **shoot the crap, shoot the shit** *tr.* to chat and gossip. (Caution with *crap, shit*.) □ *Let's get together sometime and shoot the bull.* □ *You spend too much time shooting the crap.*

shoot the crap See the previous entry.

shoot the dozens See *play the dozens*.

shoot the shit See *shoot the bull*.

shorts AND **case of the shorts** *n.* the lack of money. (Always with *the*.) □ *Here I am with a case of the shorts again.* □ *The shorts always come around at the end of the month.*

shot **1.** *n.* a try at something. □ *Go ahead. Give it another shot.* □ *Have a shot at this problem.* **2.** *mod.* exhausted; ruined. □ *I really feel shot today.* □ *Here's your pen back. It's shot anyway.* □ *This thing is shot. Let's get a new one.* **3.** *n.* a rocket launching. □ *The shot was canceled because of the weather.* □ *This shot, like the last, was a total failure.*

shot down **1.** *mod.* demolished; destroyed. □ *Her idea was shot down after all her work.* □ *I felt shot down, even though I was sure of what I was getting into.* **2.** *mod.* rejected by a young woman. □ *Tiffany is a cruel chick. I was shot down from day one.* □ *Fred's shot down, thanks to his best girl. He'll get over it.*

shove off   See *push off*.

shredded   *mod.* alcohol intoxicated. (Collegiate.) □ *We are all too shredded to drive home. What shall we do?* □ *I believe that each of us is shredded enough to fly home. Let's vote on that.*

shuck   [ʃək] **1.** *n.* an insincere person. □ *The guy's a shuck. Don't believe a thing he says!* □ *Who needs a shuck for a legislator?* **2.** *tr. & in.* to kid someone; to tease someone. □ *Cool it! I'm just shucking.* □ *Stop shucking me!* **3.** *tr.* to swindle someone; to deceive someone. □ *The con man shucked a number of people in the town before moving on.* □ *He was going to shuck the mayor, but people were beginning to talk, so he blew town.* **4.** *n.* a hoax. □ *What a stupid shuck!* □ *How could you fall for that old shuck?*

shutters   *n.* the eyelids. □ *Her shutters dropped slowly, and she was asleep.* □ *She blinked those yummy shutters over those bedroom eyes, and my knees turned to mush.*

shwench   [ʃʍɛntʃ] *n.* a female freshman. (Collegiate.) □ *A couple of giggling shwenches showed up to cheer on the team.* □ *There's a shwench in my English class who knows more than the prof.*

sicks   *n.* nausea; vomiting. □ *Oh, man, I got the sicks.* □ *He's at home with the sicks.*

sick (up)   *in.* to empty one's stomach; to vomit. □ *I think I'm going to sick up. Isn't there supposed to be a barf bag in one of these seat pockets?* □ *He's got to sick, and there's no air sickness bag. Help!*

sicky   *n.* someone who seems mentally deranged. □ *The dame's a sicky. Watch out for yourself.* □ *Some sicky drew these obscene pictures on the wall.*

side *n.* a side of a record. □ *Let's cruise over to Sam's pad and hear some sides.* □ *Now here's a side you may remember.*

signify **1.** *in.* to cause trouble for fun; to stir things up. (Black.) □ *Why's that dude signifying over there?* □ *What are all these cats signifying about anyway?* **2.** *in.* to try to look more important than one really is; to brag. (Black.) □ *See that dude signify like somebody important?* □ *First you gotta learn to signify.*

silk *n.* a Caucasian. (Black.) □ *Some silk was over here, looking around sort of suspicious.* □ *He told his mama that if she doesn't treat him better, he's gonna bring some silk home for dinner and let her see what the neighbors think.*

silks *n.* clothing. □ *Look at the silks on that dude!* □ *I gotta get some new silks before spring.*

silky *mod.* smooth; unctuous. □ *Beware of anybody that silky.* □ *What a silky character. He could talk his way into the heart of some unsuspecting chick.*

silver bullet AND **magic bullet** *n.* a specific, failsafe solution to a problem. (From the notion that a silver bullet is required to kill a werewolf.) □ *I'm not suggesting that the committee has provided us with a silver bullet, only that their advice was timely and useful.* □ *Okay, I've got the magic bullet you need for your problem. Your favorable vote on the pork storage units for my district would be greatly appreciated, of course.*

sin-bin *n.* a van fitted with bedding as a place for necking and lovemaking. □ *Wally said he was saving his money to buy a sin-bin so he could have more fun on dates.* □ *Some rusty old sin-bin was parked in front of the house when I got there.*

sink *tr.* to swallow some food or drink. □ *Here, sink a bite of this stuff.* □ *Larry stopped at a tavern to sink a short one.*

skag AND **scag** [skæg] **1.** *n.* a rotten thing or person. □ *Don't be such a skag. Who do you think you are?* □ *Gary has become* *more of a scag than I can stand.* **2.** *n.* a very ugly woman. (Collegiate.) □ *What a skag! I wouldn't be seen with her.* □ *She looks like a scag without makeup.*

skank AND **scank** [skæŋk] **1.** *n.* an ugly (young) woman. (Collegiate.) □ *What a skank she is! Give her a comb or something.* □ *Look at her! Is she a skank or what?* **2.** *in.* to appear ugly. □ *My face is skanking like mad. Must be the zits.* □ *Both sisters skank. Must be hereditary.*

skanky ['skæŋki] *mod.* ugly; repellent, usually said of a woman. (Collegiate.) □ *She is so skanky! That grody hairdo doesn't help either.* □ *What's wrong with being a little skanky? It's what you can do with your brain that counts.* □ *She's skanky, nonetheless.*

skat [skæt] *n.* beer. □ *How about some skat, chum?* □ *You got any pretzels to go with the skat?*

skeet *n.* a blob of nasal mucus. (Collegiate.) □ *God, Fred, there's a gross skeet hanging outa your nose!* □ *That wasn't stew; that was skeets!*

skeevy ['skivi] *mod.* sleazy and disgusting. □ *This is a skeevy joint. Let's get out.* □ *Your coat looks so skeevy. Is it old?*

skid-lid *n.* a motorcycle helmet. □ *The law has no business telling me I gotta wear a skid-lid.* □ *Don't you use a skid-lid?*

skin 1. *n.* a dollar bill. □ *This ticket cost me a couple of skins—and it's not worth it.* □ *You got a skin for the toll booth?* **2.** AND **skinhead** *n.* someone with a shaved or bald head. □ *Who's the skin with the earrings?* □ *That skinhead looks stoned.* **3.** *tr.* to cheat or overcharge someone. □ *The guy who sold me this car really skinned me.* □ *We skinned him on that stock deal.*

skin a goat *tr.* to empty one's stomach; to vomit. □ *Ralph went out to skin a goat.* □ *Was my cooking so bad that everybody had to skin a goat?*

skinhead See under *skin*.

Skin me! *exclam.* "*Give me some skin!*"; "Shake my hand!" (Originally black.) ☐ *Hey, man, skin me!* ☐ *Hey, old buddy. Don't walk on! Skin me!*

skins *n.* drums. (Musicians. The same as *hides*.) ☐ *Andy can really make the skins talk.* ☐ *Buddy could beat those skins like nobody's business.*

skrag [skræg] *tr.* to murder someone. (Underworld.) ☐ *These thugs tried to skrag me, I swear.* ☐ *Marlowe wanted to skrag him right then and there.*

skulled *mod.* alcohol or drug intoxicated. ☐ *He's too skulled to drive.* ☐ *He had got himself skulled in less than 20 minutes.*

skurf [skɚf] *in.* to skateboard. (From the words *skate* and *surf*.) ☐ *He skurfed from city hall to the post office.* ☐ *My mom won't let me skurf anymore.*

sky *in.* to travel (to somewhere) in an airplane. ☐ *I decided to sky down to Orlando for the weekend.* ☐ *Let's sky to New York and then go on to London.*

slam **1.** *tr.* to criticize someone or something. ☐ *Please don't slam my car. It's the best I can do.* ☐ *The secretary was slamming the boss in one room, and the boss was slamming the secretary in another.* **2.** *n.* a criticism. ☐ *Harry took another slam at the sales record the sales force had produced for the meeting.* ☐ *I don't want to hear another nasty and hateful slam at my sister. Is that clear?*

slam-dancing *n.* a style of punk dancing where the dancers jump about, bumping into each other, trying to knock each other down. ☐ *Haven't you about had enough of that juvenile slam-dancing?* ☐ *I hurt my shoulder doing some slam-dancing.*

slam dunk   1. *tr.* & *in.* to force a basketball into the basket from above. (See also *jam*.) □ *Wilbur slam dunked another one, raising the score from 108 to 110.* □ *Wilbur slam dunked his way to fame and riches.* **2.** *n.* an act of making a basket as in sense 1. □ *Another slam dunk and Wilbur ties the score again!* □ *The goal will probably not withstand another slam dunk.*

slammer   1. *n.* a jail. □ *I got out of the slammer on Monday and was back in by Wednesday.* □ *The slammer in this town is like a hotel.* **2.** *n.* a slam dunk. □ *He really has that slammer perfected!* □ *It's another slammer for Wilbur!*

slam some beers   *tr.* to drink beer; to drink a number of beers. □ *Fred and Larry went out to slam some beers.* □ *Let's slam some beers sometime.*

sleaze AND **sleez**   [sliz] **1.** *n.* a low and despicable person. □ *God, what a sleaze! How can anybody be so skanky?* □ *You'd expect to find a sleaze like that in a sleazoid joint like this.* **2.** *n.* something worthless; junk. □ *I won't sell sleez like that! I won't even have it in my store.* □ *Look at this sleaze—and look at the price! Outrageous!* **3.** *in.* to act low; to be sexually promiscuous. □ *She looks like the type who will sleaze and lie to get her own way.* □ *She earned quite a reputation sleazing around with just anybody.*

sleazebag   *n.* a repellent person or place. □ *I won't go into a sleazebag like that.* □ *Who is the sleazebag leaning against the wall?*

sleazeball   *n.* a repellent person. □ *He's okay if you're into sleazeballs.* □ *Who is that sleazeball with the earring?*

sleaze-bucket   *n.* a repellent person, thing, or place. □ *Gad, what a sleaze-bucket! Let me out of here!* □ *Gee, Sue, your date's a real sleaze-bucket!*

sleazo(id)   1. ['slizo AND 'slizoid] *mod.* low; disreputable; sleazy. □ *Let's get out of this sleazo joint.* □ *This place is really sleazo.*

□ *Who wants a sleazoid car with no back seat?* **2.** *n.* a sleazy person. □ *Who is this sleazoid?* □ *Who was that sleazo I saw you with last night?*

sleepwalk *n.* a movement toward something without effort. (A movement that could be done "in one's sleep." See *cakewalk, walk*.) □ *Getting the degree was a sleepwalk. Getting a job was hell.* □ *It was no sleepwalk, but it didn't make me slave away either.*

slime **1.** *n.* a worthless person; a low and wretched person. □ *What a slime that guy is!* □ *Who is the slime over there with the greasy hair?* **2.** *n.* degrading matters; corrupt people or situations. □ *I don't want to be involved in slime like that.* □ *The press uncovered even more slime at city hall.*

slime bag AND **slime bucket, slimebag, slimeball** *n.* a despicable person, usually a male. (See *slime*.) □ *Gee, a slime bag like that in the same room with me! Yuck!* □ *Who's the slime bucket in the 1962 Bonneville?*

slimeball See the previous entry.

slime bucket See *slime bag*.

Slip me five! See *Give me (some) skin!*

slip someone five *tr.* to shake someone's hand. □ *Billy slipped me five, and we sat down to discuss old times.* □ *Come on, man, slip me five!*

slop(s) *n.* bad beer; inferior liquor. □ *Why do we have to drink slops like this? Can't Tom afford to give his guests something decent?* □ *Tom's slop is better than water—dishwater anyway.*

slosh **1.** *n.* beer; liquor. □ *How about a glass of slosh?* □ *No slosh for me. Just plain water.* **2.** *tr. & in.* to drink liquor, including beer; to drink to excess. □ *Are you going to slosh gin all night?* □ *I slosh just because I like the taste.*

sludgeball ['slədʒbɑl] *n.* a despicable and repellent person. □ *Mike is such a sludgeball! Why do you keep seeing him?* □ *He's no sludgeball; he's eccentric.*

smacker 1. *n.* the face. □ *What a gorgeous smacker on that chick.* □ *She ought to give that ugly smacker back to the horse before it runs into something.* **2.** *n.* a dollar. (Underworld.) □ *You got a couple of smackers for the tollbooth?* □ *Don't waste your hard-earned smackers on junk like like that.* **3.** *n.* a kiss. □ *He planted a smacker square on her lips. She kicked him in the shins for his trouble.* □ *Marlowe was greeted at the door by a lovely, cuddly chick in a nightie—eyes closed and lips parted for a better-than-average smacker. He really wished—just for a moment—that he hadn't rung the wrong doorbell.*

smarmy ['smɑrmi] *mod.* insincere and obsequious. □ *He's obnoxious, but brazen rather than smarmy.* □ *He's a smarmy creep.* □ *The guy is so smarmy, I can't stand him.*

smarts *n.* intelligence. □ *She's got plenty of smarts, but no spunk.* □ *I got the smarts to do the job. All I need is someone to trust me.*

smash *n.* wine. (Black. Because it is made from smashed grapes.) □ *I got a bottle of smash in my car.* □ *This is great smash for a buck twenty-five.*

smashed *mod.* alcohol or drug intoxicated. □ *He was so smashed he couldn't stand up.* □ *Molly can drink a lot without ever getting smashed.*

smash hit *n.* a play, movie, musical, etc., that is a big success. □ *Her first book was a smash hit. The second was a disaster.* □ *A smash hit doesn't always make people rich.*

smear *tr.* to defeat someone; to outscore someone. □ *We smeared them 50-20.* □ *They said they would smear us, but we smeared them.*

smeller *n.* [someone's] nose. □ *I think my smeller's gone bad because of my cold.* □ *He's got a fine strawberry on the end of his smeller.*

smile AND **smiler, smiley** *n.* a drink of liquor; liquor. □ *Come over and join me for a smiley.* □ *Here, have a smiler on me.*

smoke **1.** *n.* a tobacco cigarette; a pipe; a cigar. □ *I think I'll have a smoke now.* □ *You got a smoke I can owe you?* **2.** *n.* the act of smoking anything smokable, including drugs. □ *I need a smoke—of anything.* □ *I'm going to stop here for a smoke.* **3.** *n.* exaggeration; deception. (See *blow smoke*.) □ *That's not a report. That's just smoke.* □ *If the smoke is too obvious, they'll just get suspicious.*

smoke eater *n.* a fire fighter. □ *A couple of off-duty smoke eaters wandered around the store doing a little shopping.* □ *The smoke eaters took a long time getting there.*

smokin' ['smokən] *mod.* really *hot*; overpowering. □ *Those threads on that dude are really smokin'.* □ *If you wanna hear some smokin' vinyl, just stay tuned.*

smoking gun *n.* the indisputable sign of guilt. □ *Mr. South was left holding the smoking gun.* □ *The chief of staff decided that the admiral should be found with the smoking gun.*

smurf [smɚf] **1.** *n.* someone who "cleans" ill-gotten money by buying cashier's checks at banks and shifting funds from place to place. (Underworld. From the name of a type of cartoon character.) □ *I think the guy at the first window is a smurf. He's in here twice a week with $9,500 in cash each time.* □ *Did you get a good look at this alleged smurf?* **2.** *tr. & in.* to shift illicit money from place to place to conceal its origin. (Underworld.) □ *I smurf for a living. It doesn't pay much, but you meet some very interesting people.* □ *I smurfed a fortune for a famous drug kingpin and got 14 years up the river—with some very interesting people.*

smurfbrain ['sməˈfbren] *n.* a simple-minded person. (A smurf is an innocent little cartoon character.) □ *You can be such a smurfbrain!* □ *You're not a smurfbrain, I suppose?*

smurfed [smərft] *mod.* having to do with a bank that has been used to launder money. (See smurf.) □ *The teller came slowly into the office. "I think we were smurfed," she said.* □ *See that this cash is smurfed by Friday.*

snap **1.** *n.* a snapshot. □ *I got some good snaps of the fish you caught.* □ *Here's a snap of my brother.* **2.** *in.* to go crazy. □ *Suddenly Walter snapped and began beating her savagely.* □ *His mind snapped, and he's never been right since.* **3.** *n.* an easy thing to do. (Always with *a*.) □ *Nothing to it. It's a snap.* □ *The whole thing was a snap.*

snap one's cookies *tr.* to vomit; to regurgitate. □ *I think I'm gonna snap my cookies.* □ *Some jerk snapped his cookies on the sidewalk.*

snit, in a See *in a snit.*

snitzy ['snɪtsi] *mod.* classy; ritzy. □ *This is a pretty snitzy place—tablecloths and everything.* □ *Tiffany is too snitzy for me.*

snookered ['snʊkərd] *mod.* cheated; deceived. □ *He became snookered skillfully and quickly. It was almost a pleasure.* □ *I got snookered at the service station.*

snoozamorooed ['snuzəməˈrud] *mod.* alcohol intoxicated. □ *Man, was she smoozamorooed!* □ *He went and got himself snoozamorooed before the wedding.*

snow **1.** *n.* deceitful talk; deception. □ *No snow, okay? I want straight talk.* □ *All I heard for an hour was snow. Now, what's the truth?* **2.** *tr.* to attempt to deceive someone. □ *Don't try to snow me!* □ *You can try to snow me if you want, but I'm onto your tricks.* **3.** *n.* a powdered or crystalline narcotic: morphine, heroin, or cocaine. (Now almost always the latter.) □ *Now, snow* *is almost old-fashioned.* □ *The price of snow has come down a lot as South America exports more of it.*

snow job *n.* a systematic deception. □ *You can generally tell when a student is trying to do a snow job.* □ *This snow job you call an explanation just won't do.*

snuff it *tr.* to die. □ *The cat leapt straight up in the air and snuffed it.* □ *I was so sick they thought I was going to snuff it.*

S.O.B. *n.* a "son of a bitch"; a despised person, usually a male. (Crude. Also a rude and provocative term of address. Never an acronym.) □ *Tell that S.O.B. to mind his own business.* □ *Look here, you S.O.B., get out!*

sofa spud ['sofə 'spəd] *n.* someone who spends a great deal of time sitting and watching television. (A play on *couch potato*.) □ *Sofa spuds have been getting a lot of attention in the newspapers.* □ *These sofa spuds usually watch sports on television.*

software rot *n.* an imaginary disease that causes computer programs to go bad over a long period of time. (Computers.) □ *I guess software rot finally got to my program!* □ *What you have here is not a bug, but just plain old software rot.*

So gross! *exclam.* "How disgusting!" (California. See *gross*.) □ *He put chocolate syrup on his pie! So gross!* □ *He's barfing! So gross!*

soldier 1. *n.* a liquor bottle; an empty liquor bottle. (Compare to *dead soldier*.) □ *Toss your soldier into the garbage, please.* □ *There was a broken soldier on the floor and a cap on the table.* 2. *n.* a whole tobacco cigarette. □ *The old man almost fell over trying to pick up the soldier from the sidewalk.* □ *"Look, Jed. A soldier. My lucky day!" said the old soak to his buddy.*

solid 1. *mod.* good; great; *cool*. □ *Man, this music is solid!* □ *Listen to that solid beat.* 2. *mod.* consecutive; consecutively. □

Larry ate for four solid days. □ *Then he "had the flu" for three days solid.*

soul kiss **1.** *n.* a kiss where the kissers' tongues interact; a *French kiss.* □ *He tried to give me a soul kiss, but I pulled away.* □ *Yes, a soul kiss sounds silly—till you try it with somebody you really like.* **2.** *in.* [for two people] to kiss with interacting tongues. □ *They were soul kissing and making noises.* □ *The creep had bad breath and wanted to soul kiss!*

sounds *n.* music; records. □ *I got some new sounds. Ya wanna come over and listen?* □ *Man, these sounds are massive!*

sozzle ['sɑzl̩] *in.* to drink to excess. □ *The guys are sozzling over at John's place.* □ *I wish you'd stop coming home every night and sozzling to oblivion.*

space See under *space out.*

spaced (out) AND **spacy** *mod.* silly; giddy. □ *I have such spaced-out parents!* □ *He's so spaced!* □ *I love my spacy old dad.*

space out **1.** *n.* a giddy person. (Usually **space-out.**) □ *Terry is becoming such a space-out!* □ *What a space out you are!* **2.** AND **space** *in.* to become giddy; to become disoriented. □ *She is spacing again. She doesn't even know where she is.* □ *I spaced out after the long climb.*

space someone out AND **space out someone** *tr.* to cause someone to become giddy. □ *The whole business just spaced me out.* □ *The spectacle spaced out the entire audience.*

spacy See *spaced (out).*

spastic *mod.* overly responsive; out of control. □ *She can get so spastic when I come in late.* □ *Tell the spastic jerk to shut up.* □ *My dad's spastic when it comes to drugs.*

spaz [spæz] **1.** *n.* a fit or an attack; a strong reaction to a bad or funny situation. □ *My father had a spaz when he heard.* □ *Take it easy! Don't have a spaz.* **2.** *n.* a total jerk; someone who overreacts to something. (Not used for a congenitally spastic condition.) □ *Some spaz is in the other room screaming about a stolen car.* □ *Relax! You don't need to be a spaz.*

spaz around *in.* to waste time; to mess around. □ *You kids are always spazzing around. Why don't you get a job?* □ *We're just spazzing around. Leave us alone.*

spaz out 1. *in.* to overreact to something; to become overly excited about something. □ *I knew you would spaz out! It's not that bad!* □ *Come on, don't spaz out!* **2.** *n.* an emotional display. (Usually **spaz-out**.) □ *There's no need for a spaz-out!* □ *She threw a hell of a spaz-out.*

specs [spɛks] *n.* eyeglasses; spectacles. □ *I broke my specs.* □ *I need specs to find where I left my specs.*

speeder *n.* a speeding ticket. □ *The cop that gave Mary a speeder Wednesday gave her another one Friday.* □ *Actually, that's three speeders in one week, counting the one she got Monday.*

spiff *n.* extra money paid to a salesperson to sell certain merchandise aggressively. (See also *push money*.) □ *The manufacturer supplied a little spiff that even the store manager didn't know about.* □ *I got about $300 last month in spiff for selling some low-grade shoes.*

spiffed out *mod.* nicely dressed up; decked out. □ *I like to get all spiffed out every now and then.* □ *Wow, you look spiffed out! Where are you going?*

spiffed up *mod.* dressed up, brushed up, and polished up nicely. □ *See if you can get yourself a little spiffed up before we get to the front door. We wouldn't want the Wilmington-Thorpes to* *think you only have one suit.* □ *The house doesn't have to be too spiffed up for the Franklins. They are used to clutter.*

spiffy ['spɪfi] *mod.* excellent. □ *This is a real spiffy place you've got here, Sam.* □ *Come have a look at my spiffy new car.* □ *Doesn't look so spiffy to me.*

spike *tr.* to puncture an idea. □ *I explained the plan, but the boss spiked it immediately.* □ *I hate to see my ideas spiked like that.*

spiked **1.** *mod.* having to do with a drink with alcohol added; having to do with a punch with an alcoholic content. □ *Is the punch spiked? I want some without.* □ *We have spiked punch only.* □ *Carl's breakfast orange juice is usually spiked.* **2.** *mod.* having to do with hair that stands up straight. □ *His spiked hair wouldn't look so bad if it wasn't orange.* □ *Both orange and spiked is too much.* □ *Is spiked hair a fad or the way of the future?*

spinach *n.* money. (Because it is green.) □ *How much spinach you got on you?* □ *Look at this! One hundred dollars in good old American spinach!*

split *in.* to leave. □ *Look at the clock. Time to split.* □ *Let's split. We're late.* □ *I've got to split. See you later.*

spook **1.** *tr.* to frighten or startle someone or something. □ *Something I did spooked the teller, and she set off the silent alarm.* □ *Don't spook the cattle. They'll stampede.* **2.** *n.* a spy; a C.I.A. (U.S. Central Intelligence Agency) agent. □ *I just learned that my uncle had been a spook for years.* □ *Fred is training to be a spook, but don't tell anybody.*

spook factory *n.* the C.I.A. (U.S. Central Intelligence Agency,) in Washington, D.C., where spies are said to be trained. □ *Tom got a job in the spook factory.* □ *Does the spook factory pay very well?*

spot 1. *n.* a small drink of liquor. □ *I'll just have a spot, please.* □ *Just a spot for me, too.* 2. *n.* a nightclub; a night spot. □ *It was a nice little spot, with a combo and a canary.* □ *We went to a spot with a jukebox for entertainment.*

spot someone (something) 1. *tr.* to give an advantage to someone. □ *I'll spot you 20 points.* □ *No need to spot me. I'm the greatest!* 2. *tr.* to lend someone something. □ *Can you spot me a few bucks?* □ *I can spot you a whole hundred!*

spring for something AND **bounce for something** *in.* to treat (someone) by buying something. (See also *pop for something*.) □ *I'm bouncing for pizza. Any takers?* □ *Ralph sprang for drinks, and we all had a great time.*

spud [spəd] 1. *n.* a potato. □ *I'd like a few more spuds.* □ *Mashed spuds are the best of all.* 2. *n.* vodka, presumed to be made from potatoes. □ *How about a glass of spud?* □ *She keeps a big jug of spud in the refrigerator and drinks it like water.*

spunk [spəŋk] *n.* courage. □ *Show some spunk. Get in there and stand up for your rights.* □ *I have the spunk, but I don't have the brains.*

square 1. *mod.* old-fashioned; law-abiding; stodgy. □ *Man, you are really square.* □ *I come from a very square family.* 2. *n.* a person who behaves properly. □ *You are a square if I ever saw one.* □ *Ask that square what her favorite kind of music is.* 3. AND **square joint** *n.* a tobacco cigarette, compared to a marijuana cigarette. □ *You got a square on you?* □ *No, thanks. I've heard that them squares will give you cancer.* 4. *tr.* to settle or to make something right. □ *Let's talk about squaring this matter.* □ *Will 20 bucks square the matter?*

square joint See under *square.*

squat (See also *cop a squat, diddly-squat, (doodly-)squat.*) 1. *in.* to sit (down). □ *Come on in and squat for a while.* □ *Squat over here by the fire.* 2. *n.* nothing. (See *diddly-squat.*) □ *I worked all* *day on this, and she didn't pay me squat.* □ *I earn just a little more than squat, but I am very pleased with my life.*

squeal *in.* to inform (someone about something). □ *Who squealed to the cops?* □ *Molly squealed on us.*

squeeze **1.** *n.* liquor. (Black. See *grape(s)*.) □ *Let's stop on the way and get some squeeze.* □ *Freddie, where is your squeeze?* **2.** *tr.* to put pressure on someone. □ *The mob began to squeeze Carl for money.* □ *The tight schedule squeezed us all.* **3.** *n.* a tight situation; a situation where pressure is felt. □ *I'm in sort of a squeeze. Can you wait a month?* □ *When the squeeze is over, we'll be able to get squared away.* **4.** *n.* one's lover. (Black.) □ *I'll see if my squeeze wants to go.* □ *Get your squeeze, and let's go sink a few.*

squib [skwɪb] *n.* a notice; a small advertisement. □ *There was a squib in the paper about your project.* □ *I read a squib about that yesterday.*

squid [skwɪd] *n.* an earnest student. (Collegiate.) □ *This whole campus is populated by squids and nerds.* □ *I'm no squid. I went out on a date last month.*

squiff [skwɪf] *n.* a drunkard. □ *It's no fun living with a squiff.* □ *Is there anything that can be done for a confirmed squiff?*

squiff out *in.* to collapse from drink. □ *Hank squiffed out at midnight, right on the dot.* □ *She kept from squiffing out because she didn't trust her date.*

squirrel **1.** *n.* a strange or eccentric person. □ *Martin can be such a squirrel.* □ *Freddie is a squirrel, but I love him.* **2.** *n.* a car engine's horsepower. □ *What kind of squirrels you got under the hood?* □ *I got 440 squirrels and a whole bunch of carburetors.*

squirts *n.* a case of diarrhea. (Always with *the*.) □ *He's got the squirts and can't go out.* □ *What do you take for the squirts?*

squooshy ['skwuʃi AND 'skwuʃi] *mod.* soft; squishy. □ *I can't stand squooshy food!* □ *Mush is supposed to be squooshy.* □ *I like to walk barefooted in squooshy mud.*

stanza ['stænzə] *n.* an inning in baseball or some other division of a ball game. □ *He's doing better than he was in the last stanza.* □ *Jerry Clay is pitching again in this stanza.*

starched AND **starchy** *mod.* alcohol intoxicated. (Compare to *stiff.*) □ *Man, was he starched!* □ *No, he wasn't quite stiff, but he was starched.*

stay loose See *hang loose.*

steam **1.** *tr.* to anger someone. □ *She steamed him by being two hours late.* □ *The professor steamed the class with the long assignment.* **2.** *in.* to be angry. □ *She was absolutely steaming.* □ *They steamed for a while and then did as they were told.*

steamed (up) **1.** *mod.* angry. □ *Now, now, don't get so steamed up!* □ *She is really massively steamed.* **2.** *mod.* alcohol intoxicated and fighting. □ *He was really steamed—and could hardly stand up.* □ *By midnight, Larry was too steamed to drive home, and he had to spend the night.*

steam someone's beam *tr.* to make someone angry. □ *Being stood up really steams my beam!* □ *Come on, don't steam your beam. Remember how hard times are now.*

stems *n.* legs. □ *Look at the stems on that dame!* □ *My feet are sore, and my stems ache all the time.*

step off the curb *in.* to die. □ *Ralph almost stepped off the curb during his operation.* □ *I'm too young to step off the curb.*

stern *n.* the posterior. □ *The little airplane crashed right into the stern of an enormous lady who didn't even notice.* □ *Haul your stern over here and sit down.*

stiff 1. AND **stiffed** *mod.* alcohol intoxicated; dead drunk. □ *Kelly was too stiff to find his keys.* □ *She knows how to stop drinking before she gets stiff.* 2. *n.* a drunkard. □ *Some stiff staggered by—belching clouds of some beery smell.* □ *The guy's a stiff, and you want to run him for mayor? Even in this town that's going too far.* 3. *n.* a corpse. (Underworld.) □ *They pulled another stiff out of the river last night. Looks like another mob killing.* □ *They took me into a room full of stiffs to identify Walter's body.* 4. *tr.* to fail to tip someone who expects it. □ *Ya know, you can tell right away when a guy's gonna stiff you—ya just know.* □ *I guess I get stiffed two or three times a day.*

sting 1. *tr.* to cheat or swindle someone; to overcharge someone. □ *That street merchant stung me, but good.* □ *They are likely to sting you in any of those hockshops.* 2. *n.* a well-planned scheme to entrap criminals. □ *The sting came off without a hitch.* □ *It was a good sting and shouldn't have failed.* 3. *tr.* to entrap and arrest someone. □ *The feebies stung the whole gang at once.* □ *"We've been stung!" they hollered.*

stinger *n.* the drawback; the catch; the hitch. □ *Now, here's the stinger.* □ *Sounds good, but what's the stinger?*

stink 1. *in.* to be repellent. □ *This whole setup stinks.* □ *Your act stinks. Try another agent.* 2. *n.* a commotion. □ *The stink you made about money has done no good at all. You're fired.* □ *One more stink like that and out you go.*

stinker 1. *n.* an unpleasant or wicked person. □ *Jerry is a real stinker. Look what he did!* □ *What stinker messed up my desk?* 2. *n.* a serious problem. □ *This whole business is a real stinker.* □ *What a stinker of a problem.*

stink on ice *in.* to be really rotten. (So rotten as to reek even when frozen.) □ *This show stinks on ice.* □ *The whole idea stank on ice.*

stinkpot 1. *n.* a baby with a dirty diaper. (Also a term of address.) □ *Jimmy's a stinkpot. Better change him.* □ *Come here, you lit-*

tle stinkpot. I'll fix you. **2.** *n.* anything smelly. □ *What are you barbecuing in this old stinkpot?* □ *Why don't you drive this stinkpot into a service station and get it tuned?*

stoked (on someone or something) *mod.* excited by someone or something. (Compare to *stokin'*.) □ *We were stoked on Mary. She is the greatest.* □ *Everyone is stoked on spring.* □ *Now, don't get too stoked, you are the one who has to run.*

stoked out *mod.* exhausted. □ *I ran all the way and got stoked out.* □ *Alex is totally stoked out.*

stokin' *mod.* excellent; wild. □ *That car is really stokin'.* □ *We had a stokin' time at Fred's house.*

stone *mod.* completely; totally. (See additional examples in the following entries.) □ *This lecture is stone dull.* □ *I am stone mad at you.*

stoned (out) *mod.* alcohol or drug intoxicated. □ *Fred is really stoned out.* □ *I have never seen anybody so stoned who could still talk.*

stone fox *n.* an attractive woman; a very sexy woman. □ *She is a stone fox if I ever saw one.* □ *Who is that stone fox I saw you with last night?*

stone groove *n.* something really cool; a fine party or concert. □ *This affair is not what I would call a stone groove. Stone beige, maybe.* □ *Ted's do was a stone groove.*

stonkered ['stɔŋkəd] **1.** *mod.* killed. □ *The car crashed into him and he was stonkered for sure.* □ *He was stonkered before the plane hit the ground.* **2.** *mod.* alcohol intoxicated. □ *My buddy here is stonkered and needs a ride, and can I have one, too?* □ *Wally was stonkered beyond any help.*

storked *mod.* pregnant. □ *She got herself good and storked. Now what?* □ *I hear that Molly is storked again.*

straight **1.** *mod.* honest; unembellished. □ *This is the straight truth.* □ *Have I ever been anything but straight with you?* **2.** *n.* a tobacco cigarette; a tobacco cigarette butt. (As opposed to a marijuana cigarette.) □ *No, I want a straight. That pot makes me sneeze.* □ *Can I bum a straight off you?* **3.** *mod.* having to do with undiluted liquor. □ *I'll take mine straight.* □ *Make one straight with a little ice.*

straight (dope) *n.* the true information. □ *He gave us the straight dope.* □ *I want the straight dope. I can take it.*

straight low *n.* the absolute truth; the true lowdown on something. □ *Can you give me the straight low on this mess?* □ *Nobody ain't gonna tell no warden the straight low; you can be sure of that.*

straight up **1.** *mod.* upright. □ *A fine guy—really straight up.* □ *She is one of the most straight up brokers in town.* **2.** *mod.* without ice; neat. □ *I'll have a bourbon, straight up, please.* □ *No, not straight up. Just a little ice.*

strap *n.* an athlete, not necessarily male. (From *jockstrap.*) □ *A whole gang of straps came in the bar and ordered milk.* □ *The guy's a strap all right, but he's not dumb.*

street **1.** *n.* the real, free world, as opposed to prison. (Always with *the.*) □ *The street just isn't the same as stir.* □ *It's good to be back on the street.* **2.** *n.* Wall Street in New York City. (Always with *the.*) □ *The street doesn't seem to believe the policy makers in Washington.* □ *If you want excitement and stress, the street is the place to be.*

streeter *n.* an urban "street person." □ *These streeters have to be bright and clever just to survive.* □ *A couple of streeters taught me how to get a meal for nothing.*

street smart *mod.* wise in the ways of urban life; wise in the ways of tough neighborhoods. □ *Freddy was street smart at age eight.* □ *Bess wasn't street smart enough to survive by herself.*

street smarts *n.* the knowledge and ability to survive on the urban street. □ *If you don't have street smarts, you won't last long out there.* □ *You either pick up street smarts, or you don't.*

stress **1.** *in.* to suffer annoyance; to experience stress. □ *I'm stressing again! Please don't annoy me!* □ *Clare finds that she is stressing more and more about little things.* **2.** *tr.* to annoy or bother someone. □ *Don't stress Wally! He's had a hard day.* □ *The whole affair about my beemer stressed me a whole lot.* (More at *stressed.*)

stressed *mod.* upset; annoyed. □ *Come on, man, don't get stressed! It's only a gag.* □ *I am really stressed. I need a vacation.*

stroke *tr. & in.* to flatter someone; to soothe and comfort someone. □ *She strokes everybody to keep them on her side during the bad times.* □ *Stop stroking me, man! I can face the world!*

stud [stəd] *n.* a human male viewed as very successful with women. (From the term for a male horse used for breeding purposes.) □ *Fred thinks he is a real stud.* □ *Man, look at that stud over there. Think he's going steady with anyone?*

studhammer *n.* a male who is successful sexually with women. □ *Alex is a real studhammer.* □ *The guy thinks he is a studhammer, but he is just a jerk.*

stud-muffin *n.* a really good-looking guy; a *stud.* □ *Who's the stud-muffin with Sally?* □ *Did you see that stud-muffin come in?*

Stuff a sock in it! *exclam.* "Shut up!" (That is, stuff a sock in your mouth.) □ *I've heard enough. Stuff a sock in it!* □ *Stuff a sock in it! You are a pain.*

stumper *n.* a shoe. (Black. Usually plural. See *stumps.*) □ *Make those stumpers shine!* □ *You like my new stumpers?*

stumps *n.* a person's legs. □ *My stumps are sore from all that walking.* □ *You need good strong stumps to do that kind of climbing.*

style *in.* to show off; to strut around. (Black.) □ *Look at that brother style!* □ *Why don't you style over here and meet my man?*

suave [swɑv] *n.* personal polish and smoothness. □ *Man, does that guy ever have suave!* □ *You need some suave to carry off this sham.*

suck **1.** AND **suck something up, suck up something** *tr.* to drink beer or liquor. □ *Let's go out and suck a few up.* □ *Yeah, I'll suck one with ya.* **2.** *in.* [for someone or something] to be bad or undesirable. □ *This movie sucks!* □ *I think that the whole business sucks.*

sucker **1.** *n.* a dupe; an easy mark. □ *See if you can sell that sucker the Brooklyn Bridge.* □ *The sucker says he doesn't need a bridge, thank you.* **2.** *tr.* to trick or victimize someone. □ *That crook suckered me. I should have known better.* □ *They suckered him into selling half interest in his land.* **3.** *n.* an annoying person. (Also a rude term of address.) □ *Look, sucker, get out of my way!* □ *I am really sick of that sucker hanging around here.* **4.** *n.* a gadget; a thing. □ *Now, you put this little sucker right into this slot.* □ *Where is that sucker that looks like a screw?*

suck face *tr.* to kiss. (Compare to *swap spits*.) □ *The kid said he was going out to suck face. It sounds awful.* □ *Sally said she didn't want to suck face.*

suck (some) brew AND **suck (some) suds** *tr.* to drink beer. (See also *quaff a brew*.) □ *Wanna go suck some brew?* □ *I'm tired of sucking suds. Got any whiskey?*

suck (some) suds See the previous entry.

sucky *mod.* poor; undesirable. □ *This is the suckiest movie I ever saw.* □ *This food is sucky. It is really vile!*

suds **1.** *n.* beer. (See also *bust (some) suds, in the suds, suck (some) suds.*) □ *How about some suds, Bill?* □ *I can't get enough suds.* **2.** *in.* to drink beer. □ *How 'bout going out and sudsing for a while?* □ *They were sudsing when they should have been studying.*

suit *n.* a businessman or businesswoman; someone who is in charge. □ *This suit comes up and asks to go to the airport.* □ *A couple of suits checked into a working-class hotel and caused some eyebrows to raise.*

sunshades *n.* sunglasses. (See also *shades.*) □ *Where are my sunshades? Did you borrow them again?* □ *I left my sunshades in the car.*

superfly *mod.* excellent; wonderful. □ *This dude is really superfly.* □ *I don't care about this superfly friend of yours. If he doesn't have a job, I don't want you seeing him anymore. Ya hear?*

superjock **1.** *n.* an excellent athlete. □ *Mike is a real superjock. He plays four sports.* □ *All those superjocks get special meals and tutors to help them pass their classes.* **2.** *n.* a very well-built man regardless of athletic ability. □ *My boyfriend is a superjock, and does he look good!* □ *No nerd has ever been a superjock.*

super-strap *n.* an earnest and hardworking student. (As compared to a *jock, strap, superjock.*) □ *He's just a super-strap and he doesn't do anything but study.* □ *I couldn't be a super-strap even if I had the brains. I just don't care that much.*

surf *mod.* wonderful; with it. (California.) □ *This party is, like, surf.* □ *This not what I would call a surf day.*

swacked [swækt] *mod.* alcohol intoxicated. □ *Molly is too swacked to drive home. Can somebody give her a lift?* □ *He* *walked straight out of the office and went straight into the bar with the intention of getting swacked.*

swallow **1.** *n.* a puff of cigarette smoke. □ *He took just one swallow and started coughing.* □ *Can I have a swallow of your fag?* **2.** *tr.* to believe or accept something. (Compare to *eat*.) □ *Did they actually swallow that?* □ *Nobody's gonna swallow that nonsense.*

swap spits *tr.* to kiss with someone. □ *A couple of kids were in the car swapping spits.* □ *Tiffany and Wilbur were off somewhere swapping spits, I guess.*

sweat **1.** *tr. & in.* to fret (about something) while waiting for an outcome. □ *Come on, don't sweat it. It'll work out.* □ *This whole promotion business really has me sweating.* **2.** *n.* trouble; bother. □ *I can handle it. It won't cause me any sweat.* □ *You really caused a lot of sweat around here.*

swift **1.** *mod.* smart and clever. □ *Excuse my brother. He's not too swift.* □ *Dave is doing well in school. He's swift, and he likes his classes.* **2.** *mod.* sexually fast or easy, usually said of a woman. □ *Molly is swift they say, but I find her to be a perfect lady.* □ *Clare is not only swift, she has a reputation.*

swing **1.** *in.* [for someone] to be up to date and modern. □ *Tom really swings. Look at those blue suede shoes!* □ *I used to swing, but then age and good taste overtook me.* **2.** *in.* [for a party or other event] to be fun or exciting. □ *This party really swings!* □ *I've never been to a gathering that swings like this one.* **3.** *in.* to be involved in sexual fads, group sex, or the swapping of sexual partners. □ *Carol says that Tom, Ted, and Alice swing. How does she know?* □ *There is a lot less swinging going on since these strange diseases have appeared.*

swipe **1.** *tr.* to drink liquor rapidly and to excess; to bolt a drink of liquor. □ *Ted swiped a quick one and ran out the door.* □ *Fred sat at the bar and swiped two gins and ate an egg.* **2.** *n.* inferior or homemade liquor. □ *This swipe is gross. I'd rather drink* *water.* □ *I can't stand the swipe they serve here.* **3.** *tr.* to steal something. □ *Carl swiped a pack of cigarettes from the counter.* □ *Somebody swiped my wallet!* **4.** *n.* a blow or an act of striking someone or something. □ *Bob got a nasty swipe across the face.* □ *The cat gave the mouse a swipe with its paw.*

swish [swɪʃ] **1.** *mod.* overly fancy; effeminate; displaying effeminacy. □ *The lobby of the theater was a little swish, but not offensive.* □ *Who is your swish little friend?* **2.** *n.* elaborate decoration; effeminacy. □ *There's a little too much swish here. Get rid of the gold drapes.* □ *What this place needs is more swish. Hang some baubles here and there.*

switch *n.* a switchblade knife. □ *They found a switch in his pocket when they searched him.* □ *Carl was arrested for carrying a switch.*

swoozled AND **swozzled** ['swuzl̩d AND 'swɑzl̩d] *mod.* alcohol intoxicated. □ *How can anybody be so swozzled on three beers?* □ *Those guys are really swoozled!*

T

tabbed *mod.* well dressed. (Black.) □ *That dude is well tabbed.* □ *She's really tabbed in some nice threads.*

tag **1.** *n.* a name. □ *I know the face, but I forgot the tag.* □ *Everybody knows that tag well.* **2.** *n.* a car license plate or sticker. □ *The car had Kansas tags and was towing a trailer.* □ *Don't forget to get a new tag for this year.*

take a dirt nap *tr.* to die and be buried. □ *I don't want to end up taking a dirt nap during this operation.* □ *Isn't Tom a little young to take a dirt nap?*

take a hike AND **take a walk** *tr.* to leave; to beat it. □ *Okay, I've had it with you. Take a hike! Beat it!* □ *I had enough of the boss and the whole place, so I cleaned out my desk and took a walk.*

take a walk See the previous entry.

take five *tr.* to take a five-minute break. □ *Okay, gang, take five. Be back here in five minutes, or else.* □ *She told them to take five, but they turned the five into fifty.*

taken AND **had, took** **1.** *mod.* cheated; deceived. (Correct grammar is usually avoided in the slang senses of these words.) □ *I counted my change and I knew I was taken.* □ *You were really took, all right.* □ *I was had, for sure!* **2.** *mod.* drug intoxicated; unconscious from drugs. □ *The guy in the corner booth was taken and crying in his beer.* □ *His eyes were bloodshot, his* *hands were shaking—he was had.* **3.** *mod.* dead. □ *I'm sorry, your cat is taken—pifted.* □ *Your cat's took, lady, tough luck.*

take names *tr.* to make a list of wrongdoers. (Often figuratively, as with a schoolteacher whose major weapon is to take names and send them to the principal.) □ *The boss is madder than hell, and he's taking names.* □ *Gary is coming by to talk about the little riot last night, and I think he's taking names.*

take someone or something out AND **take out someone or something** **1.** *tr.* [with *someone*] to block someone, as in a football game. □ *I was supposed to take out the left end, but I was trapped under the center.* □ *Okay, Andy, you take out the center this time.* **2.** *tr.* [with *something*] to bomb or destroy something. □ *The enemy took out one of the tanks, but not the one carrying the medicine.* □ *The last flight took out two enemy bunkers and a radar installation.* **3.** *tr.* [with *someone*] to date someone. □ *I hope he'll take me out soon.* □ *She wanted to take him out for an evening.*

take the spear (in one's chest) *tr.* to accept full blame for something; to accept the full brunt of the punishment for something. □ *The admiral got the short straw and had to take the spear in his chest.* □ *I sure didn't want to take the spear.*

taking care of business *tr.* doing what one is meant to do; coping with life as it is. (Black.) □ *If the dude is taking care of business, what else do you want out of him?* □ *Walter is taking care of business. Back in a minute.*

talking head *n.* a television news reader or announcer whose head and neck appear on the screen. □ *I've had it with talking heads. I can read the paper and learn as much in 20 minutes.* □ *Some of those talking heads make millions a year.*

talk on the big white phone *in.* to vomit into a toilet. □ *One more beer and I'm gonna have to go talk on the big white phone.* □ *She was talking on the big white phone all night.*

tall **1.** *mod.* high on drugs; intoxicated with marijuana. (Drugs.) □ *When Jerry gets a little tall, he gets overwhelmed with a sense of guilt.* □ *She seems a little tall. What's she on?* **2.** *mod.* high quality. □ *This is one tall pizza, man.* □ *You're bringing in some tall ideas, man.*

tall in the saddle *mod.* proud. (Often with *sit.*) □ *I'll still be tall in the saddle when you are experiencing the results of your folly.* □ *Despite her difficulties, she still sat tall in the saddle.*

tank **1.** AND **tank up** *in.* to drink too much beer; to drink to excess. □ *The two brothers were tanking up and didn't hear me come in.* □ *Let's go out this Friday and tank awhile.* **2.** *tr. & in.* to lose a game deliberately. □ *Wilbur would never tank.* □ *The coach got wind of a plan to tank Friday's game.* **3.** *in.* for something to fail. □ *The entire stock market tanked on Friday.* □ *My investments did not tank when the market collapsed.*

tanked **1.** AND **tanked up** *mod.* alcohol intoxicated. □ *She was too tanked to drive.* □ *That old codger is really tanked.* **2.** *mod.* defeated; outscored. □ *The team was tanked again—20 to 17.* □ *I just knew we'd get tanked today.*

tap dance like mad *in.* to be busy continuously; to have to move fast to distract someone. □ *When things get tough, Congress tap dances like mad.* □ *Any public official knows how to tap dance like mad and still seem honest.*

taped [tept] *mod.* finalized; settled. (As if one were taping a package.) □ *I'll have this deal taped by Thursday. Then we can take it easy.* □ *Until this thing is taped, we can't do anything.*

tap out *in.* to lose one's money in gambling or in the financial markets. □ *I'm gonna tap out in about three more rolls—just watch.* □ *I really tapped out on that gold mining stock.* (More at *tapped.*)

tapped [tæpt] **1.** AND **tapped out** *mod.* broke. □ *The consumer is just about tapped. Don't expect much buying in that sec-*

tor. □ *I'm tapped out. Nothing left for you or anybody else this month.* **2.** AND **tapped out** *mod.* exhausted. □ *I need a nap. I'm tapped out.* □ *I've had it. I'm tapped.* **3.** AND **tapped out** *mod.* ruined. □ *We are tapped. That really did it to us.* □ *The project is completely tapped out.*

tawny ['tɔni] *mod.* excellent. □ *Who is throwing this tawny party anyway?* □ *This pizza is, like, tawny!*

technicolor yawn *n.* vomit. □ *This garbage will bring on a few technicolor yawns if we serve it.* □ *Who did the technicolor yawn in the bushes?*

tee someone off AND **tee off someone** *tr.* to make someone angry. □ *That really teed me off!* □ *Well, you sure managed to tee off everybody!*

T.G.I.F. **1.** *interj.* "Thank God it's Friday." □ *It was a rough week. T.G.I.F.* □ *Everybody was muttering T.G.I.F. by Friday afternoon.* **2.** *n.* a party held on Friday in honor of the end of the workweek. □ *Everyone is invited to the T.G.I.F. tonight.* □ *Terry has a T.G.I.F. in his room every evening.*

there, in See *in there.*

the way it plays *phr.* the way it is; the way things are. □ *The world is a rough place, and that's the way it plays.* □ *It's tough, but it's the way it plays.*

third wheel *n.* an extra person; a person who gets in the way. (Such a person is as useful as a third wheel on a bicycle.) □ *I feel like such a third wheel around here.* □ *Well, let's face it. We don't need you. You are a third wheel.*

thou [θɑʊ] *n.* one thousand. □ *I managed to get a couple of thou from the bank, but I need a little more than that.* □ *It only costs four thou. I could borrow it from my uncle.*

threads *n.* clothing. □ *When'd you get new threads, man?* □ *Good-looking threads on Wally, huh?*

throat *n.* an earnest student; a "cutthroat" student. (Collegiate.) □ *Merton is not a throat! He's not that smart.* □ *All the throats got A's, of course.*

throw a map *tr.* to empty one's stomach; to vomit. □ *Somebody threw a map on the sidewalk.* □ *I felt like I was going to throw a map.*

throw one's cookies See *toss one's cookies.*

throw one's voice *tr.* to empty one's stomach; to vomit. □ *Wally's in the john throwing his voice.* □ *Another drink of that stuff and Don'll be throwing his voice all night.*

throw something back AND **throw back something** *tr.* to eat or drink something. □ *Did you throw back that whole pizza?* □ *Jed threw back a quick snort and went on with his complaining.*

throw up one's toenails AND **throw one's toenails up** *tr.* to wretch; to vomit a lot. □ *It sounded like he was throwing up his toenails.* □ *Who's in the john throwing up her toenails?*

thunderbox *n.* a portable stereo radio, often played very loudly in public. □ *Someday I'm going to smash one of these thunderboxes!* □ *Why not get a thunderbox of your own?*

thunder-thighs *n.* big or fat thighs. (Cruel. Also a rude term of address.) □ *Here comes old thunder-thighs.* □ *Here, thunder-thighs, let me get you a chair or two.*

tick *n.* a minute; a second. □ *I'll be with you in a tick.* □ *This won't take a tick. Sit tight.*

ticked (off) *mod.* angry. □ *Wow, was she ticked off!* □ *Kelly was totally ticked.*

ticker 1. *n.* a heart. ☐ *I've got a good strong ticker.* ☐ *His ticker finally gave out.* **2.** *n.* a watch. ☐ *My ticker stopped. The battery must be dead.* ☐ *If your watch runs on a battery, can you really call it a ticker?*

ticket 1. *n.* the exact thing; the needed thing. ☐ *Her smile was her ticket to a new career.* ☐ *This degree will be your ticket to a bright and shining future.* **2.** *n.* a license. ☐ *I finally got a ticket to drive a big truck.* ☐ *I showed her my ticket, and she let me off with a warning.*

Time (out)! *exclam.* "Stop talking for a minute!" (A way of interrupting someone.) ☐ *Time! I have something to say.* ☐ *Just a minute! Time out! I want to speak!*

time to cruise *n.* "Time to leave." ☐ *See ya. It's time to cruise.* ☐ *Time to cruise. We're gone.*

tinsel-teeth *n.* a nickname for someone who wears dental braces. (Also a term of address.) ☐ *Tinsel-teeth is having a hard time talking.* ☐ *Well, tinsel-teeth, today's the day your braces come off.*

tints *n.* sunglasses. ☐ *Somebody sat on my tints.* ☐ *I have to get some prescription tints.*

toast 1. *n.* a drunkard. ☐ *The old toast stumbled in front of a car.* ☐ *A couple of toasts tried to get us to buy them drinks.* **2.** *mod.* excellent. (Black.) ☐ *This stuff is toast!* ☐ *Your silks are real toast.* **3.** *mod.* done for; in trouble. ☐ *If you don't get here in 20 minutes, you're toast.* ☐ *I told him he was toast for not being there.*

tokus AND **tukkis, tuchus** ['tokəs AND 'tʊkəs] *n.* the buttocks. (Yiddish.) ☐ *She fell right on her tokus!* ☐ *Look at the tukkis on that fat guy.*

took See *taken.*

tool **1.** *n.* an earnest student. (Compare to *power tool*.) ☐ *Of course he's a tool. See the plastic liner in his pocket?* ☐ *Merton is a tool, and he's proud of it.* **2.** *n.* a dupe; someone who can be victimized easily. ☐ *They were looking for some tool to drive the getaway car.* ☐ *Who's the tool with the briefcase?* **3.** *in.* to speed along (in a car). (Compare to *tool around*.) ☐ *We were tooling along at about 75 when the cop spotted us.* ☐ *I was tooling, and nobody could catch me.*

tool around *in.* to drive or cruise around. (Compare to *tool*.) ☐ *We tooled around for a while and then rented a horror flick.* ☐ *Let's tool around on the way home.*

toot **1.** *n.* a binge or a drinking spree. ☐ *Harry's on a toot again.* ☐ *He's not on one again. It's the same old toot.* **2.** *tr. & in.* to drink copiously. ☐ *She could toot booze from dusk to dawn.* ☐ *They tooted and tooted till they could toot no more.* **3.** *n.* an emotional state of some kind; an obsessive act or display. ☐ *She's on a toot about how nobody loves her anymore.* ☐ *Those toots wore everybody out.*

top, blow one's See *blow a fuse*.

torqued [tɔrkt] *mod.* angry; *bent*. ☐ *Sure I was torqued. Who wouldn't be?* ☐ *Now, now! Don't get torqued!*

toss **1.** *in.* to empty one's stomach; to vomit. ☐ *I was afraid I was going to toss.* ☐ *She tossed right there on the steps and ran away.* **2.** *tr.* to throw something away. ☐ *Toss it. It's no good.* ☐ *I'll toss this one. It's all scratched.* **3.** *tr.* to search someone. (Underworld.) ☐ *The cops tossed him and found nothing.* ☐ *The feds have a special way of tossing somebody for drugs.*

toss one's cookies AND **throw one's cookies, toss one's lunch, toss one's tacos** *tr.* to empty one's stomach; to vomit. ☐ *Right then and there, with no warning, he tossed his cookies.* ☐ *If you feel like tossing your cookies, please leave quietly.*

toss one's lunch See the previous entry.

toss one's tacos See *toss one's cookies*.

toss something off AND **toss off something** **1.** *tr.* to do something quickly without much time or effort. □ *It was no big deal. I tossed it off in 30 minutes.* □ *We can toss off the entire order in —let's say—three hours.* **2.** *tr.* to drink something quickly. □ *She tossed off a scotch in one big swig.* □ *He tossed it off and ordered another.* **3.** *tr.* to ignore criticism; to ignore defeat or a setback. □ *She just tossed it off like nothing had happened.* □ *How could she just toss it off?*

totalled **1.** *mod.* wrecked; damaged beyond repair. (From *totally wrecked*.) □ *The car was totalled. There was nothing that could be saved.* □ *There's a place in the city that will buy totalled cars.* **2.** *mod.* alcohol intoxicated. □ *Tom was too totalled to talk.* □ *Jed was totalled and couldn't see to pay the bill.*

totally *mod.* absolutely; completely. (Standard. Achieves slang status through overuse.) □ *How totally gross!* □ *This place is totally dull.*

to the max *mod.* maximally. (California. See *max, grody to the max*.) □ *She is happy to the max.* □ *They worked to the max their whole shift.*

tough something out *tr.* to carry on with something despite difficulties or setbacks. □ *Sorry, you'll just have to tough it out.* □ *I think I can tough it out for another month.*

trammeled ['træmḷd] *mod.* alcohol intoxicated. (Collegiate.) □ *Jim came home trammeled and was sick on the carpet.* □ *Wow, is she trammeled!*

tranny ['træni] *n.* an automobile transmission. □ *It looks like you get a new tranny, and I get 900 bucks.* □ *What kind of tranny does that hog have?*

trans [trænts] *n.* an automobile. (From *transportation.*) □ *I don't have any trans—I can't get myself anywhere.* □ *What are you using for trans these days?*

trash **1.** *tr.* to throw something away. □ *Trash this stuff. Nobody will ever use it.* □ *I'll take it. Don't trash it.* **2.** *n.* a low, worthless person; worthless people. □ *The guy is trash! Stay away from him.* □ *Running around with that trash—no wonder he's in trouble.* **3.** *tr.* to vandalize something. □ *Somebody trashed the statue with spray paint.* □ *Who trashed my room?*

trashed *mod.* alcohol or drug intoxicated. (Collegiate.) □ *They were trashed beyond help.* □ *Let's all get trashed and raid the girl's dorm.*

tree!, Go climb a See *Go chase yourself!*

trip (See also *bum trip, down trip, good trip, lay a (heavy) trip on someone, lay a guilt trip on someone, round tripper.*) **1.** *n.* a prison sentence; a trip to prison. (Underworld.) □ *Yeah, me and Lefty both was on a little trip for a few years.* □ *I had a short trip, so what?* **2.** *n.* intoxication from a drug. (Drugs.) □ *Me and Sid went on a little trip.* □ *The trip was great, but once was enough.* **3.** *n.* an annoying person or thing. □ *Class was a trip today.* □ *She is such a trip.* **4.** *in.* to leave. (Black.) □ *I gotta trip, man.* □ *Time to trip. See ya.*

trounce [traunts] *tr.* to beat someone; to outscore someone. (Sports.) □ *They really trounced us.* □ *Western trounced Eastern for the 47th year in a row.*

Trust me! *exclam.* "Believe me!"; "Honestly!" □ *It's true! Trust me!* □ *He actually said it just like Tom told you. Trust me!*

Tsup? *interrog.* "What's up?"; "What is happening?"; "What have you been doing?" □ *Hi! Tsup?* □ TONY: *Tsup?* TIFFANY: *Like, nothing.*

tube **1.** *n.* a can of beer. (See *crack a tube.*) □ *Toss me a tube, will ya?* □ *How many tubes do you think we ought to get for tonight?* **2.** *n.* the inner curve of a tall wave. (Surfing. See *tubular.*) □ *I'm waiting for the best tube.* □ *A good tube will do, won't it?* **3.** *in.* to fail; to *go down the tube(s).* □ *The whole plan tubed at the last minute.* □ *I tubed, and I'm sorry.* (More at **tube it.**) **4.** *n.* a television set. □ *What's on the tube tonight?* □ *The tube is in the shop, so I read a book.* **5.** *n.* a cigarette. □ *You got a tube I can bum?* □ *There's a pack of tubes in my jacket.*

tubed *mod.* alcohol intoxicated. (See *tube*, sense 1.) □ *They were both tubed and giggling.* □ *You really look tubed, man!*

tube, in a See *in a tube.*

tube it *tr.* to fail a test. (See *tube.*) □ *I tubed it, and I'll probably get a D in the course.* □ *I was afraid I'd tube it, so I studied my head off.*

tube steak *n.* a frankfurter or a wiener. □ *Are we having tube steak again for dinner?* □ *I could live on tube steak. Nothing is better!*

tub of guts See the following entry.

tub of lard AND **tub of guts** *n.* a fat person. (Cruel. Also a rude term of address.) □ *Who's that tub of guts who just came in?* □ *That tub of lard can hardly get through the door.*

tubular *mod.* excellent. (Surfing and later general youth slang. Having to do with a *tube* [wave] that is good to surf in.) □ *That pizza was totally tubular!* □ *This whole week is, like, tubular.*

tuchus See *tokus.*

tude [tud] *n.* a bad "attitude." □ *Hey, you really got a tude, dude.* □ *Are you pulling a tude with me?*

tukkis See *tokus.*

tunes *n.* a record; a record album. □ *I got some new tunes. Wanna come over and listen?* □ *The old tunes are good enough for me.*

turd **1.** *n.* a lump of fecal material. (Caution with *turd*.) □ *There is a dog turd on the lawn.* □ *There are some little mouse turds in the kitchen.* **2.** *n.* a wretched person. (Caution with *turd*. Also a provocative term of address.) □ *You stupid turd!* □ *The guy acts like a real turd most of the time.*

turkey **1.** *n.* a failure; a sham. □ *This whole business is a turkey.* □ *The turkey at the town theater closed on its first night.* **2.** *n.* a stupid person. □ *Who's the turkey who put the scallops in the scalloped potatoes?* □ *You are such a turkey!*

turn belly-up AND **go belly-up** **1.** *in.* to fail. □ *I sort of felt that the whole thing would go belly-up, and I was right.* □ *The computer—on its last legs anyway—turned belly-up right in the middle of an important job.* **2.** *in.* to die. (As a fish does when it dies. See *belly-up*.) □ *The cat was friendly for a moment before she turned belly-up.* □ *Every fish in Greg's tank went belly-up last night.*

turnoff *n.* something that repels someone. □ *The movie was a turnoff. I couldn't stand it.* □ *What a turnoff!*

turn turtle *in.* to turn over, as with a ship. (When a ship is upside down in the water, its hull looks like the shell of a huge turtle.) □ *The old dog finally turned turtle, and that was the end.* □ *The car struck a pole and turned turtle.*

turn up one's toes AND **turn one's toes up** *tr.* to die. □ *The cat turned up its toes right after church. Ah, the power of prayer.* □ *I'm too young to turn my toes up.*

tweased [twizd] *mod.* alcohol intoxicated. □ *Jim came in a little tweased last night.* □ *How tweased can anybody get on two beers?*

tweeked [twikt] *mod.* alcohol intoxicated. (Collegiate.) □ *They're not really bombed—just tweeked a little.* □ *Fred was too tweeked to stand up.*

twerp See the following entry.

twirp AND **twerp** [twɚp] *n.* an annoying runt of a person. (Also a term of address.) □ *Look, you twirp, get out!* □ *Some little twerp threatened to kick me in the shin.*

twit *n.* an irritating and stupid person. (Also a term of address. See also *in a twit.*) □ *Get out of here, you twit!* □ *Don't be such a twit all the time!*

twofer ['tufɚ] *n.* an item that is selling two for the price of one. □ *Here's a good deal—a twofer—only $7.98.* □ *Everything in this store is a twofer. I only want one of these. Do I have to bring a friend who wants one, too?*

two-time *tr.* to deceive one's lover. □ *Sam wouldn't two-time Martha. He just wouldn't!* □ *Sam would and did two-time Martha!*

two-time loser *n.* a confirmed *loser.* □ *Poor Carl is a two-time loser.* □ *Merton is a two-time loser, or at least he looks like one.*

two umlauts ['tu 'umlɑuts] *n.* a Löwenbräu (brand) beer. □ *I'll take a two umlauts.* □ *Calling a beer "two umlauts" is the most contrived bit of slang I have ever heard of.*

U

uke See *(y)uke.*

umpteen ['əmptin] *mod.* many; innumerable. □ *I've told you umpteen times not to feed the cat right out of the can.* □ *There are umpteen ways to do this right. Can you manage to do one of them?*

umpteenth See the following entry.

umpty-umpth AND **umpteenth** ['əmpti'əmpθ AND 'əmp'tintθ] *mod.* thousandth, billionth, zillionth, etc. (Represents some very large, but indefinite number.) □ *This is the umpty-umpth time I've told you to keep your dog out of my yard.* □ *This is the umpteenth meeting of the joint conference committee, but still there is no budget.*

units, (parental) See *(parental) units.*

unlax [ən'læks] *in.* unwind and relax. □ *I just can't wait to get home and unlax.* □ *Unlax, man. Take it easy.*

up 1. *mod.* happy; cheery; not depressed. □ *I'm up today. Let's celebrate.* □ *This is not an up party. Let's cruise.* **2.** *tr.* to increase something. □ *She tried to up the price on me, thinking I wouldn't notice.* □ *The bank upped its rates again.*

upchuck ['əptʃək] **1.** *tr. & in.* to vomit (something). □ *Wally up-chucked his whole dinner.* □ *Who upchucked over there?* **2.** *n.*

vomit. □ *Is that upchuck on your shoe?* □ *There is still some up-chuck on the bathroom floor.*

up for grabs 1. *mod.* available for anyone; not yet claimed. □ *It's up for grabs. Everything is still very chancy.* □ *I don't know who will get it. It's up for grabs.* 2. *mod.* in total; chaos. □ *This is a madhouse. The whole place is up for grabs.* □ *When the market crashed, the whole office was up for grabs.*

up for something *mod.* agreeable to something. □ *I'm up for a pizza. Anybody want to chip in?* □ *Who's up for a swim?*

up front 1. *mod.* at the beginning; in advance. □ *She wanted $200 up front.* □ *The more you pay up front, the less you'll have to finance.* 2. *mod.* open; honest; forthcoming. (Usually **up-front**) □ *She is a very up-front gal—trust her.* □ *I wish the sales-man had been more up-front about it.* 3. *mod.* in the forefront; under fire (at the front). □ *You guys who are up front are gonna get the most fire.* □ *You two go up front and see if you can help.*

uptight *mod.* anxious. □ *Dave always seems uptight about some-thing.* □ *He is one uptight guy.* □ *Don't get uptight before the test.*

urp See *earp.*

U.V.s ['ju'viz] *n.* "ultraviolet" rays from the sun; sunshine. □ *I wanna get some U.V.s before we go home.* □ *Watch out for those U.V.s.*

V

vanilla **1.** *mod.* plain; dull. □ *The entire production was sort of vanilla, but it was okay.* □ *No more vanilla music, please.* □ *The vacation was vanilla, but restful.* **2.** *n.* a Caucasian. □ *Some vanilla's on the phone—selling something, I guess.* □ *That vanilla is looking at you sort of cop-like.*

V-ball *n.* volleyball. (Compare to *B-ball*.) □ *You wanna play some V-ball?* □ *Playing V-ball is one of the best forms of exercise.*

veg (out) [vɛdʒ ɑʊt] *in.* to cease working and take it easy; to vegetate. □ *Someday, I just want to veg out and enjoy life.* □ *I think I'll just veg this weekend.*

vest *n.* an important businessman or businesswoman. (See *suit*.) □ *One of the vests complained to the management about the way I cleaned his office.* □ *Some vest jumped out the window this afternoon.*

vette [vɛt] *n.* a Corvette automobile. □ *I'd rather have a vette than a caddy.* □ *Vettes aren't as popular as they once were.*

vibes [vɑɪbz] *n.* vibrations; atmosphere; feelings. (Usually with *good* or *bad*.) □ *I just don't get good vibes about this deal.* □ *The vibes are just plain bad.*

vic [vɪk] **1.** *n.* a victim. (Streets. See *vivor*.) □ *We're all vics, but we all keep going.* □ *Harry is a con artist, not a vic.* **2.** *n.* a convict. □ *Carl is a vic, but nobody cares much.* □ *We try to give* *the vics a chance at employment where they won't be treated badly.*

vicious ['vɪʃəs] *mod.* great; excellent. □ *Man, this burger is really vicious.* □ *That guy is one vicious driver, all right.*

vines *n.* clothing. (Black.) □ *I like those smokin' vines you're in.* □ *Good-looking vines on that guy, right?*

vinyl ['vaɪnl] *n.* phonograph records. □ *This is one of the best tunes on vinyl.* □ *I got some new vinyl. Come over and listen.*

vivor ['vaɪvɚ] *n.* a survivor; a street person who manages to survive. (Streets. Compare to *vic*.) □ *Harry's a vivor, and I like him.* □ *She's no champ, but she's a vivor.*

viz [vaɪz] *n.* Levis; blue jeans. □ *How do you like my new viz?* □ *Those viz are too tight for her.*

vomity ['vamɪdi] *mod.* nasty. (Crude.) □ *What is this vomity stuff on my plate?* □ *Is that what you call vomity?* □ *That is a really vomity idea!*

W

wad [wɑd] *n.* a bundle of money; a bankroll. (Originally underworld.) □ *I lost my wad on a rotten horse in the seventh race.* □ *You'd better not flash a wad like that around here. You won't have it long.*

wailing AND **whaling** *mod.* excellent. (Teens.) □ *Man, that's wailing!* □ *What a whaling guitar!*

walk **1.** *n.* something easy. (Always with *a*. See *cakewalk, sleepwalk*.) □ *That game was a walk!* □ *What a walk! I've never had such an easy time of it!* **2.** *in.* to walk out on someone. □ *They had a big fight, and he walked.* □ *Much more of this and I'm going to walk.* **3.** *in.* to walk away from something unharmed. □ *It couldn't have been much of an accident. Both drivers walked.* □ *It was a horrible meeting, but when it was over I just walked.*

walk heavy *in.* to be important. (Black.) □ *Harry's been walking heavy since he graduated.* □ *Why have you been walking heavy, man?*

walkover *n.* an easy victory; an easy task. (From sports.) □ *The game was a walkover. No problem.* □ *Learning the computer's operating system was no walkover for me.*

walk tall *in.* to be brave and self-assured. □ *I know I can walk tall because I'm innocent.* □ *You go out on that stage and walk tall. There is no reason to be afraid.*

waltz *n.* an easy task. ☐ *The job was a waltz. We did it in a day.* ☐ *The coach promised them that the game would be a waltz.*

wanabe AND **wanna be** ['wɑnə bi OR 'wənə bi] *n.* someone who wants to be something or someone. (The term is associated with Madonna, the singer.) ☐ *All these teenyboppers are wanabes, and that's why we can sell this stuff to them at any price.* ☐ *A wanna be came by selling chances on a raffle.*

waste *tr.* to kill someone. (Underworld.) ☐ *Reggie had orders to waste Carl.* ☐ *The mob's triggers sped by in a car and wasted four pushers.*

wasted **1.** *mod.* dead; killed. ☐ *Carl didn't want to end up wasted.* ☐ *That's silly. We all end up wasted one way or another.* **2.** *mod.* alcohol or drug intoxicated. ☐ *I really feel wasted. What did I drink?* ☐ *I've never seen a bartender get wasted before.*

way rad *mod.* quite excellent. (California. See *rad*.) ☐ *Oh, Tiff! That's way rad!* ☐ *You are? Way rad!*

weed **1.** *n.* tobacco; a cigarette or cigar. ☐ *I've about given up weed.* ☐ *This weed is gonna be the death of me.* **2.** *n.* marijuana; a marijuana cigarette. ☐ *This is good weed, man.* ☐ *This weed is green, but decent.*

weeds *n.* clothing. ☐ *Good-looking weeds you're wearing.* ☐ *These weeds came right out of the catalog. Would you believe?*

weird out *in.* to become emotionally disturbed or unnerved; to *flip (out)*. ☐ *The day was just gross. I thought I would weird out at noon.* ☐ *I weirded out at the news of Frankie's death.*

wet rag See the following entry.

wet sock AND **wet rag** *n.* a *wimpy* person; a useless *jerk*. (See also *rubber sock*.) ☐ *Don't be such a wet sock! Stand up for your rights!* ☐ *Well, in a tight situation, Merton is sort of a wet rag.*

whaling See *wailing*.

What's going down? *interrog.* "What's happening?" □ *I can't figure out what's going down around here.* □ *Hey, man, what's going down?*

What's happ(ening)? *interrog.* "Hello, what's new?" (See also *Tsup?*) □ *Hey, dude! What's happening?* □ *What's happ? How's it goin'?*

What's shakin' (bacon)? *interrog.* "How are you?"; "What is new?" □ *What's shakin' bacon? What's going down?* □ *Hi, Jim. What's shakin'?*

What's the deal? See the following entry.

What's the scam? AND **What's the deal?** *interrog.* "What is going on around here?" (See *scam.*) □ *There's a big rumpus down the hall. What's the scam?* □ *I gave you a twenty, and you give me five back? What's the deal? Where's my other five?*

What's up? *interrog.* "What is going on?"; "What is happening?" (See also *Tsup?*) □ *Hi, Jim! What's up?* □ *Haven't seen you in a month of Sundays. What's up?*

wheel *tr. & in.* to drive a car. (Black.) □ *I'm gonna wheel over later this afternoon.* □ *Let's wheel my heap over to Marty's place.*

wheels *n.* transportation by automobile. □ *I gotta get some wheels pretty soon.* □ *I'll need a ride. I don't have any wheels.*

w(h)enchy ['wɛntʃi OR 'ʌɛntʃi] *mod.* bitchy; snotty. (Collegiate.) □ *I really wish you wouldn't be so wenchy with me!* □ *What's the matter with that wenchy chick?* □ *Then she began to get whenchy, so I left.*

whenchy See *wenchy*.

vhitebread *mod.* plain; dull. □ *Naw, the whole thing is too whitebread.* □ *If I wanted a whitebread vacation, I'd have gone to the beach.*

whiz 1. *n.* a talented or skilled person. □ *She's a real whiz with stats.* □ *I'm no math whiz, but I can find your errors.* **2.** *in.* to urinate. (Caution with topic.) □ *I gotta stop here and whiz.* □ *You can't whiz in the park!*

whole ball of wax *n.* everything; the whole thing. (Always with *the.*) □ *Well, that just about ruins the whole ball of wax.* □ *Your comments threatened the whole ball of wax, that's what.*

whole enchilada [. . . ɛntʃəˈlɑdə] *n.* the whole thing; everything. (From Spanish. Always with *the.*) □ *Nobody, but nobody, ever gets the whole enchilada.* □ *Carl wants the whole enchilada.*

wicked *mod.* excellent; impressive. □ *Now this is what I call a wicked guitar.* □ *Man, this wine is wicked!*

wimp out (of something) *in.* to *chicken out (of something)*; to get out of something, leaving others to carry the burden. □ *Come on! Don't wimp out now that there's all this work to be done.* □ *Ted wimped out on us.*

wimpy *mod.* weak; inept; square. □ *You are just a wimpy nerd!* □ *Come on, don't be so wimpy.*

wing *in.* to travel by airplane. □ *We winged to Budapest to attend a conference.* □ *They winged from there to London.*

wing it *tr.* to improvise; to do something extemporaneously. □ *I lost my lecture notes, so I had to wing it.* □ *Don't worry. Just go out there and wing it.*

winks *n.* some sleep. □ *I gotta have some winks. I'm pooped.* □ *A few winks would do you good.*

wired 1. *mod.* nervous; extremely alert. □ *The guy is pretty wired because of the election.* □ *I get wired before a test.* 2. AND **wired up** *mod.* alcohol or drug intoxicated. □ *Ken was so wired up he couldn't remember his name.* □ *Tiff is, like, totally wired up.*

wired into someone or something *mod.* concerned with someone or something; really involved with someone or something. □ *Mary is really wired into classical music.* □ *Sam and Martha are totally wired into one another.*

wombat ['wɑmbæt] *n.* a strange person; a *geek.* (Collegiate.) □ *Why does everybody think Merton is such a wombat?* □ *Who's the wombat in the 1957 Chevy?*

wonk [wɔŋk] *n.* an earnest student. (Collegiate.) □ *Who's the wonk who keeps getting the straight A's?* □ *Yes, you could call Merton a wonk. In fact, he's the classic wonk.*

wonky ['wɔŋki] *mod.* studious. (Collegiate.) □ *Merton is certainly the wonky type.* □ *You ought to get a little wonky yourself.*

woody *n.* a wooden surfboard; a surfboard. □ *Who's the guy with the woody on his head?* □ *Get your woody, and let's get moving.*

worship the porcelain god *tr.* to empty one's stomach; to vomit. (Collegiate.) □ *Somebody was in the john worshiping the porcelain god till all hours.* □ *I think I have to go worship the porcelain god. See ya.*

wrinkle-rod *n.* the crankshaft of an engine. □ *You need a new wrinkle-rod, lady.* □ *A wrinkle-rod'll set you back about $199, plus installation charges, of course.*

wrongo ['rɔŋo] 1. *mod.* wrong. □ *You are totally wrongo.* □ *Wrongo, wrongo! You lose the game!* 2. *n.* an undesirable thing or person; a member of the underworld. □ *The guy's a total* *wrongo. He's got to be guilty.* □ *This whole business is a complete wrongo.*

wuss(y) ['wʊs(i)] *n.* a *wimpy* or weak person. □ *Don't be such a wuss. Stand up for your rights.* □ *Wussies like you will never get ahead.*

Y

yank 1. *tr.* to harass someone. (See also *yank someone around*.) □ *Stop yanking me!* □ *Yank the guy a little, and see what that does.* 2. *n.* a Yankee; a U.S. soldier. (Sometimes capitalized.) □ *I don't care if you call me a yank. That's what I am.* □ *Hey, Yank! What's new?*

yank someone around *tr.* to harass someone; to give someone a hard time. (Compare to *jerk someone around*.) □ *Listen, I don't mean to yank you around all the time, but we have to have the drawings by Monday.* □ *Please stop yanking me around.*

yank someone's chain *tr.* to harass someone; to give someone a hard time. (As if one were a dog wearing a choker collar, on a leash.) □ *Stop yanking my chain!* □ *Do you really think you can just yank my chain whenever you want?*

yeaster *n.* a beer-drinker. □ *A couple of yeasters in the back of the tavern were singing a dirty song.* □ *Who's the yeaster with the bloodshot eyes?*

york [jork] 1. *in.* to empty one's stomach; to vomit. □ *He ate the stuff, then went straight out and yorked.* □ *Who yorked in the flower pot?* 2. *n.* vomit. □ *Is that york I see on the living-room window?* □ *Hey, Jimmy! Come out in the snow and see the frozen york!*

yu(c)k [jək] 1. *n.* someone or something disgusting. (Also a term of address.) □ *I don't want any of that yuck on my plate!* □ *Who is that yuk in the red bandanna?* 2. *exclam.* "Horrible!"

(Usually **Yuck!**) □ *Oh, yuck! Get that horrible thing out of here!* □ *Yuck! It looks alive!* **3.** *n.* a joke. □ *Come on! Chill out! It was just a yuck.* □ *Not a very good yuk if you ask me.*

yu(c)ky AND **yukky** ['jəki] *mod.* nasty. □ *What is this yucky pink stuff on my plate?* □ *This tastes yukky.*

(y)uke [juk] **1.** *in.* to empty one's stomach; to vomit. (Collegiate. Compare to *puke*.) □ *I think somebody yuked in the backseat, Tom.* □ *My friends wouldn't uke in my car!* **2.** *n.* vomit. (Collegiate.) □ *That is uke on the floor, isn't it?* □ *Tell me that the stuff in the backseat isn't yuke!*

Z

za [zɑ] *n.* pizza. (Collegiate.) □ *I'm gonna spring for some za.* □ *Who wants some of this za?*

zap **1.** *tr.* to shock someone. □ *That fake snake zapped me for a minute.* □ *The incident zapped me, but good.* **2.** *tr.* to impress someone. □ *My big idea really zapped the boss. I may get a raise.* □ *I like to have something to zap the board with at every meeting.* **3.** *exclam.* "Wow!" (Usually **Zap!**) □ *Zap! I did it again!* □ *He said, "Zap!" indicating that he really liked the present, I guess.*

zapped **1.** *mod.* tired; exhausted. □ *I'm too zapped to go on.* □ *I'm way zapped. Good night.* **2.** *mod.* alcohol or drug intoxicated. □ *We all got zapped and then went home.* □ *Marty is too zapped to stand up.*

zarf [zɑrf] *n.* an ugly and repellent male. □ *Ooo, who is that zarf who just came in?* □ *That zarf is Merton, and he makes all A's, and he helps me with my homework, so just shut up!*

zero *n.* an insignificant person; a nobody. □ *Pay her no mind. She is a zero around here.* □ *I want to be more in life than just another zero.*

zip **1.** *n.* nothing. □ *There was no mail today. Nothing. Zip.* □ *I got zip from the booking agency all week.* **2.** *n.* a score or grade of zero. □ *Well, you got zip on the last test. Sorry about that.* □ *The prof said that zip is better than nothing, but I don't see how* *it could be.* **3.** *n.* vigor; spunk. □ *Put some zip into it. It's too ho-hum.* □ *This whole thing lacks the zip it needs to survive.*

zit [zɪt] *n.* a pimple. □ *Don't squeeze your zits on my mirror!* □ *That is one prize-winning zit on your nose.*

zonk [zɔŋk] **1.** *tr.* to overpower someone or something. □ *We zonked the dog with a kick.* □ *It took two cops to zonk the creep.* **2.** *tr.* to tire someone out. □ *The pills zonked me, but they made my cold better.* □ *Jogging always zonks me.* (More at *zonked (out)*.)

zonked (out) AND **zounked (out)** [zɔŋkt... AND zaʊŋkt...] **1.** *mod.* alcohol or drug intoxicated. □ *She's too zonked to drive.* □ *Jed was almost zounked out to unconsciousness.* **2.** *mod.* exhausted; asleep. □ *She was totally zonked out by the time I got home.* □ *I'm zounked. Good night.*

zonk out *in.* to collapse from exhaustion; to go into a stupor from drugs or exhaustion. □ *I'm gonna go home and zonk out.* □ *I went home after the trip and just zonked out.*

zot(z) [zat(s)] *n.* zero; nothing. □ *I went out to get the mail, but there was zot.* □ *All I got for a raise was little more than zotz.*